GOOD AND FAITHFUL SERVANT

Stewardship in the Orthodox Church

GOOD AND FAITHFUL SERVANT

Stewardship in the Orthodox Church

Edited by

ANTHONY SCOTT

ST VLADIMIR'S SEMINARY PRESS
CRESTWOOD, NEW YORK 10707
2003

Library of Congress Cataloging-in-Publication Data

Good and faithful servant : stewardship in the Orthodox Church / edited by
    Anthony Scott.
    p. cm.
  Includes bibliographical references.
  ISBN 0-88141-255-4 (alk. paper)
   1. Stewardship, Christian.   2. Orthodox Eastern Church—Doctrine.
  I. Scott, Anthony (Anthony L.)

BV772.G585 2003
248'.6'0882819—dc22

2003058793

CONTENTS

FOREWORD

I thank God that Father Anthony Scott had the vision to bring together Orthodox academics, theologians, and clergy to contribute to this much-needed book on stewardship in the Orthodox Church. Several of the contributors to this book pointedly explain that all we have—our time, our talent, and our treasure—comes from God and that God owns everything. That is a very difficult concept for most people to grasp, especially for Orthodox Christians, both those who migrated from abroad and those born in this country.

We might ask: Why are our friends in Protestant and Roman Catholic communities years ahead of us as regards the concept of stewardship? I know that some will say that it is because we are an "immigrant church." However, I submit that we now have several generations of American-born Orthodox Christians. How does one explain the thousands of American-born Orthodox Christian men and women in all professions and fields of employment, from the highest levels as chief executives to the lowest levels, who contribute more of their time, talent, and treasure to their colleges, to their kids' sports teams, or to their country club rather than to their church and its salvific mission?

In my opinion, we the laypeople—parents and grandparents—and the clergy—including the hierarchs—have failed in our duty to teach our children and those in our sphere of influence what it means to be an Orthodox Christian. It has only been within the past ten years that I have heard discussions about stewardship in its broadest form. Many of our spiritual fathers are uncomfortable discussing or preaching on the subject. Yet, our salvation depends upon living our lives as faithful stewards. What is going to happen to our children and grandchildren if they do not learn about stewardship? Shouldn't the topic be given a high priority?

During the period from 1991 to 1997, I had the privilege of being co-chair of the $20 million capital campaign for St Vladimir's Orthodox Theological Seminary. Additionally, in 1996, the dean of our cathedral and I started our parish stewardship program, just the two of us. Moreover, for the past five years I have been the stewardship chair of the Western American Diocese of the Serbian Church. In 1982, following the teaching of our Lord that it is better to give than to receive, my wife and I formed a small, private family foundation, the Obren B. & Marilyn Gerich Foundation.

During these many years, I have experienced much joy and much frustration related to these assignments. I have had the joy of watching St Vladimir's Seminary exceed its $20 million goal. I had the joy of dealing, for several years, with a 92-year-old Russian widow from Southern California who faithfully contributed hundreds of dollars to her parish, to her parish in her homeland, to her first parish in the United States (Minneapolis), to St Vladimir's Seminary, and yet who had only two dresses to her name and reused the envelopes that her bills came in! Ultimately she gave 50 percent of her home to the seminary and 50 percent to her parish in Minneapolis. Every night, despite failing eyesight, she spent an hour reading from her large-print Bible.

I also experienced the frustration as stewardship chair of our cathedral: watching people give $1.00 per week in the collection plate and call that tithing! When I asked about a sacrificial, annual stewardship commitment, the typical response was, "Why do I need to pay more money, since I pay my dues of $150 per year?"

Why are these two real examples—which I have experienced over and over again—so different? I submit that the Russian widow's life was Christ-centered, while the other situation reminds me of the Gospel story of the beggar Lazarus—only in this case the Church of Jesus Christ got the left-over crumbs.

In this volume, Fr Anthony Scott describes obstructions to sacrificial giving, including the "dues" system, and in my experience, his words meet the mark (see "Orthodox America: Philanthropy and Stewardship"). Whoever initiated the "dues" system in our parishes did a great disservice to the entire Church. Members feel that paying dues to the parish is the same as paying dues at their country club or other clubs, but they are incorrect. At a country club, a budget is prepared which covers all of the operating costs, maintenance reserves, and planned improvements. That total is then divided by the number of members in order to calculate the amount of the dues required for that year. That is not what happens at our parishes.

In most parishes, "dues" bear no relationship to the total operating budget. In my parish, our annual budget is approximately $550,000, without provision for replacement reserves, missions, charitable works, and so forth. We have five hundred "dues-paying members." Our dues should be $1,100 per person per year. Instead they are $204! It is not difficult to see how deceptive and inoperable a dues system is.

Likewise, "Forty Sentences," by Fr Thomas Hopko, is not relaxing reading for those of us who profess to be Christians. I personally found it to be convicting. I found that several of "the sentences" made particularly painful demands upon my current perspective, if I were really serious about my life and if I were concerned about where I would spend eternity. Consider Sentence 16: "Stewardship extends to every aspect of our life and work in the world. . . . Humans are to be stewards of all that they are and have, which comes from their divine Master. . . . They are to care first for their own souls and bodies, then for those of their family members . . . then for all people. . . . They are to care also for the earth, the plants and the animals, the fish of the sea and the birds of the air." Other chapters in this book pricked my conscience and challenged me as well.

I must admit that when the time arrived for me to show leadership as co-chair of St Vladimir's capital campaign by making a seven-figure gift, it was not easy. I have committed my life to our Lord and Savior, but giving away one-third of my "pie"—was that smart? I came up with all kinds of scenarios where I might need the money for my own use, but in the end the Scripture teaching "To whom much is given much is expected" (Lk 12.48) kept recurring in my conscience. Also, what about the Lord's promise that he would take care of my needs and me: "Be anxious for nothing"(Mt 6.31–33)? Did I really believe that? And how about the Sunday Eucharistic prayer, which for me is one of the most important: "For a good account before the awesome, dreaded judgment seat of Christ." I must admit that God has returned that gift two-fold, or as we Americans haughtily would say, "My net worth increased due to my brilliance."

Dr John Barnet ("Stewardship and the New Testament") points out that "the drive toward self-sufficiency eventually overcomes all other motivations, including one's charitable intentions toward his neighbor." He quotes Martin Hengel in saying that property represents both "a dangerous threat and a supreme obligation." As I thought about those words, I felt uneasy. First, the threat to accumulate, "to build more barns," and to make certain that I never run out of goods opposes the concept that my time, talent, and treasure are a "supreme obligation" to be a good and faithful servant and to love my neighbor as myself. It is a continual struggle.

And, even when the fear of disbursing assets is overcome, the sin of pride rears its head. Because it has not been common for Orthodox Christians to make significant gifts to the parish, the diocese, or the seminaries, when one does make such a gift, much ado and praise is poured on the donor. I suspect that many donors struggle with Jesus' teaching in Matthew 6.1: "Take care! Don't do your good deeds publicly, to be admired, for then you will lose the reward from your Father in heaven."

This book addresses all those pitfalls, as well as providing edifying and instructive correctives: Professor Jaroslav Pelikan's exposition about stewardship in the ante-Nicene, pre-Constantinian Church ("Stewardship of Money in the Early Church: A Close Reading of *Who Is the Rich Man that Shall Be Saved*, by Clement of Alexandria"); Dean John H. Erickson's explanation of fundamental social and political influences on financial matters in Orthodox parishes ("Historical Perspectives on Orthodox Stewardship in America"); and the Very Reverend Fr Stanley Harakas's outline of primary ethical dimensions of stewardship ("Ethics and Stewardship"). Dr Paul Meyendorff places stewardship within the liturgical context ("Offering You 'Your Own of Your Own'"); Fr Demetrios Constantelos discusses "Some Aspects of Stewardship of the Church of Constantinople"; Dr Susan Ashbrook Harvey relates stewardship to "Healing the Christian Body"; and Bishop Hilarion Alfeyev, within the context of the mores of the society of St Gregory of Nazianzus, argues the point, "Stewardship as a Way to Deification." From the late Fr Michael Prokurat's "Stewardship and Tithe in the Old Testament" to Dn John Chryssavgis's "The Power of Detachment in Early Monastic Literature," this volume spans and explores a great many aspects of stewardship.

Throughout, I am reminded that stewardship encompasses more than money. It is my total life, my time, my talents, and my treasure. For most Americans, especially those of us in the business world, we are measured by how much money we have and how many "toys" we own. Why would you want to give away some of your toys or money to help your neighbor? Who would buy the annual *Forbes* magazine of the richest 400 men and women in America if it had only one entry: "The richest person—God . . . Net Worth—EVERYTHING!"

This book made me hearken back to the memory of my late father, who had three years of education in Yugoslavia, who never made more than $700 per month, who worked for the same company forty-eight years, who was married for forty-seven years, who dedicated his time and meager treasure to God and his Church, and who died at age 92 as a peaceful and happy man, free from cholesterol medication and heart palpitations, and ignorant of the medication valium. For forty years, he and his wife lived in the same 900-square foot home, for which he paid $4,000. He never had a family foundation, was not being continually pursued by development officers and fundraisers, and was not on any boards. He lived a long life full of peace and love. He lived in the fullness of his faith and knew what was everlasting.

Orthodox Christians have much to learn and a long way to go. I pray that this book will be the basis for a new way of thinking and for new direction in our Holy Church. I highly recommend that every hierarch, priest, and parish council member read it. Every parish bookstore should have copies for sale, and every parish library should have a copy on the shelf. In addition, there are now several clergymen and laypeople who are conducting workshops and giving seminars on stewardship. Parishes and dioceses should avail themselves of these gifted people.

In my opinion stewardship can no longer be ignored. What is at stake is more than parish budgets: It is the future of our church in America. Matthew 19.21, the "Parable of the Rich Man," burns in my heart. I can only plead for God's mercy and continually recite the Jesus prayer, "Lord Jesus Christ, Son of God, have mercy on me a sinner."

BRIAN GERICH
Trustee of St Vladimir's Orthodox Theological Seminary
Senior Vice President of Public Storage, Inc.

STEWARDSHIP OF MONEY IN THE EARLY CHURCH

A Close Reading of Who Is the Rich Man that Shall Be Saved? *by Clement of Alexandria*

———◆———

JAROSLAV PELIKAN[*]

I n any serious discussion of Christian "stewardship" as something more substantial than a scriptural-sounding euphemism for begging or fund-raising, the early, i.e., the ante-Nicene or pre-Constantinian, Church must have a certain pride of place, either because it is the repository of the normative Catholic Tradition on which all subsequent periods of Christian history have drawn or, alternately for the more radical forms of Protestantism, because it was there that the true Church "fell" by adopting the so-called apostolic norms of episcopacy and dogma that have vitiated the authenticity of its witness ever since. When it is "Orthodox stewardship" that is under investigation, the special prominence in this period both of acknowledged spokesmen for Orthodoxy such as Irenaeus of Lyons and of brilliant but controversial theological virtuosos such as Origen of Alexandria makes it obligatory to examine its proto-Orthodox witness, not only, as many of us have been doing for a long time, for the earliest doctrinal and creedal efforts to find formulas by which to give

*Dr Jaroslav Pelikan is Sterling Professor of History *Emeritus* at Yale University. He is the author of more than thirty books and is widely acknowledged as one of the most important living historians of Christian doctrine.

voice to the Church's faith in the Holy Trinity or the mystery of the Word made flesh, but also for the earliest theoretical and practical endeavors of construing the interrelations between the Church and the social and political order, including the sticky problem of private property.[1] The primitive communism described in the words of the Acts of the Apostles, "Now the company of those who believed were of one heart and soul, and no one said that any of the things which he possessed was his own, but they had everything in common"[2]—especially because it is followed in Acts by the grim account of how Ananias and Sapphira were punished for deviating from it[3]—has drawn the interest of those modern Christian movements, such as the Social Gospel in liberal Protestantism and Liberation Theology in Roman Catholicism, who have tried to find in the early Christian attitude toward money and property a third possibility beyond the tired old antitheses between capitalism and socialism.

But it has become a commonplace of modern discussions about the relation of Christianity to politics to observe that neither the writers of the New Testament nor the other Christian authors of the first two or three centuries, in their considerations of the puzzling directive of Christ in the Gospel of Matthew about the difference between what was to be "rendered to Caesar" and what was to be "rendered to God,"[4] had quite prepared their readers for the serious possibility, which became a political reality with the fourth-century conversion of Constantine and the subsequent legislation of Theodosius, that Caesar would actually become a member of the Church and a guardian of the Church—indeed, even a bishop of sorts, as the emperor Constantine (although he had not yet been baptized at the time) said to the assembled episcopate of the Church when, as reported by Eusebius, he "let fall the expression 'that he himself too was a bishop,' addressing them in my hearing in the following words: 'You are bishops whose jurisdiction is within the church; I also am a bishop, ordained by God to oversee whatever is external to the church.' "[5] (Precisely what was "within" and what was "external" remained quite unclear, especially if one considers, for example, the role of Christian emperors and empresses,

---

[1]S. Giet, "La doctrine de l'appropriation des biens chez quelques-uns des Pères," *Recherches de science religieuse* 49 (1948):55–91.

[2]Acts 4.32.

[3]Acts 5.1–11.

[4]Mt 22.21.

[5]Eusebius, *The Life of Constantine* 24 (NPNF-II 1:546).

"equal to the apostles," in the seven ecumenical councils of the Church, beginning with Constantine himself at Nicaea.)

In a similar though not quite identical way, as Otto Schilling has shown in the most comprehensive monograph on the question,[6] those same early Christian writers, in their parallel considerations of the closely connected saying in the Gospel of Matthew about why it was "hard for a rich man to enter the kingdom of heaven" and easier for a camel to pass through the eye of a needle,[7] addressed their discussions of Christian stewardship of money chiefly to an audience for many of whom the primary problem was not money but the lack of it. In the apt words of Adolf von Harnack,

> This resolute renunciation of the world was really the first thing which made the church competent and strong to tell upon the world. Then, if ever, was the saying true: "He who would do anything for the world must have nothing to do with it." Primitive Christianity has been upbraided for being too unworldly and ascetic. But revolutions are not effected with rosewater, and it was a veritable revolution to overthrow polytheism and establish the majesty of God and goodness in the world—for those who believed in them, and also for those who did not. This could never have happened, in the first instance, had not men asserted the vanity of the present world, and practically severed themselves from it.[8]

This situation helps to explain why in this pre-Constantinian period, as Ernst Troeltsch put it in his pioneering work on *The Social Teachings of the Christian Churches*, "the problem of property . . . was only solved amid much hesitation and uncertainty," and even that not for a very long time.[9] But it is noteworthy that in his notes to that generalization Troeltsch, amid various other references to primary and secondary sources, was obliged to add that "the only work which deals with the problem directly is . . . that of Clement: *Can a Rich Man Be Saved?*"—a historical judgment that, on

---

[6]Otto Schilling, *Reichtum und Eigentum in der altchristlichen Literatur* (Freiburg im Breisgau: Herder, 1908).

[7]Mt 19.23–24.

[8]Adolf von Harnack, *The Mission and Expansion of Christianity in the First Three Centuries*, James Moffett, tr., Introduction by Jaroslav Pelikan (New York: Harper Torchbooks, 1961), 98.

[9]Ernst Troeltsch, *The Social Teachings of the Christian Churches*, Olive Wyon, tr., Introduction by H. Richard Niebuhr (New York: Harper Torchbooks, 1960), 115.

balance, must still be seen as holding true.[10] Occupying as it does this truly unique and even isolated position within the writings of the ante-Nicene Fathers of the Church, the treatise by Clement of Alexandria (d. ca. 215)–which, though written in Greek, is often referred to by the Latin title *Quis dives salvetur*[11]–may therefore serve as a convenient point of organization for the present study of the Christian stewardship of money in the ante-Nicene or pre-Constantinian Church.[12]

THE CHRISTOCENTRIC PRESUPPOSITIONS OF CHRISTIAN STEWARDSHIP

In this attempt to formulate a Christian interpretation of money–as in their ethical thought generally, and even in their doctrinal thought–the Christian apologetics and Christian theology of the second and third centuries were intent on making two quite distinct and yet complementary points: to assert the newness and qualitative difference of the gospel of Jesus Christ as the decisive and final revelation of God, which had taken place "in these last days,"[13] but also to affirm its continuity with the noblest intuitions and deepest aspirations, pagan as well as Jewish, that had preceded it: consequently, not only with the prophecy of Isaiah that "a virgin shall conceive and bear a Son,"[14] but with the prophecy of Vergil (which many of them, such as St Augustine, claimed to have been borrowed from Isaiah) that "now the Virgin descends" to give birth to a Child who would be the bringer of peace to the world.[15] Being, as Eric Osborn has shown, the founder of Christian philosophy,[16] Clement, in a well-known parallelism based on St Paul's discussion of the proper function of the law of Moses,[17]

---

[10]Two older studies are still quite useful: Franz Xaver Funk, "Clemens von Alexandrien über Familie und Eigentum," *Theologische Quartalschrift* 53 (1871):427–49; and L. Paul, "Welcher Reiche wird selig werden?" *Zeitschrift für wissenschaftliche Theologie* 44 (1901):504–44.

[11]See comments and bibliography in Johannes Quasten, *Patrology* (4 vols.; Westminster, Md.: The Newman Press, 1951–86), 2:15–16.

[12]Clement of Alexandria, *Who Is the Rich Man that Shall Be Saved?* (ANF 2:591–604). Because this is, therefore, in one sense a one-source paper despite its other references, I have, in citing the treatise, adopted–but also adapted–this translation, giving the paragraph number in brackets, so that the passages can be located in any of the other editions.

[13]Heb 1.2.

[14]Isa 7.14.

[15]Vergil, *Eclogues* IV.4–63.

[16]Eric Francis Osborn, *The Philosophy of Clement of Alexandria* (Cambridge: Cambridge University Press, 1957).

[17]Gal 3.23–26.

carried this program so far as to suggest that "before the advent of the Lord, philosophy was necessary to the Greeks," because it "was a 'schoolmaster [*paidagōgos*]' to bring 'the Hellenic mind,' as the law [brought] the Hebrews, 'to Christ.'"[18]

When he came from his broad (if not always profound) reading of classical and Hellenistic Greek literature to discuss the Christian attitude toward money and property and what was meant by denying the world for Christ, therefore, Clement was quite aware of the many striking parallels to be found between Christian and pre-Christian asceticism, Jewish and even pagan—parallels that were close enough to induce the church historian Eusebius, a century or so after Clement, to identify as Christian monks of the apostolic era a Jewish community of ascetics who went into the desert and "renounced their property," as they had been described by Philo of Alexandria in his treatise *On the Contemplative Life*.[19] "Nor was the renunciation of money and property and the bestowal of it on the poor or needy a new thing, for many did so before the Savior's advent, some because of the leisure [thereby obtained] for learning and others for empty fame and vainglory, as the Anaxagorases, the Democriti, and the Crateses [11]," Clement freely acknowledged. When Christ said that it was easier for a camel to pass through the eye of a needle than for a rich man to be saved, this saying required careful attention and study: it had to be interpreted within its total context in the text of the Gospels rather than narrowly or myopically, as was the wont of some [4], and it had to be "apprehended in a scholarly way [*mathēmatikōs*]" lest it be distorted or misunderstood [18]. If there was to be a mature case for a Christian view of money and for the responsible Christian use of property (which would probably serve as a capsule definition of stewardship), therefore, it could not be based simplistically on the absolute renunciation of money and property: the world had not really needed Christ and His gospel to learn about that. "Why then command as new, as divine, as alone life-giving, what did not save those of former days?" What was there about the commandment of Christ that was new and special, and even peculiar to the "new creation"[20] [12]?

Clement's answer to his own question about the uniqueness and newness of Christ was quite clear and unequivocal, more so, it must be admitted,

[18]Clement of Alexandria, *Stromata* I.5 (ANF 2:305).
[19]Eusebius, *Church History* II.xvii (NPNP-II 1:117–19).
[20]Cf. 2 Cor 5.17; Gal 6.15.

than those of several other Christian theologians and apologists during these centuries, at any rate as they are known to us through their writings. For him, what was "new, divine, and alone life-giving" about the Christian stewardship of money and property was its grounding in the person and work of Jesus Christ, which meant not merely an obedience to the teachings of the four Gospels about money and an imitation of Christ's example in treating it (although both of those were, of course, an indispensable element in it), but above all the acceptance of the gift of grace and of new life through His death and resurrection. For to a superficial observer—like Origen's opponent, Celsus, who paraphrased the invitation of the gospel as "Whoever is a sinner, whoever is unwise, whoever is a child, and, in a word, whoever is a wretch, the kingdom of God will receive him!"[21]—the persons to whom Christian stewardship gave its money or property might appear to be "ragged, or ugly, or feeble." But that was a shallow judgment that ignored the deeper reality, for "within dwells the hidden Father, and His Son [*pais*], who died for us and rose with us [33]." In a summons that manifested Clement's training in classical Greek rhetoric, with its emphasis on *pathos* as the emotional "frame of mind" of the hearer,[22] as well as his own profoundly Christocentric piety, he appealed:

> For each of us He gave His life—the equivalent for all. From us He demands the same in return, for one another. And if we owe our lives to the brethren, and have made such a mutual compact with the Savior, why should we go on hoarding and shutting up worldly goods, which are beggarly, alien to us, and transitory [37]?

With the coming of Christ in His life, death, and resurrection, this "divine transaction [32]" and unprecedented exchange had turned the whole human system of money and property completely upside down, not by outlawing it or banishing it (which would, in a sense, have been too easy and, besides, would not have worked, as the earlier forms of asceticism had already demonstrated [12]), but by a radical and fundamental revaluation of the moral and spiritual currency itself.

Money and property, therefore, were in and of themselves morally neutral. They were "instruments which are of good use to those who know the

---

[21]As quoted by Origen, *Against Celsus* III.59 (Henry Chadwick, tr.).
[22]Aristotle, *Rhetoric* I.ii.3 1356a.

instrument [14]." The analogy that Clement cited in the present treatise was physical beauty and good looks: "It is not on account of handsomeness of body that anyone shall live or, on the other hand, perish [18]." An even more appropriate analogy, as is evident from his other writings, was human reason and intelligence.[23] The New Testament, and above all St Paul,[24] had warned against its pride and pretension as vigorously and as frequently as it warned against the delusions of wealth; and this biblical warrant had been used in Clement's day (and, alas, not only in his day!) as a justification for Christian anti-intellectualism. But Clement recognized that these warnings did not invalidate the use of reason and intelligence, and even of logic, and he urged that "those who hunt after the connection of the divine teaching must approach it with the utmost perfection of the logical faculty."[25] For in the mystery of the divine dispensation or *oikonomia* (the etymological origin of the English words "economy" and "economics"), the logical faculty and a pleasing appearance and even money could become either demonic or divine: "If you use it skillfully, it is skillful; if you are deficient in skill, it is affected by your lack of skill, *being itself devoid of blame*. Such an instrument is money [14]."

Nor was Clement, in articulating these philosophical and theological presuppositions about money and property, too squeamish to become quite specific about their concrete implications for Christian stewardship in the real world. He spelled out those implications in a lengthy and specific set of definitions of the mysterious title from the first of the Beatitudes that opened the Sermon on the Mount, "Blessed are the poor in spirit, for theirs is the kingdom of heaven."[26] The genuinely "poor in spirit" was

> he who holds possessions, and gold, and silver, and houses, as the gifts of God; and ministers from them to the God who gives them for the salvation of men; and knows that he possesses them more for the sake of the brethren than his own; and is superior to the possession of them, not the slave of the things he possesses; and does not carry them about in his soul, nor bind and circumscribe his life within them, but is ever laboring at some good and divine work, even if he should at some time

[23]H. Richard Niebuhr, *Christ and Culture* (New York: Harper, 1951), has put this entire issue into a new light by setting Clement into the context of a comprehensive taxonomy.

[24]1 Cor 1.17–2.16.

[25]Clement of Alexandria, *Stromata* I.28 (ANF 2:340–41).

[26]Mt 5.3.

or another be compelled to lose them, and is able with a cheerful mind to bear their removal equally with their abundance [16].

In this remarkable passage, which could probably without a great deal of difficulty be transported into any era of Christian history (and, for that matter, into any Christian confession), Clement set forth five component and tightly interrelated principles of the Christian stewardship of money and property.

THE OPERATIVE PRINCIPLES OF CHRISTIAN STEWARDSHIP

Money was a gift of God, and therefore not intrinsically evil.

Implicit in this first assertion, however, was a rejection of the most widespread heresy in the ante-Nicene Church, a dualism (shared by Marcion and many of the Gnostics) between Creation and Redemption that would have separated the realm of divine grace from the material world of stuff, of sexual intercourse, and of reptiles and insects.[27] Behind this dualism was an even more profound metaphysical separation between the Creator and the Redeemer, between the lesser God who had made the visible world and the Father of Jesus Christ. When so many of the early creeds began with some form of the affirmation, "I believe in God the Father Almighty, Maker of heaven and earth," to quote the so-called Apostles' Creed of the West, they were, at least by implication, declaring it to be the faith of the Orthodox and Catholic Church that "the Creator" of the physical world and "the Father" of Jesus Christ were not two separate beings, but one and the same God. Although Christian Orthodoxy properly and unequivocally repudiated this dualism, also in the later and more sophisticated form that it took in the Manichaean heresy, what could be styled a "soft dualism" often reasserted itself within the life of the Church, in an exaltation of the "spiritual" that depreciated or even despised the material world, above all the world of sexuality but also the world of things—and the world of money. Therefore it has been necessary over and over for the Orthodox Christian interpretation of the stewardship of money to reaffirm Clement's proposition that "possessions, and gold, and silver, and houses [are] the gifts of God." In Clement's commonsensical rhetorical question, "If no one had anything, what room would be left among men for giving [13]?" Or, as he

---

[27]Tertullian, *Against Marcion* I.xiv.1 (ANF 3:281).

phrased the same concern more profoundly on the basis of the doctrine of God the Creator, "Why should money have ever sprung from the earth at all if it is the author and patron of death [26]?"

Like all other gifts, money and property were here to be used in freedom for the service of "the God who gives them for the salvation of men."

In "the divine and mystic wisdom [5]" of this salvation, the God who made all things but who needed none of them nevertheless required them of His servants, though only by their own free and unconstrained choice. "For God compels not (for compulsion is repugnant to God)"; rather, "the choice depends on the man as being free, but the gift on God as the Lord [10]." To a degree that some of his editors and interpreters, particularly those who held to a doctrine of the bondage of the human will, have found theologically embarrassing, Clement of Alexandria emphasized that "to save the unwilling is the part of one exercising compulsion, but to save the willing that of one showing grace," so that in this sense "God conspires with willing souls" to save them by His grace [21]. Against both of the extreme attitudes toward money—"neglecting salvation, as if they had already been foredoomed" or "condemning [money] as a traitor and an enemy to life"— the high art of the Christian life was to "learn in what way and how to use money and obtain life," which consisted in "rendering only this small tribute of gratitude for the greatest benefits, and being unable to imagine anything else whatever by way of recompense to God, who needs nothing [27]." Gerard Manley Hopkins was to formulate this same imperative in his poem "Morning, Midday, and Evening Sacrifice" of 1879:

> This pride of prime's enjoyment
> Take as for tool, not toy meant
> And hold at Christ's employment.[28]

That was the paradoxical divine-human transaction [32], in which the divine Donor solicited voluntary gifts from the recipients of His bounty as though He were in need of the very things that He had created and had given to them in the first place.

---

[28]*Poems of Gerard Manley Hopkins* (3rd ed.; London: Oxford University Press, 1948), 88.

*The ground of the paradox of Christian stewardship was that the God who became
incarnate in Jesus Christ, and who required that He alone be worshiped and
served, demanded this service "more for the sake of the brethren."*

As Christ's classification of the "greatest commandments" in response to a
critical inquirer made clear,[29] followed as it was three chapters later in
Matthew's Gospel by the word of the Son of Man at the Last Judgment,
"Truly, I say to you, as you did it to one of the least of these my brethren,
you did it to me,"[30] the identification of the beneficiaries of Christian stewardship as those "within [whom] dwells the hidden Father, and His Son,
who died for us and rose with us [33]," implied a direct correlation between
"loving Christ" and "loving and caring for those who have believed in Him
[30]." Quite simply and evangelically put, "we owe our lives to the brethren
[37]." In his effort to resolve the challenge of Christ's lesson about how difficult it was for a rich man to enter the kingdom, Clement of Alexandria
anticipated many of the themes of Christian stewardship that are associated, for example, with the preaching of St John Chrysostom to the rich
and powerful, as Blake Leyerle has recently systematized these.[31] With
Christian believers throughout history, Clement took Christ's parable of
the Good Samaritan as a supreme paradigm for selfless generosity.[32] In
keeping with the Christocentric emphasis of his message that "for each of
us He gave His life [37]," Clement grounded the moral imperative of this
parable in an interpretation that saw Christ Himself as the ultimate Good
Samaritan, who found a wounded humanity lying by the side of the road
and in His compassion bound up its wounds and healed it with His wine
and oil [29].

But Clement could also apply the paradigm to the exceedingly practical requirements of Christian stewardship in the here and now of his hearers, by pointing out something that was obvious about the narrative of the
Good Samaritan, or that at any rate became obvious once it had been
pointed out by Clement: that before he ever found the man half-dead by
the side of the road, the Samaritan already "came provided with such things
as the man in danger required," which included not only the medicinal
wine and oil, but also the "money for the innkeeper, part given now and

[29]Mt 22.37–40.
[30]Mt 25.40.
[31]Blake Leyerle, "Chrysostom on Alms-Giving," *Harvard Theological Review* 87
(1994): 29–47.
[32]Lk 10.30–37.

part promised [28]." To the Good Samaritan, but also by extension to every Christian steward, therefore, the searching question applied: "If no one had anything, what room would be left among men for giving [13]?" This insight was what made it possible for the Good Samaritan or any other Christian steward to practice stewardship without excessive anxiety or constant calculation about whether its recipients were truly worthy of it (as though anyone had ever been worthy of the compassion of Christ!): "In the uncertainty of ignorance it is better to do good to the undeserving for the sake of the deserving, than by guarding against those that are less good to fail to meet [the needs of] the good [33]." That was why, in the Pauline triad of "faith, hope, love," it was love that was said to be "the greatest."[33] For both faith and hope would eventually attain their goals, while love, in this life and then in the life everlasting, would only go on growing [38], without ceasing and, as especially St Gregory of Nyssa was to emphasize, without ever reaching satiety.

The Christian steward possessed—and gave—money and property in such a manner as to be "superior to the possession of them."

Such generosity—which could even, at the risk of anachronism, be styled "disinterested benevolence"—was made possible by the Christian's divinely sovereign attitude toward wealth. Such an attitude was based on a strict hierarchy of values, in which the supreme position was occupied not by property or cash, but by those "riches which deify and which minister everlasting life [19]." This characteristically (though not exclusively) Eastern Christian definition of salvation as *theōsis*, deification by being made "partakers of the divine nature,"[34] is often dismissed as a remnant of Neoplatonism and as a mystical and otherworldly quietism that severs the moral nerve; and undeniably it has sometimes been that. But Clement's use of it shows how eminently practical it could be, for it represented a "liberation from" that was also a "liberation for," which was able to put money in its place—and that place was the service of God "and all mankind," in the words of the Liturgy of St John Chrysostom. These authentic "riches which deify" were what made someone "free, unsubdued, free of disease, unwounded by wealth," regardless of external circumstances; that "superiority to the possession of" money and property meant that "one is able in

[33]1 Cor 13.13.
[34]2 Pet 1.4.

the midst of wealth to turn from its power," to "practice self-discipline, and
to seek God alone, and to breathe God and walk with God [26]."

*The Christian steward was one who was able to manage money and property
in such a way as "to be able with a cheerful mind to bear their loss equally
with their abundance."*

For contrary to the conventional wisdom, be it that of the smug and self-
satisfied or that of the false species of ascetic, both of these extreme circumstances, abundance of money no less than loss of money, could be a snare.
It was the "superiority to the possession of them" that would enable the
Christian steward, whether rich or poor, to "escape the superfluity of riches
and the difficulty they interpose in the way of life, and to be able to enjoy
the eternal good things [39]." As Clement pointed out very vividly at the
beginning of his treatise, it was shallow and sycophantic to "bestow lauda-
tory addresses on the rich," because even without any help from such flat-
tery "wealth is of itself sufficient to puff up and corrupt the souls of its
possessors, and to turn them from the path by which salvation is to be
attained [1]." But he went on to remind his hearers as well that "it is no great
thing or desirable to be destitute of wealth if [this happens] without a special object [11]." Therefore he denounced the rich man "who carries his
riches in his soul, and instead of God's Spirit bears in his heart gold or land,
and is always acquiring possessions without end, and is perpetually on the
lookout for more [17]." It was a "spurious wealth" to transform the meaning and purpose of life into such "outward possession, which is transitory
and perishing, and now belongs to one, now to another—and in the end to
nobody at all [19]!" But it was also a spurious and "wretched" poverty to
"have no part in God, and still less in human property, and not to have
tasted the righteousness of God [17]." For all the painful economic and
social contrast between the comfort of the rich and the plight of the poor,
to which Clement was not by any means insensitive, they were therefore in
fact very much alike, in that both of them were "the slaves of the things that
they possessed [or did not possess but wanted to, as the case may be], carrying them about in their souls and binding and circumscribing their lives
within them [16]."

SOME IMPLICATIONS FOR THE HISTORY AND THE PRACTICE OF ORTHODOX STEWARDSHIP

At just about the time that Clement wrote this little masterpiece, the social and economic situation of the Church was beginning to change. It would be more than a century before Constantine and his successors gave the Church its legal rights as a "religion that is permissible [*religio licita*]," and then increasingly preferential treatment as the state religion of the Roman empire. But already during the reign of the Roman emperor Commodus (180–92), according to the report of Eusebius,

> our condition became more favorable, and through the grace of God the churches throughout the entire world enjoyed peace, and the word of salvation was leading every soul from every race of man to the devout worship of the God of the universe. So that now at Rome many who were highly distinguished for wealth and family turned with all their household and relatives unto their salvation.[35]

Although this amelioration of conditions was only temporary, having been followed by persecutions under Emperors Decius and then Diocletian, it does seem that the development, with Clement of Alexandria, of a distinctively Christian understanding of money and of its stewardship came none too soon, to be able to minister to the needs also of this new Christian constituency.

But in the long run, as later chapters in this book will document at some length, the conversion of Constantine brought to the Christian East not only the end of persecution, at least for a brief respite before other persecutors and other martyrs arose, but also some highly ambiguous consequences, not least in the area of the stewardship of money. Orthodox Christianity had welcomed the relief brought by toleration, but also the privileged status within political society that followed—at least until a change of official policy that turned against Orthodox teaching demonstrated yet again the fickleness of rulers and the abiding timeliness of the warning from the Psalms in the Liturgy, "Put not your trust in princes."[36] There is good reason to argue that only with the Iconoclastic Controversies

---

[35]Eusebius, *Church History* V.xxi.1 (NPNF-II 1:239).

[36]George Huntston Williams, "Christology and Church-State Relations in the Fourth Century," *Church History* 20-III (1951): 3–33; 20-IV: 3–26.

of the seventh, eighth, and ninth centuries did Byzantine Orthodoxy fully confront the dimensions of the problem, and of the need to protect its administrative autonomy even and especially against interference by an Orthodox ruler. Central to this need was not only political authority but economic power. As long as the Church was dependent for its livelihood on revenues collected by the State, that administrative autonomy, and with it the freedom to teach and pray, would always be in some sort of jeopardy.

Ironically, therefore, the success of modern anticlericalism and rationalism in undoing the alliance of Church and State proved to be an unexpected blessing for the Church, not only by setting it free from meddling by politicians, but by setting it free for a recovery of dynamic elements from its Tradition that had often been neglected because they did not seem to be needed. It is surely not a coincidence that the development of Christian stewardship as not only a strategic but a sacramental force in the life of all the churches took place in a context where the Church could no longer rely on a steady stream of income from "church taxes" or even from "dues" to carry out its ministry. In this "post-Constantinian" universe, therefore, the distinctive features of the "pre-Constantinian" context of the second and third centuries have drawn a new interest and acquired a new relevance. And in that setting, the modest little treatise by Clement of Alexandria, *Quis dives salvetur*, Latin title and all, with its vigorous emphasis on stewardship as a matter of free choice rather than of constraint, can, please God, find its voice again.

STEWARDSHIP AND THE TITHE IN THE OLD TESTAMENT

MICHAEL PROKURAT*

"All shall give as they are able, according to the blessing of the Lord your God that He has given you." (Deut 16.17)

"Do not grow weary when you pray, do not neglect to give alms." (Sir 7.10)

"With every gift show a cheerful face, and dedicate your tithe with gladness." (Sir 35.11)

"Prayer with fasting is good, but better than both is almsgiving with righteousness." (Tob 12.8)

"Thus also in spiritual things, one serves God and labors in believing and ordering his own life well, and another in undertaking the care of strangers, and another in the patronage of the needy. Even for the Apostle's own tithe, Stephen's company served God in being guardians of the widows, others in teaching the word, wherein Paul was also, serving in the preaching of the Gospel. And this was his mode of service: For it was to this that he was appointed." (St John Chrysostom, *Homily on Romans* 1.9)

*The Very Rev Michael Prokurat was a pastor and priest for thirty-three years, professor of Sacred Scripture at the University of St Thomas, and editor and primary author of *The Historical Dictionary of the Orthodox Church*. Fr Michael fell asleep in the Lord on July 23, 2003.

S tewardship commands a prevalent place as a multifaceted theme throughout the Old Testament. Whether we focus our attention on the divine prerogatives of stewardship, the care and dominion over creation given to men and women, human responsibilities in handling their time-treasure-talents, or the transformation of humanity and creation through this ministry, the topic remains extremely broad. For example, in surveying only one small part of the Bible, the book of Genesis, one could variously describe stewardship as the toil of Adam and Eve before and after the Fall, the tithe accepted by Melchizedek at Salem (Jerusalem), or the sacrifice of Isaac by Abraham. In view of this breadth, we shall limit our inquiry to focus on Old Testament attitudes toward stewardship as sacrificial giving, especially tithing.

PRESUPPOSITIONS

Devotional and philanthropic practices appear widespread in Biblical cultures ranging over a millennium, from the time of David until the time of Jesus. Stewardship, sacrificial giving, and tithing all may be found in the Old Testament but are not always easily recognizable. Some references are explicit and easy to understand, but many of the most important ones are hidden within the unexpressed cultural attitudes and beliefs or are presuppositions to the ancient Near Eastern world.

Beliefs and attitudes ancient people held but did not always articulate or explain constitute presuppositions of the biblical world. They might seem strange to us, or they might appear to us as the way things are "supposed to be" but are not. They might even be current beliefs and attitudes of people of faith, but in any case, they are not the same as the beliefs and attitudes of secular America today. For these reasons they deserve special comment.

The first important presupposition held throughout biblical times is that God possesses everything, or in contemporary terms, "owns all of it": land, people, animals, environment, and so forth. In brief, God owns everything because He created it. It all belongs to Him. And since that is so, a related presupposition follows: His people believe that they receive everything from His hand as a gift—to care for during earthly life and then to be returned.

What a strange concept for Americans who are intent on being owners of as many consumer goods as possible! Most Americans would be quick to point out that they own their own land, home, car, furniture, and so on. It belongs to them by legal right, and they will show you the documents to prove it. When they die, it will be passed on to their children or someone else. It is their right! People in biblical times, whatever their religion, saw their world in relation to God (or gods), and personal "rights" took a back seat to both divine and community interests.

We also observe that during biblical times most land was not inhabited, and no one claimed to own it.[1] People lived in small cities and towns and went out to farm by hand what little land they developed and cultivated. Today all the land on earth appears to be owned by someone, and it is not God. Historically this attitude is very recent, approximate to the time in the nineteenth century when cartographers and national leaders compiled a complete, accurate map of the world; and then they proceeded to draw lines, portioning it out among modern nations.

However, two distinct attitudes in the ancient world evolved as regards the deity and ownership, and these are reflected in the Garden of Eden story in Genesis. The first attitude, proper to Christians and Jews, is that creation—including even our own life—is a gift from God, to be accepted and cared for with proper attention, with our stewardship. The gift giver is obviously God, and the beneficence of the gift is dependent on Him completely. The man and the woman in the Garden enjoyed this relationship with God and creation until the Fall, when their attitude changed.

The second attitude, which came with the Fall, claimed that human beings were solely in control of creation and themselves. They put themselves first, in place of God, and consequently there was "hell to pay." This theme occurs throughout Genesis 1–11: beginning with the prototypical man and woman, Adam and Eve, moving in ever expanding circles through the nuclear family (Cain and Abel), the larger family unit, the community, the city, and ending in the representative mega-culture of the day, Babel. In each instance human beings put themselves in place of God—exercising the ultimate sin of pride—and were punished because of it. Nevertheless, in every case God was merciful and provided a way for salvation. Thus, responsible stewardship could be restored with repentance.

These biblical presuppositions, including the belief that all human beings belong to God, are foreign to people today, in spite of the fact that

---

[1]For a discussion of the theological significance of "the land" in the Old Testament, see Walter Brueggemann, *The Land* (Philadelphia: Fortress Press, 1977).

we have specific reminders of them in our language and culture. For example, when a child is born, most parents—even if they are not believers—recognize that this life is a gift from God. In many of the world's cultures, including American culture, it is commonplace to answer the child's question, "Where did I come from?" with the serious response, "From God." Similarly, traditional Judeo-Christian law, Western and Eastern, makes it illegal to take a human life, even one's own, because that life properly belongs to God and is not the "property" of the individual or state. Giving the state the right to take human life—whether through abortion, euthanasia, capital punishment, or any other means—is tantamount to giving the state God's right, or to put it another way, is tantamount to making the government into a god.

Many ancient cultures took this understanding of "divine rights" to its logical, but most extreme, conclusion: human sacrifice. On occasion the practice is referred to in the Bible among the People of God, in spite of the clear prohibition indicated in the story of Abraham's near sacrifice of his son Isaac in Genesis 22.[2] While the topic of human sacrifice is much too complex to treat here, the basic sensibility that all human life belongs to God is upheld in Scripture, though in a form that prohibits sacrificial murder. Within the story of the Passover (Exodus 12–13) we learn that all the firstborn of both humans and animals belong to God but that humans are "redeemed" through an appropriate, substitutionary sacrifice.[3]

About half of the text of the first five books of the Bible (the Pentateuch, or Torah) consists of various laws central to which are the laws of sacrifice. Although Christians no longer perform these different sacrifices, the dynamics that motivate them are instructive to our understanding of stewardship. In different forms, the most important of these sacrifices are blood sacrifices. The ancient Hebrews viewed blood concretely, as equivalent to life itself: take away the blood and life is gone (Lev 17.10–16; similarly, Gen 9.4–6). Since they believed that all life comes from God, blood—or life itself—was the sacrifice appropriate to God alone. Humans were forbidden

[2]This is the tenth reading prescribed for the vespers and Divine Liturgy of Great and Holy Saturday, the paschal baptismal service. The same reference occurs in the prayer for the paschal blessing of meats.

[3]The Church's liturgical cycle calls for the reading of this text—and others similar to it—first at Great Vespers of the feast of the Meeting of the Lord. By so doing the compilers of the lectionary imply that even Jesus had to be sacrificially redeemed according to the precepts of the Mosaic Law.

from using blood for any purpose other than sacrifice to God (Deut 15.23). Life, in this way, was offered up to God without involving any human sacrifice; rather, animal sacrifices were substituted.

Finally, people living in ancient times allowed the sensibility that God literally possesses humanity to shape their culture and daily lives (and the same may be said of Christians today). They called themselves "servants" of God and based their entire sacrificial system, both the priesthood and the sacrifices themselves, on this understanding. Similarly, Christian liturgical services use the same terminology of "servants" to describe the faithful. Further, everything dedicated or gifted to God was based on the premise that He already owned it. He did not really need sacrifice and gifts to exist, but gave them to us for our own existence. Today, as then, we enjoy a proper relationship with Him—and the gifts—when we offer them back to God. And God, of course, gives them back to us. A review of the books of the Old Testament provides us with specific tenets of sacrificial giving.

THE PENTATEUCH

Leviticus 27

Chapters 17 through 26 of the book of Leviticus are a corpus of laws known as the Holiness Code, based upon the central theme of holiness. The People of God, Israel, are expected to be holy, even as God is holy. In a lengthy appendix to the Holiness Code (chapter 27) religious vows regarding people and property represent "the commandments that the Lord gave to Moses for the people of Israel on Mount Sinai" (27.34). Among them one finds vows of years of service, vows of animal sacrifices (other than firstlings, which automatically belong to God, as in Ex 13.11–16), vows of houses, vows of inheritance and landholdings, and tithes. Although tithes are grouped with vows, the tithes are not vowed, since their portioning off and dedication to God is assumed and expected.

These ancient practices legitimately parallel to contemporary forms of giving.[4] For instance, vows of human years of service comprise what we today might call ministry and community service. Vows of animals and produce, by which they measured their livelihood as an agricultural society before the invention of money, equal payment in-kind. Vows of houses and

---

[4]Although social and religious institutions of the Old Testament differ in significant ways from those of contemporary Western culture, they are similar enough in intent to be seen as comparable.

inheritance can be compared to contemporary bequests. And vows of landholdings and assessments parallel living trusts. Tithes of herds and flocks
and produce of fields and orchards are, again, payment of one-tenth of their
labors in-kind, much as we might give a tithe of our paycheck. In each case
the tithes are considered "holy to the Lord."

Numbers 18

The eighteenth chapter of the book of Numbers explains how a tithe from
Israel is to go to the Levites, who have no tribal inheritance of their own.
Aaron and the Levites served as priests and ministers of the sanctuary. The
chapter falls within the division including chapters 1 through 25, describing
the time "in the wilderness" (which is the Hebrew name of the book of
Numbers), before they arrived on Mount Sinai.

As part of a larger episode of forty years, this section of the story tells
of murmuring against God and a refusal to take possession of the land.
These complaints, the murmurings, extended to issues of leadership and
priestly service, whereupon the Lord, through a budding rod of almond,
chose Aaron and the ancestral house of Levi to serve in the sanctuary and
in the tent of meeting, respectively. No other tribe or Israelite had this
prerogative, on pain of death. In exchange, Aaron and the Levites bore
the responsibility for any offenses connected with the priesthood and the
sanctuary.

Aaronic priests and their families made their living by offering all the
sacrifices, which (except for those parts burned entirely) became their possession. In contrast to many other cultures, the Israelites did not believe
that their sacrifices physically satisfied their deity, but rather that their sacrifices supported their priests.[5] The Levites, who did not perform sacrifices,
lived off tithes, while a tithe of what the Levites received, or a "tithe of the
tithe," also went to the Aaronic priests.

Neither the priests nor the Levites had an allotment of land among the
Israelites, but only sacrifices and tithes. Because of this arrangement, the
priests and Levites maintained an economic advantage over the rest of the
tribes, even though they were not landowners. This was so if only for the
fact that their (one) tribe lived off the best portions and received ten per

---

[5]Bernhard W. Anderson. Annotated note on Lev 2.2–3, in Bruce M. Metzger and Roland
E. Murphy, eds., *The New Oxford Annotated Bible with the Apocryphal/Deuterocanonical Books:
New Revised Standard Version* (New York: Oxford University Press, 1991) 127.

cent of what the other eleven tribes produced. Thus, among the Israelites there was an expectation that the religious leadership performed a valuable service before God and that their reward for this service provided them with a high standard of living—with more wealth than their fellow Israelites. One may contrast this attitude with those churches and Christians today who expect—or even force—their clergy to live at a lower standard of living than the average parishioner.

Deuteronomy 12.1–31

The book of Deuteronomy is presented as three farewell addresses of Moses. It is most probably the "book of the law," i.e., a scroll, found in the Temple of Jerusalem during the reign of King Josiah (2 Kgs 22–23), which was used to help centralize worship in Jerusalem in the reform of 621 B.C. However, the descriptions of tithing found in chapters 12, 14, and 26 have more to teach us.

Chapter 12 is found within the second address of Moses (chapters 5 through 28).[6] It describes the centralization of worship, a theme distinctive of and important to the book. Instructions are repeated here about how to avoid idolatry, how to slaughter and eat meat, and most especially, how to make sacred donations. Herein is a surprise.

Many educated Christians understand that their weekly donations in church are an integral part of liturgy —a personal, vowed offering in the context of the eucharistic meal. This eucharistic offering is representative of our entire week's work, given as part of the thanksgiving of the Communion service. Very few—even among the clergy—are aware of the fact that this same understanding is found in the Old Testament!

> But you shall seek the place that the Lord your God will choose out of all your tribes as His habitation to put His name there. You shall go there, bringing there your burnt offerings and your sacrifices, your tithes and your donations, your votive gifts, your freewill offerings, and the firstlings of your herds and flocks. And you shall eat there in the presence of the Lord your God, you and your households together, rejoicing in all the undertakings in which the Lord your God has blessed you. (Deut 12.5b-7)

---

[6]Reading part of Exodus 12 is prescribed for the vespers and Divine Liturgy of Great and Holy Saturday.

This passage directs the Israelites to go to the appointed place where God dwells, to take all their sacred donations emblematic of their life's work, and to eat there with other households in the presence of God. How strikingly similar this is to the Christian eucharistic assembly, wherein there is also "rejoicing in all the undertakings in which the Lord your God has blessed you."

Deuteronomy 14.1–15.23

In the pericope of Deuteronomy 14.1–15.23 we have a description of the way of life of a holy people. Since a tithe is due the landowner (Gen 28.22; Lev 27.30; Am 4.4)—and the Lord owns the land of Israel—Israel is the steward who pays the annual tithe to God.[7] Besides a tithe of firstlings of herd and flock, the people are responsible for a tithe of "wheat, wine, and oil," representing what we Americans would call the "meat and mashed potatoes" of the Mediterranean diet. These three foods occur as a thematic group throughout the Old Testament, even from the early poetic texts (e.g., Gen 27.28), and represent human agricultural bounty. The same symbolism is preserved in Orthodox Christian liturgical practice on the eve of the feasts, when wheat, wine, and oil are blessed. Having been offered by the faithful, the bounties of the land are distributed back to the people in celebration of the feast.

Nevertheless, Deuteronomy 14 goes beyond this practice and introduces a conversion of the tithe into money (literally: "silver") so that it might be transported more easily. Thus, the monetary tithe is a very old practice stemming from the recognition that the Lord "owns everything" and receives the steward's tithe due the landowner. In this case, the "landowner" is the Creator.

Deuteronomy 14.27–29 modifies and expands the Israelite understanding of the tithe to a central sanctuary (usually identified with Jerusalem) by introducing an important new provision. Every three years the tithe is distributed to the poor and needy. This group includes not only widows and orphans, as we would expect, but also destitute resident aliens and the local Levites who have neither an inheritance of land (that is, an agricultural

---

[7]For Christians, the "New Israel," see the similar prayers for "Offering First Fruits" and the "Sanctification of Fragrant Herbage." These prayers in the Eastern Church are said at the feasts of the Transfiguration (August 6) and the Dormition (August 15), and are directly related to offering the agricultural tithe found in the Old Testament (on which the name "first fruits" itself is based).

inheritance) nor a salary from the central sanctuary. The Levites here might be described as country clergy who had lost their livelihood.[8] The reason given for this provision is: "so that the Lord your God may bless you in all the work that you undertake" (v. 29). The implication is that if the community neglects the poor and needy, God has no reason to bless the work of that community. Chapter 26 of Deuteronomy records two short liturgies for tithing: the initial liturgy offers first fruits with the priest at the central sanctuary; the tithe to the poor and needy in the local community. Each liturgy ends with a prayer that recognizes that the Lord has given the people "a land flowing with milk and honey" (vv. 9, 15), and they in turn express their thanks with the tithe.

As we read through the Pentateuch, the impression we get—indeed, the impression we are meant to have about sacred donations—is that Abraham the patriarch was the first to pay tithes of the spoils of war (cf. Psalm 110). The patriarch Jacob soon followed at the sanctuary of Bethel, promising a tithe of everything received (Gen 28.18–22). Second, in the wilderness on the way to Mount Sinai (Num 18), the Lord commanded that tithes be given to the Levites. Next, the Lord commanded Moses on Mount Sinai that the people of Israel give sacrificially, their tithes and more. Last, Moses explained extensively in Deuteronomy how—by and to whom—these gifts were to be given.

THE PROPHETS

Before proceeding to a consideration of sacrificial giving and tithing in the prophets, a contextual note is in order. Although the references to tithing in the prophets are confined to two, and citations of sacrificial giving are limited, the few number of references by no means indicates a blind spot in the prophetic books. The preoccupation of the prophetic books with issues of social and economic justice makes this clear and emphatic. Many of the social justice issues have to do with the distribution of food and wealth, especially notable in reference to the welfare of widows and orphans. The Major Prophets—Isaiah, Jeremiah, and Ezekiel—and many of the twelve Minor Prophets brought such concerns forward in the book of Deuteronomy.

Further, these references do not designate individual charity, terms in which we Americans usually think, but communal charity. For this reason

[8]Gerhard von Rad, *Deuteronomy. Old Testament Library*, Dorothy Barton, tr. (Philadelphia, Pa.: Westminster Press, 1966), 103.

the prophetic admonitions to social justice toward the widows and orphans and others marginalized in society do not coincide with sacrificial giving simply on an individual basis. The sin against the widows and orphans—that is, their systematic exploitation and impoverishment—was all the more serious because of its communal or corporate character.

Amos 4

In the fourth chapter of the pre-exilic prophet Amos, which might be read as a unit, sacrificial giving and tithing are mentioned (4.4), but as characteristic of vain piety. Amos said that such piety was practiced in vain because the Israelites (in this instance focusing attention on the behavior of the women) oppress the poor and needy and engage in luxurious excesses.[9] Amos described this sacrificial piety ironically as sin, in spite of its frequency and intensity: the oppressive rich brought sacrifices daily and tithes every three days. Thank offerings and freewill offerings were in abundance and announced publicly (4.4–5), and the people delighted in presenting all these sacrificial gifts to the Lord. However, when these offerings were presented in the sanctuaries of Bethel and Gilgal, Amos labeled them "transgressions." The reason these otherwise salvific actions were considered transgressions was the sinful community context in which they were given, given even as the needy and poor were crushed. Moreover, while the needy were being oppressed, those enjoying luxuries were characterized callously as ordering around their spouses, "Bring me something to drink!" (Am 4.1).

As sacred as the sacrificial gifts and tithes were thought to be, their effects could not overcome the social injustice that destroyed real people, poor people. Amos prophesied that these transgressors, in spite of their tithes, would be led away into captivity as slaves. When Assyria invaded and destroyed Samaria and Israel some years later in 721 B.C., so they were. Later prophets, including Jesus, understood that Amos' prophecy against pious excess and hatred for the poor may judge every generation.

Malachi 3.6–12

"Will anyone rob God? Yet you are robbing me! But you say, 'How are we robbing you?' In your tithes and offerings! You are cursed with a curse, for you are robbing me—the whole nation of you!" (Mal 3.8–9)

---

[9]For example, the couches of the Samaritan householders were so expensively ornamented that they were inlaid with carved ivory.

References to tithing in Malachi 3.8, 10 are part of the question-and-answer "instruction," known as the literary genre *torah*, characteristic of the book. The whole work, dating from the first half of the fifth century B.C., is titled a prophetic "oracle" and might have some continuity with the oracles at the end of the book of Zechariah.[10] Certainly the content of Malachi, relating to proper support of the Lord's house, is reminiscent of several oracles of the prophet Haggai, the late sixth century B.C. contemporary of Zechariah. Both encourage people to return to the Lord and to evidence their return by the appropriate gifts—gifts given to the Lord's house.

The language Malachi used is very strong, comparing the withholding of tithes to robbery, no less than the robbery of God. Subsequently, withholding tithes—the same tithes ordered in the laws of Leviticus 27 and Numbers 18—resulted in a curse. The curse was connected with various aspects of crop failure. Likewise, Haggai had drawn attention to the farming crisis of an earlier generation resulting from their neglect of the Lord's Temple in Jerusalem (Hag 1.5–11). Both Haggai and Malachi prophesied that cheating God results in a curse, the cessation of God's blessing in agricultural collapse.

THE WRITINGS
Nehemiah 13.1–31

In the middle of the fifth century B.C. Nehemiah traveled to Jerusalem from Persia and, following upon the religious reforms of Ezra a generation before, proceeded to rebuild the walls of the city. This building program allowed Jerusalem to reclaim its position as a religious and political capital, which it had lost in the Babylonian destruction a century and a quarter earlier (587 B.C.). To this effect, the officials, the Levites, the priests, and all the faithful of Jerusalem entered into a covenant to uphold the Law of God (Neh 9.38–10.39; similarly, 12.44–47). Since there was no longer a monarchy to support the Temple or to enforce the Mosaic laws sustaining the less fortunate, it fell to the leaders and people to pay for the Temple services, sacrifices, and philanthropy according to the prescribed norms.[11] These laws seem to have been constantly violated during the ministries of the prophets Haggai and Malachi. Prominent in the renewed covenant was a

[10]Joseph Blenkinsopp, *A History of Prophecy in Israel* (Louisville, Ky.: The Westminster Press, 1996), 209.

[11]This situation is reminiscent of the Russian Church after the Russian Revolution, when the czar no longer supported the churches. The people had to accept the responsibility themselves for maintaining the institution.

voluntary temple tax, offerings of first fruits and firstborn, the tithes for the Levites, and the tithe of the tithes for the Temple.

Nehemiah made a second administrative trip to Jerusalem at the behest of the Persian emperor Artaxerxes about a decade after his first visit (between 433–423 B.C.). During this second visit he reaffirmed the previous, agreed upon covenant that the people had disobeyed—violated especially in the collection of the tithes of wheat, wine, and oil for the Levites, singers, and gatekeepers, and the contributions for the priests. New faithful treasurers were appointed for the distribution of the tithe to the temple staff, which recently had been neglected. In addition to the tithe, special attention was paid to reaffirming the observance of the Sabbath and cleansing the priesthood and the people from foreign cultic influences. Today we may be reminded of the *diaspora* churches spread throughout the world, tempted by influences "foreign" to Christianity and struggling with the occasional administration that is less than honest.

2 Chronicles 31.1–21

Just as three chapters in 2 Kings describe Hezekiah (715–687 B.C.) as a good king, four chapters in 2 Chronicles continue this tradition and compare him with the later reformer King Josiah (640–609 B.C.). The Chronicler, writing about 400 B.C., used chapter 31 to describe the stewardship Hezekiah exercised in his religious reform.

After breaking down the shrines to foreign gods in Judah, he re-established the service of the priests and Levites with contributions from his own possessions. Further,

> he commanded the people who lived in Jerusalem to give the portion due to the priests and Levites, so that they may devote themselves to the law of the Lord. As soon as the word spread, the people of Israel gave in abundance the first fruits of grain, wine, oil, honey, and of all the produce of the field; and they brought in abundantly the tithe of everything. The people of Israel and Judah who lived in the cities of Judah also brought in the tithes of cattle and sheep, and the tithe of the dedicated things that had been consecrated to the Lord their God, and laid them in heaps. (2 Chr 31.4–6)

As the story unfolds, the stewardship reform was so successful that Hezekiah systematized it, building storage chambers in the Temple where the tithes and dedicated contributions were gathered for distribution. Teams of Levitical overseers were appointed to allot the gifts proportionately: temple offerings for the sustenance of the priests and Levites serving from throughout the land.

The Chronicler's evaluation of Hezekiah's successful stewardship may be summarized in his own words:

> Hezekiah did this throughout all Judah; he did what was good and right and faithful before the Lord his God. And every work that he undertook in the service of the house of God, and in accordance with the law and the commandments, to seek his God, he did with all his heart; and he prospered. (2 Chr 31.20–21)

Sirach 3.30–4.10; 29.8–13; 35.1–26

Two centuries before Jesus of Nazareth, another Jesus, the son of Sirach, wrote a Hebrew book of wisdom[12] similar to Proverbs. His grandson translated his flowing wisdom poetry into Greek after 132 B.C. (from the Prologue to Sirach), and we know this book variously as the "Wisdom of Jesus, Son of Sirach (ben Sira) " or "Ecclesiasticus." Three sections of the book are devoted to sacrificial giving, with an overall orientation toward almsgiving for the poor.

The first two sections on almsgiving actually address the needs of the poor. The ethical theme of "righteousness" found throughout Scripture is identified with almsgiving in Sirach, "almsgiving atones for sin" (3.30). What the classical prophets saw as the cause of the widow and the orphan, Sirach also puts forward, giving explicit instructions: "Do not add to the troubles of the desperate; or delay giving to the needy" (4.3). He articulates a theology of the poor foreign to contemporary thought: Be gracious to the poor, if only because they have no voice in society. Accordingly, God Himself listens to them and is their Redeemer (or Avenger). When they curse their oppressors, God hears them (35.14–26; 4.5–6; cf. Deut 15.9–10). The second section affirms that almsgiving to the poor is a commandment of the Law: "Help the poor for the commandment's sake, and in their need do not send them away empty-handed" (29.9, as an explanation of Deut 15.7–11). The extended meaning of this duty is that sacrificial giving becomes a spiritual treasury against evil (29.11–13; Tob 12.8–10).

---

[12]"Wisdom" is *chokmah* in Hebrew and *sophia* in Greek.

The last section under consideration (35.1–13) expands the image of keeping the Law through almsgiving rather than Temple sacrifice. Not only does almsgiving fulfill righteousness, but also constitutes a spiritual substitute for offerings on the altar.[13] This perspective is a profound advancement on attitudes of mechanistic sacrifice to the gods (or God) as a bribe, wherein a "quid pro quo" was expected. Sirach evaluated the attitude and psychology of philanthropy as well: "With every gift show a cheerful face, and dedicate your tithe with gladness" (35.11). Just as in the book of Deuteronomy and the later teachings of Jesus, offerings were required to correspond to a movement of the heart within the giver.

Tobit 4.1–21; 12.1–22; 14.1–15

About the same time as Sirach composed his book in Hebrew, the Jewish author of Tobit wrote with a similar emphasis on common wisdom and its morality—by means of the story of a spiritual quest. Three sections of the book mention sacrificial giving and, just as with the message of Sirach, anticipate Gospel maxims on the same topic (Mt 6.2–4). Classical Judaism's focus on righteousness, morality, and sacrificial giving was adopted in its entirety by Christianity and then developed.

Tobit 4.1–21 emphasizes the importance of proportional giving for everyone, whether rich or poor: "If you have many possessions, make your gift from them in proportion; if few, do not be afraid to give according to the little you have" (v. 8). Similarly chapter 14, Tobit's deathbed counsel, insists that this teaching is to be kept throughout all generations: "Your children are also to be commanded to do what is right and to give alms, and to be mindful of God and to bless His name at all times with sincerity and with all their strength" (14.9).

Other admonitions in the book encourage people to pay wages fairly, to give food to the hungry, and to clothe the naked, reminding us of later teachings of Jesus on the same topics. But one of the most striking admonitions—one accepted in the Pauline writings and by St. John Chrysostom—is to "give all your surplus as alms" (4.16). This charitable principle, that the "extra" of our labors rightly belongs to the poor, has been all but forgotten in Western culture. It might be viewed as a deleted half-verse of Scripture, deleted in America's so-called Protestant work ethic. This "ethic" was

[13]See also Tobit, chapter 4.

identified by the famous sociologist Max Weber and was said to be a Biblical principle—mentioned throughout Scripture and encapsulated in one verse in Ephesians—to "work hard and prosper." But the verse, and the "ethic," were cut short: " . . . let them labor and work honestly with their own hands, *so as to have something to share with the needy* (emphasis mine)."

CONCLUSION

In reiterating points drawn from Old Testament readings as regards stewardship and the tithe, we come to some striking conclusions. First, Christians and Jews see creation—including our own life—as a gift from God, to be accepted and cared for with proper attention, by stewardship. Second, the People of God did not believe that their sacrifices physically satisfied their deity, but rather that they supported their priests. The Israelites valued the service before God performed by their religious leadership, and their reward for this service was a good standard of living. Third, the gathered Israelite family (mimicked by the Christian eucharistic assembly) were to go to the appointed place where God dwells, to take all their sacred donations emblematic of their life's work, and to eat there with other households in the presence of God. Fourth, Old Testament symbolism is preserved in Eastern liturgical practice on the eve of the feasts, when the tithed wheat, wine, and oil are blessed. In both the Old and New Covenants the faithful offer the bounties of the land, and the wheat, wine, and oil are distributed back to the people in celebration of the feast. Fifth, the ancient, monetary tithe stems from the recognition that the Lord "owns everything" and receives the steward's tithe due the landowner. Deuteronomy modifies and expands the Israelite understanding of the tithe to Jerusalem by introducing an important new provision: Every three years the tithe is distributed to the poor and needy. The implication is that if the community neglects the poor and needy, God has no reason to bless the work of that community. Sixth, the theological and ethical theme of "righteousness" found throughout Scripture is identified with almsgiving in Sirach: " almsgiving atones for sin." Not only does almsgiving fulfill righteousness, but it also may constitute a spiritual substitute for offerings on the altar. Seventh, the Prophets, including Jesus, understood that Amos' prophecy against pious excess and hatred for the poor judges every generation. Both prophets Haggai and Malachi prophesied that cheating God results in a curse: the cessation of God's blessing in agricultural collapse. But one of the most striking admonitions found later in the Writings—one accepted in the Christian Church—was to "give all your surplus as alms."

FURTHER READING

The interested reader might consult any of a number of helpful resources listed below, but before doing so is encouraged to go back and read the biblical citations listed herein in their entirety. For the purposes of this chapter, the Old Testament text served as the primary source.

Anderson, Bernhard W. *Understanding the Old Testament*. 4th ed. Englewood Cliffs, N. J.: Prentice-Hall, 1997.

Bulgakov, Sergei. "Orthodoxy and Economic Life," in *The Orthodox Church*. Translated by Lydia Kesich. Crestwood, N.Y.: St. Vladimir's Seminary Press, 1988. Less helpful is Bulgakov's first discussion in print of the "Divine Sophia" in the "Sophic Economy," chapter 4 of his *Philosophy of Economy* (recently translated into English by Ekaterina Evtukhova), which he identifies with the world soul, prototypical humanity, the Body of Christ, and the Church—a rather wide-ranging definition!

Farmer, William R., ed. *The International Bible Commentary*. Collegeville, Minn.: The Liturgical Press, 1998.

Florovsky, Georges. "St. John Chrysostom: the Prophet of Charity." Tuckahoe, N.Y.: *St Vladimir's Seminary Quarterly* 4, Number 3&4 (1955): 37–42.

Haran, Menahem. *Temples and Temple Service in Ancient Israel*. Winona Lake, Ind.: Eisenbrauns, 1985.

Harrington, Daniel J. *Invitation to the Apocrypha*. Grand Rapids, Mich.: Eerdmans, 1999.

Hierarchs of the Standing Conference of the Canonical Orthodox Bishops in the Americas. *And the Word Became Flesh and Dwelt Among Us, Full of Grace and Truth: A Pastoral Letter on the Occasion of the Third Christian Millennium*. Brookline, Mass.: Holy Cross Orthodox Press, 2000.

Matthews, Victor H., and Don C. Benjamin. *Social World of Ancient Israel, 1250–587 BCE*. Peabody, Mass.: Hendrickson Publishers, Inc., 1993.

"Orthodox Perspectives on Creation," Tuckahoe, N.Y.: *St Vladimir's Theological Quarterly* 33.4 (1989) 331–49.

Stewardship Ministries Resources, Greek Orthodox Archdiocese. http://ww2.goarch.org/goa/departments/stewardship/resources/welcome.html

Vaux, Roland de. *Ancient Israel*. 2 vols. New York: McGraw-Hill, 1961.

Wilson, J. Christian. "Tithe," in *The Anchor Bible Dictionary*, vol. VI. Edited by David Noel Freedman. New York: Doubleday, 1992, 578–580.

STEWARDSHIP AND THE NEW TESTAMENT

JOHN BARNET*

A SCRIPTURAL UNDERSTANDING OF PROPERTY

For as long as there has been history, there has been private property; for as long as there has been private property, there have been wealth and poverty. Natural law theory holds that in prehistory's Golden Age all possessions were held in common and that, in Martin Hengel's words, "the moral downfall of man began with the introduction of private property."[1] Metal working, agriculture, trade, and various crafts destroyed the paradisal condition by introducing "mine" and "thine." On the other hand, the Christian perspective, amply attested in the writings of the Church Fathers, sees private property, and therefore wealth and poverty, as a *consequence* of the Fall and not its cause. The distinction is an important one, for perspective dictates the approach with which one solves the problem of wealth and poverty: philosophy sees the solution in the eradication of private property; Christianity, in the restoration of communion with God. (Interestingly enough, in both instances private property is viewed as an unnatural condition, a condition that provokes philosophy's romantic call for a return to nature and the Fathers' admonitions that possessions are the root of all dissension.) The Christian approach—the restoration of communion with God—suggests that what is to be condemned is not property itself but the misuse of property, which makes communion with God impossible.

*Dr John Barnet is Assistant Professor of New Testament and Assistant to the Dean for Technology and Special Projects at St Vladimir's Orthodox Theological Seminary in Crestwood, NY.

[1]Martin Hengel, *Property and Riches in the Early Church: Aspects of a Social History of Early Christianity*, translated by John Bowden (Philadelphia, Pa.: Fortress Press, 1974), 4.

The possibility, indeed probability, of misusing property means that, for a Christian, property represents, again in Hengel's words, both "a dangerous threat and a supreme obligation."[2] In the first half of this chapter I shall outline the scriptural view of property as threat and obligation. In the second half of the chapter I would like to explore the limitations of the threat-obligation paradigm for the theme of stewardship, proposing instead that stewardship, or the management of property, must be rooted above all else in the New Testament conviction that private property represents the opportunity for Christian witness.

PROPERTY AS THREAT AND OBLIGATION IN THE OLD TESTAMENT

In the Old Testament one finds numerous references implying that possessions themselves are not wrong. Indeed, there are frequent allusions to the idea that possessions are actually a blessing from God, as in the examples of the blessing of Abraham and the blessing of Isaac:

> The Lord has greatly blessed [Abraham], and he has become great; He has given him flocks and herds, silver and gold, menservants and maidservants, camels and asses. (Gen 24.35)

> The Lord blessed [Isaac], and the man became rich, and gained more and more until he became very wealthy. (Gen 26.12–13)

Furthermore, the Torah protects legitimate property:

> You shall not steal. (Ex 20.15)

> You shall not covet your neighbor's house; you shall not covet your neighbor's wife, or his manservant, or his maidservant, or his ox, or his ass, or anything that is your neighbor's. (Ex 20.17)

The protection of property, however, is only one aspect of the Law; the Law also commands the love of neighbor (Lev 19.18), among whom are the poor and the sojourner: "And you shall not strip your vineyard bare, neither shall you gather the fallen grapes of your vineyard; you shall leave them for the poor and for the sojourner" (Lev 19.10). Characteristic of

---

[2]Hengel, *Property and Riches*, 69.

Jewish piety of the pre-Christian era were efforts to alleviate, if not elimi-nate, the sharpest contrasts between rich and poor. This was done through individual works of mercy and institutional welfare. Imitation of the good-ness of God, who provides all good things, was said to be the justification for individual acts of generosity. The legal basis for institutional welfare is found in Deuteronomy:

> At the end of every three years you shall bring forth all the tithe of your produce in the same year, and lay it up within your towns: and the Levite, because he has no portion or inheritance with you, and the sojourner, the fatherless, and the widow, who are with your towns, shall come and eat and be filled; that the Lord your God may bless you in all the work of your hands that you do. (Deut 14.28–29)

Also found in the Torah are regulations stipulating debt remission and land redistribution, both of which tended to benefit the poor and the downtrodden:

> At the end of every seven years . . . every creditor shall release what he has lent to his neighbor. (Deut 15.1)

> And you shall hallow the fiftieth year . . . when each of you shall return to his property. (Lev 25.10)

Scriptural regulations for debt remission and land redistribution were pos-sible, as Hengel notes, because "Yahweh was the real owner of the holy land."[3] Even the Jews were no more than sojourners on Yahweh's property, hereditary tenants entrusted with a loan for which they were accountable to God. This for the Jews was the "supreme obligation" of property.

The "dangerous threat" of property, on the other hand, may well have represented the greater concern for the Jewish community, for it struck at the very heart of Judaism as expressed in the *Shema*: "Hear, O Israel: The Lord our God is one Lord; and you shall love the Lord your God with all your heart, and with all your soul, and with all your might" (Deut 6.4–5). Only the worship of another god—an idol from Judaism's perspective of universal monotheism—could destroy the very foundation of Judaism. Yet it was

[3]Hengel, *Property and Riches*, 14.

precisely this tendency toward idolatry that constituted the dangerous threat of property. For as Luke Johnson explains, idolatry can be understood as

> the choice of treating as ultimate and absolute that which is neither absolute nor ultimate. We treat something as ultimate by the worship we pay it, meaning here, of course, neither the worship of lips or of incense but of service. Worship is service. Functionally, then my god is that which I serve by my freedom. Whatever I may claim as ultimate, the truth is that my god is that which rivets my attention, centers my activity, preoccupies my mind, and motivates my action. That in virtue of which I act is god; that for which I will give up anything else is my god.[4]

In other words, when the mind is preoccupied with possessions, regardless of whether the possessions are many or few, then the mind is closed to God. Such a person is closed to God even if he or she professes faith in God, a contradictory condition that actualizes the terrible words of the prophet Isaiah: "This people draw near with their mouth and honor me [the Lord] with their lips, while their hearts are far from me, and their fear of me is a commandment of men learned by rote" (Is 29.13). The dangerous threat of property is well illustrated in the contrasting responses to God's call of Abraham, the model of appropriate response, and Lot's wife, the example of one who responded wrongly.[5] Abraham was a wealthy man (Gen 12.5). Nevertheless, when he was called by God to an unknown land (Gen 12.1), he did not identify his life with his possessions but, in Johnson's words, "allowed his identity to be determined by the one who called him."[6] Lot's wife, on the other hand, identified her life with the wealth of her husband (Gen 13.5) and failed to obey (Gen 19.26) God's call to leave Sodom (Gen 19.17). As Johnson concludes, "She could not respond to God's call, and so lost the life that she sought to establish by what she owned."[7]

The Reappraisal of Property in the Presence of the Kingdom

The Old Testament understanding of property as threat and obligation finds expression in the New Testament as well, although it is reinterpreted

---

[4]Luke T. Johnson, *Sharing Possessions: Mandate and Symbol of Faith* (Philadelphia, Pa.: Fortress Press, 1981), 49.

[5]Johnson, *Sharing Possessions*, 60–62.

[6]Johnson, *Sharing Possessions*, 60.

[7]Johnson, *Sharing Possessions*, 62.

in the light of the gospel, as indeed is the entirety of the Old Testament Law. For, as the Apostle Paul teaches, the Law was only "our custodian until Christ came, that we might be justified by faith" (Gal 3.24). The reinterpretation of the Old Testament understanding of property is a consequence of what Hengel calls the "central significance"[8] of Christianity, namely, its emphasis on the imminence of the kingdom of God.

In the presence of the kingdom men and women are not to be anxious about their daily needs, as Jesus teaches in the Sermon on the Mount:

> do not be anxious, saying, "What shall we wear?" or "What shall we drink?" or "What shall we wear?" For the Gentiles seek all these things; and your heavenly Father knows that you need them all. But seek first His kingdom and His righteousness, and all these things shall be yours as well. (Mt 6.31–33)

Instead, they are called to witness at every opportunity that it is God, not mammon, who sustains them: "Man shall not live by bread alone, but by every word that proceeds from the mouth of God" (Mt 4.4). Therefore, for Christians, the significance of the imminence of the kingdom is that property is stripped of its idolatrous power to hold them in dependent relationship, a power that can overwhelm the concern for neighbor and make impossible the love of enemy. Certainly Jesus attacked mammon whenever it captured men's hearts. But, as Hengel writes,

> Jesus was not interested in any new theories about the rightness or wrongness of possessions in themselves, about the origin of property or its better distribution; rather he adopted the same scandalously free and untrammeled attitude to property as to the powers of the state, the alien Roman rule and its Jewish confederates. The imminence of the kingdom of God robs all these things of their power *de facto*, for in it "many that are first will be last, and the last first."[9]

In other words, for those who have eyes to see, the presence of the kingdom truly makes the things of this world irrelevant.

The claim that the imminent kingdom renders all earthly things irrelevant stands in tensive relationship with the Old Testament view that

[8] Hengel, *Property and Riches*, 29.
[9] Hengel, *Property and Riches*, 30.

property represents a blessing from God. On the one hand, it is certainly true that by accepting the support of the women who followed Him, Jesus Himself implicitly affirms the view that property is not wrong: "Mary, called Magdalene, from who seven demons had gone out, and Joanna, the wife of Chuza, Herod's steward, and Susanna, and many others, who provided for them out of their means" (Lk 8.2–3). Nevertheless, Judaism's positive assessment of property as blessing is completely transformed in the teaching of Jesus, who calls His disciples "blessed" because they see and hear what the prophets longed to see (Mt 12.16–17). While the heavenly reward of those who follow Jesus will indeed be great (Mt 19.28–29), in this life they are to expect only the subsistence provisions of those who labor for the sake of the gospel:

> Preach as you go, saying, "The kingdom of heaven is at hand." Heal the sick, raise the dead, cleanse lepers, cast out demons. You received without paying, give without pay. Take no gold, nor silver, nor copper in your belts, no bag for your journey, nor two tunics, nor sandals, nor a staff; for the laborer deserves his food (Mt 10.8–10).

God will provide for the earthly needs of the disciples, as Jesus promises everyone who seeks first God's kingdom and His righteousness (Mt 7.33): those who accept the gospel when they are evangelized by the disciples will care for them (Mt 10.11). Indeed, the disciples' dependence on the charity of others is itself to be understood as a sign of the gospel, a sign that the disciples serve only one master (Mt 23.10). On the other hand, to those who would think to find some middle ground between God and the things of this world, Jesus makes clear the impossibility of their endeavor: "No one can serve two masters; for either he will hate the one and love the other, or he will be devoted to the one and despise the other. You cannot serve God and mammon" (Mt 6.24).

Perhaps the ultimate expression of Jesus' uncompromising attitude toward possessions is found in His hard words to the rich man: "If you would be perfect, go, sell what you possess and give to the poor, and you will have treasure in heaven; and come, follow me" (Mt 19.21). Although the rich man has faithfully observed the commandments of the Law, including the commandment to love one's neighbor (Mt 19.18–20), he is unable to make the final act of radical obedience that leads to eternal life.

When the rich man rejects the invitation of Jesus, he becomes a sign of how difficult it is for a rich man to enter the kingdom, much to the astonishment of the disciples, who apparently hold the view that property is a sign of God's favor: "Who then can be saved" (Mt 19.25)? And like the rich man, many of us also turn away from this invitation, whether our possessions are many or few, before we understand the meaning of Jesus' words: "With men this [salvation] is impossible, but with God all things are possible" (Mt 19.26).

Although Jesus' demand of the rich man—that he should give his possessions to the poor—is severe, the truly radical aspect of His words is that He commands a total commitment to Himself and His path. Therefore, even if we are able to share from our abundance, like Zacchaeus who gives half of his possessions to the poor in response to the presence of the kingdom (Lk 19.8), our generosity may not be adequate, even if it fulfills the Old Testament commandment to love one's neighbor. For this commandment too is reinterpreted by Jesus, who teaches that it is not enough to give; one must be charitable in the proper spirit:

> Beware of practicing your piety before men in order to be seen by them; for then you will have no reward from your Father who is in heaven. Thus when you give alms, sound no trumpet before you, as the hypocrites do in the synagogues and in the streets, that they may be praised by men. Truly, I say to you they have received their reward. But when you give alms, do not let your left hand know what your right hand is doing, so that your alms my be in secret; and your Father who sees in secret will reward you. (Mt 6.1–4)

Indeed, so important is the hidden intention of one's piety that it becomes the sole basis for evaluating the gift; the amount itself becomes irrelevant, as Jesus teaches regarding the widow's sacrifice: "Truly I tell you, this poor widow has put in more than all of them; for they all contributed out of their abundance, but she out of her poverty put in all the living that she had" (Lk 21.3–4).

The most significant reinterpretation of Judaism's view of property, however, undoubtedly occurs as a consequence of the new understanding that Jesus brings to the greatest commandment—the commandment to love God above all else. The Old Testament truth that possessions are a "dangerous threat" (when they are mistaken for the Absolute) is clearly preserved in the teaching of Jesus, as noted previously in the pericope on serving two masters. But this truth is also reinterpreted by Jesus when He links the two great commandments of the Law: "You shall love the Lord your God with all your heart, and with all your soul, and with all your mind. This is the great and first commandment. And a second is like it, You shall love your neighbor as yourself" (Mt 22.37–39). The significance of this juxtaposition is that each commandment is to be understood in terms of the other, with the result that it is not possible to love God and hate neighbor or to love neighbor and hate God: "He who says he is in the light and hates his brother is in the darkness still. He who loves his brother abides in the light" (1 Jn 2.9–10). Indeed, the juxtaposition of these commandments reveals that the love of the needy neighbor *is* the love of God:

> Come, O blessed of my Father, inherit the kingdom of the world; for I was hungry and you gave me food, I was thirsty and you gave me drink, I was a stranger and you welcomed me, I was naked and you clothed me, I was sick and you visited me, I was in prison and you came to me. . . . Truly, I say to you, as you did it to one of the least of these my brethren, you did it to me. (Mt 25.35–36, 40)

In this passage, Jesus makes it clear that the love of neighbor, which must be manifested in concrete action (1 Jn 3.17–18), is the basis for salvation. It is not possible to state more strongly the requirement to love one's neighbor, especially the needy neighbor, nor to explain how this love is to be expressed. For Christians, this represents the "supreme obligation" of property.

STEWARDSHIP AS THE OPPORTUNITY FOR CHRISTIAN WITNESS

Most of us willingly accept the idea that Christian charity is the necessary expression of love. Yet many of us find it difficult to express concretely this love with our own possessions, whether in response to the daily request for a handout from those who we believe, rightly or wrongly, are unwilling to help themselves or the conscience-striking plea from someone in terrible distress. Regardless of the source of the request, many of us have at one time closed our hearts against our neighbor.

One explanation for our refusal to help the neighbor is that we often are unwilling to do the difficult work of determining the neighbor's true need and then acting upon that need regardless of the consequences.

Another explanation is that we have lost the scriptural understanding of possessions as a loan from God. Consequently, we come to assign more value to the things of this world than to our fellow man, a perspective that reverses the hierarchy ordained by God when He created man to have dominion over His entire creation (Gen 1.26). Thus there arises a tension born of our conflicting attitudes toward possessions and people. The nature of this tension suggests that the problem of Christian charity could be overcome by encouraging a change of attitude toward possessions on the one hand and neighbor on the other. In this section of the chapter I shall try to show, however, that an understanding of charity that emphasizes either detachment from possessions or obligation toward the neighbor is ultimately limited and therefore is not truly charity. Rather, for Christians, only that which is the free and concrete expression of the genuine love of the other can truly be called charity.

Detachment from Possessions

For a Christian, a certain detachment from possessions is a natural consequence of the realization that in the presence of the kingdom private property has no meaning. This is because the things of this world are ultimately useless in the face of an ethic that not only disregards social position, which so often accompanies distinctions of wealth and poverty, but also reverses our commonly held understanding of authority and greatness: "But Jesus called them to Him and said, 'You know that the rulers of the Gentiles lord it over them, and their great men exercise authority over them. It shall not be so among you; but whoever would be great among you must be your servant, and whoever would be first among you must be your slave'" (Mt 20.25–28). Such a reappraisal of the value of private property is reflected in the free attitude toward possessions characteristic of the Jerusalem community: "Now the company of those who believed were of one heart and soul, and no one said that any of the things which he possessed was his own, but they had everything in common" (Acts 4.32). Even the neglect of the Greek-speaking widows at the daily distribution (Acts 6.1) can be interpreted as evidence that the organization and planning of the Jerusalem community were "kept to a minimum, . . . in view of the intensive expectation of the return of Jesus."[10]

As the expectation of an imminent parousia died down, however, the

---

[10]Hengel, *Property and Riches*, 34.

early Church continued to encourage freedom from possessions as a
means "to serve God's cause, to proclaim the gospel and to serve neighbors."[11] In other words, the Church came to encourage for most a contentment with those possessions sufficient to support life, while riches
were to be used in the service of the poor, as in the following exhortation
of St John Chrysostom:

> Let us use our goods sparingly, as belonging to others, so that they may
> become our own. How shall we use them sparingly, as belonging to oth-
> ers? When we do not spend for our needs only, but give equal shares
> into the hands of the poor. If you are affluent, but spend more than
> you need, you will give an account of the funds which were entrusted
> to you.[12]

But such an understanding, however true it might be, can also be mislead-
ing, for it increases the possibility of understanding the management of
property primarily in a juridical sense, as a law or regulation to be obeyed.
In other words, it introduces the element of compulsion.

Such appears to have been the case with Ananias and Sapphira, who
withheld a portion of their possessions from the Jerusalem community
(Acts 5.1-2). One could argue, as Peter does, that they were not compelled
to give their property to the Church:

> But Peter said, "Ananias, why has Satan filled your heart to lie to the
> Holy Spirit and to keep back part of the proceeds of the land? While it
> remained unsold, did it not remain your own? And after it was sold,
> was it not at your disposal? How is it that you have contrived this deed
> in your heart? You have not lied to men but to God. (Acts 5.3-4)

Nevertheless, Ananias and Sapphira apparently felt some sort of compulsion, since they attempted to deceive the community by withholding a portion of what was intended in its entirety as a free gift. Why should they have
been reluctant to give all that they had promised? Apparently Ananias and
Sapphira felt that the portion that they withheld still had great value for

[11]Hengel, *Property and Riches*, 55.

[12]St John Chrysostom, *On Wealth and Poverty*, translated by Catherine P. Roth (Crestwood, N.Y.: St Vladimir's Seminary Press, 1984), 50.

them; however, in the face of others' expectations they were unable to express this attitude. In other words, their understanding of their place within the Jerusalem community was apparently informed by a sense of obligation, rather than being determined by the realization that in the presence of the kingdom private property has no meaning. This suggests that a model of charity that is based primarily on a contentment with sufficiency, or a detachment from possessions, is ultimately incomplete.

The Freedom of Love

While an emphasis on detachment from possessions ultimately may not serve as an adequate basis for a model of Christian charity, it does remind us that possessions offer us the opportunity to express concretely our love of neighbor. Nevertheless, as Christos Yannaras cautions, "Any good work, any objective act of virtue is justified in the Church's eyes only when its object is to manifest God, to reveal the image of God in man."[13] Or, as Scripture teaches us, acts of virtue are acceptable to God only when they "so shine before men, that they may see your good works and give glory to your Father who is in heaven" (Mt 5.14). In order to determine what sort of work reveals the image of God in man, one may begin by looking first to God Himself.

According to Yannaras, the experience of the Church has shown that God

> reveals Himself in history as personal existence, as distinctiveness and freedom. . . . The personal existence of God [the Father] constitutes His essence or being, making it into "hypostases": freely and from love He begets the Son and causes the Holy Spirit to proceed.[14]

Here we are reminded that there is no love in the Trinity without freedom, that love without freedom is not love but necessity. Consequently, for human beings to partake in true life, which is God's own life, we must existentially express our calling in personal communion and relationship with our fellow man, a relationship that must be based on the freedom of love as manifested in the relationship of personal communion of the Trinity. This means that charity, as with love itself, must be given freely. Moreover, char-

---

[13]Christos Yannaras, *The Freedom of Morality*, translated by Elizabeth Briere (Crestwood, N.Y.: St Vladimir's Seminary Press, 1984), 79–80.

[14]Yannaras, *The Freedom of Morality*, 17–18.

ity must show itself for what it truly is—an expression of love; otherwise it is not charity. In other words, charity, like love, cannot be mandated, it cannot be compelled. Otherwise, when charity is no longer a free act born of the love of neighbor, it ceases to manifest the presence of God and His kingdom.

With the Fall the element of necessity was introduced, making it impossible for us to express our calling in personal communion with our fellow man. For with the Fall, man comes to be characterized by an "existential self-sufficiency of nature bounded by individuality."[15] From that moment life became one of individual survival, rather than personal communion. It is precisely this element of necessity, this tendency toward individual self-sufficiency, that ultimately undermines a model of charity based primarily on a detachment from possessions: the drive toward individual self-sufficiency eventually overcomes all other motivations, including one's charitable intentions toward the neighbor.

The Church teaches us that this is an unnatural state, which can only be transformed from within, not merely cosmetically adjusted. Such a transformation is the aim of the gospel. But it is an aim that cannot be formalized according to a juridical model, for it is an aim that is predicated upon the freedom of the love of the Trinity. Any expectation of compulsion or necessity is not of the Trinity and therefore is not of that personal communion and relationship to which human beings are called. Moreover, this transformation is not possible through man's individual efforts. At best these efforts serve to "improve" the outer man; they leave untouched the inner man. Rather, in the words of Yannaras,

> this transformation can take place only if man is grafted into the body of Christ, the existential reality which creates life as personal communion, rather than life as individual survival. . . . It means total, bodily participation in the body of Christ; eating His flesh and drinking His blood.[16]

Participation in the body of Christ, his Church, ultimately effects the transformation of a person's heart, the seat of human understanding and intention, for it is there—in response to the gospel—that one stands before God in need of His salvation. Jesus Himself declares that He "came not to

[15]Yannaras, *The Freedom of Morality*, 81.
[16]Yannaras, *The Freedom of Morality*, 81.

call the righteous, but sinners" (Mt 9.13). Therefore, unless one first understands that one is in need of salvation, then every attempt to practice responsible stewardship, whether it be contentment with sufficiency or charity toward one's neighbor, ultimately represents merely the work of men and not, as it might otherwise be, the witness of one's salvation.

The Witness of Salvation

When the rich man rejects the invitation of Jesus to enter the kingdom, he expresses the impossibility of effecting his own salvation, despite his faithful observance of all the commandments of the Law, including the commandment to love one's neighbor. Indeed, the words of Jesus to His astonished disciples expose the fruitlessness of all human endeavors in the presence of the kingdom: "With men this [the salvation of the rich man] is impossible" (Mt 19.26). Nevertheless, Jesus adds, "But with God all things are possible" (Mt 19.26). The path of salvation that is offered by Jesus to the rich man is the path of voluntary impoverishment, the loss not only of his great possessions but also the social status that invariably accompanies great wealth.

A similar opportunity for voluntary impoverishment is presented to the centurion, a soldier of high status who declares his unworthiness before Jesus, the son of a mere carpenter (Mt 13.55): "Lord, I am not worthy to have you come under my roof; but only say the word and my servant will be healed" (Mt 8.8). Not only does the centurion implicitly know that he is powerless to fulfill his own need for the healing of his servant, he also appears to understand that he has no right to make his supplication when he confesses his unworthiness. This self-lowering on the part of the centurion recalls the private instructions of Jesus to His disciples that they should take up their crosses (Mt 10.38; 16.24), lose their lives (Mt 10.39; 16.25), humble themselves like a child (Mt 18.3–4), and become the servants of others (Mt 20.26–27). In other words, it is a self-lowering that actualizes the pattern established by Jesus Himself, who takes up His own cross (Mt 20.19), loses His own life (Mt 16.21, 23; 20.28), and comes to serve others rather than be served Himself (Mt 20.28). This pattern represents the will of His Father (Mt 26.39, 42), who raises Jesus from the dead (Mt 16.9, 23).

Voluntary impoverishment is also the posture of the Canaanite woman, who accepts Jesus' implicit characterization of her lowly status: "Yes, Lord, yet even the dogs eat the crumbs that fall from their master's table" (Mt

15.27). Furthermore, it is precisely the Canaanite woman's acceptance of Jesus' characterization of her status, her final appeal, that is considered to be the manifestation of her great faith (Mt 15.28). Like the centurion, the Canaanite woman overcomes the objection of Jesus' response, expressing the recognition of her need in the face of her unworthiness. Unlike the centurion, however, who manifests his faith in an act of self-lowering, the Canaanite woman is depicted as a thoroughly marginalized supplicant whose great faith is manifested in the acknowledgment of her low status.

CONCLUSION

Thus one comes to see that Christian charity, properly understood, is the free and concrete manifestation of one's love for the neighbor, a love that is possible only in the person whose heart has been transformed through total participation in the body of Christ, as one who stands before God in need of His salvation. Does this mean, therefore, that we are to forgo the inadequate charity of our imperfect love? No. We are to give nonetheless. We are to give to the best of our limited ability. We are to give ever mindful that our possessions must represent above all else the opportunity to witness to the salvation that is being effected in us. We are to give with the knowledge that our charity must be a sign of God's providential care. We are to give with the certainty that our voluntary impoverishment for the sake of the gospel must be a sign that we serve only one master. We are to give with humility, all the while acknowledging the inadequacy of our gift, all the while praying with the tax collector "God be merciful to me a sinner" (Lk 18.13). Such is the nature of Christian stewardship.

FURTHER READING

Chrysostom, St John. *On Wealth and Poverty*. Translated by Catherine P. Roth. Crestwood, N.Y.: St Vladimir's Seminary Press, 1984.

Hengel, Martin. *Property and Riches in the Early Church: Aspects of a Social History of Early Christianity*. Translated by John Bowden. Philadelphia, Pa.: Fortress Press, 1974.

Johnson, Luke T. *Sharing Possessions: Mandate and Symbol of Faith*. Philadelphia, Pa.: Fortress Press, 1981.

Tarazi, Paul Nadim. "Witnessing the Dynamics of Salvation," *St Vladimir's Theological Quarterly* 22 (1978): 179–91.

Yannaras, Christos. *The Freedom of Morality*. Translated by Elizabeth Briere. Crestwood, N.Y.: St Vladimir's Seminary Press, 1984.

HEALING THE
CHRISTIAN BODY

An Ancient Syriac Theme

◆───

SUSAN ASHBROOK HARVEY*

W
hen Orthodox Christians prepare to receive the Eucharist, they pray to receive the holy oblation "for the healing of soul and body." In the rich tradition that Syriac-speaking Christianity has offered to the Church, healing has been a central theme. Ancient Syriac writers often gave Christ the title of "Good Physician" or "Medicine of Life," and the Eucharist, too, was referred to frequently as "the Medicine of Life." These titles were not unique to Syriac Christianity, but their centrality to Syriac tradition is noteworthy. Noteworthy, too, is the particular way in which Syriac Christianity gave witness to how "the healing of soul and body" should be understood. It is an understanding that we would do well to recall when thinking about stewardship and its role in Christian life.

The Syriac language is a dialect of Aramaic, the language that Jesus spoke, itself a dialect of Hebrew. In Syriac the word for salvation, *hayye'*, also means "life." This double sense lends poignancy to the theme of healing, for the link between salvation and mortality is always in view. Many ancient Christians understood our present condition of human finitude to be the result of Adam and Eve's disobedience in the Garden of Eden (Gen 2–3). Mortality—the physically finite state of our bodies—was perceived to

*Dr Susan Ashbrook Harvey holds M. Litt. and Ph.D. degrees from the Centre for Byzantine Studies, University of Birmingham, England. While at Birmingham she specialized in early Syriac Christianity, working jointly between the Centre for Byzantine Studies and the Oriental Institute at Oxford. She currently is Professor of Religious Studies at Brown University, Providence, Rhode Island.

be a moral aspect of our beings as well as a physical one. The Christian prayed for the healing of soul and body because both aspects of the human person suffered in the fallen order. Without healing, we die; without salvation, we are lost. As the Syriac term evokes so well, to be saved is to have life. In healing lies the promise of salvation: the promise of eternal life.

From its earliest Christian writings, Syriac tradition repeatedly insists that healing the Christian body requires healing the *whole* body of Christ. Both the body of the individual believer and the body of the Christian community as a collective are in need of salvation. Both bodies live in a fallen state. The individual suffers hunger, thirst, illness, and death. The community suffers these same afflictions in the forms of poverty, injustice, tyranny, and war. To pray for the healing of soul and body is also to pray for a change in the human situation and condition. For ancient Syriac writers, the Christian body and the body of the Christian community were seen to be one body, each dependent on the other for its existence. This view underlies every discussion of how a Christian should live, or what activities were required for a Christian way of life. In this chapter, I wish to explore how Syriac writers understood the healing of the Christian body, as an example of how Orthodox tradition has understood the activity of stewardship.

THE FRAME OF MEMORY

The city of Edessa (called "Urhai" in Syriac, today the town of Urfa in southeastern Turkey) was one of the great centers of early Christianity. Edessa was known as "the Blessed City" because of the legend that Jesus of Nazareth Himself had placed a special blessing upon it in an exchange of letters with the city's ruler, King Abgar V Ukkama ("the Black").[1] But Edessa's privileged place was held even without the fame of such a legend. Distinguished for learned academies in Greek, Syriac, and Armenian, a center for merchants crossing the east-west trade routes, and bustling with a diverse, multi-ethnic population, Edessa was a cosmopolitan metropolis offering religious, intellectual, and cultural leadership for many centuries. In the fifth century AD, however, Edessa experienced an exceptional era of greatness. It was a time of examining Edessa's Christian experience and deciding what the distinctive contours of its legacy should be. Two products of this era deserve attention for their articulation of healing as a major

---

[1]A lively survey of Edessa's history as a Christian center may be found in J. B. Segal, *Edessa: the Blessed City* (Oxford: Clarendon, 1970).

theological theme in Syriac tradition: the *Teaching of Addai*, a long narrative claiming to recount the story of Edessa's conversion to Christianity in the first century; and the literary corpus associated with the episcopacy of Bishop Rabbula of Edessa, whose term as bishop (411–435/6) led to extensive ecclesiastical and monastic reforms.

The *Teaching of Addai* is an anonymous work written in the fifth century but claiming to be from the first century.[2] Combining a number of legends, it grants the church at Edessa the honor of apostolic origins and a venerable Christian past, which, while exaggerated, nonetheless accords with major themes of Syriac Christianity as it had developed through its first centuries. The *Teaching of Addai* tells the story of how King Abgar heard about the ministry of Jesus and wrote a letter to Him. The letter praised Jesus' mighty works, confessed Abgar's faith that Jesus must be the Son of God, petitioned that Jesus come to Edessa to heal Abgar of an illness, and invited Him to share Abgar's throne in order to escape the plots festering against him. To this letter Jesus sent a reply saying that He could not come to Edessa for it was time to end His work on earth; rather, He would send a disciple who would heal Abgar of his illness and bring the gospel teachings to the people of Edessa.[3] Subsequently, the story goes, Addai came to Edessa, healed Abgar and many others, converted the people of the city, and instituted the church there.[4]

In the Syriac account of *The Teaching of Addai*, healing is a central theme. It is a theme expressed both in individual terms (the healing of sick persons) and in social terms (the healing of the city as a community). When King Abgar first hears about the ministry of Jesus, it is the healing miracles that hold his attention, particularly the reports of Christ raising the dead. In his letter, Abgar addresses Jesus as "the Good Physician." When the apostle

[2]A bilingual Syriac–English edition is available by George Howard, *The Teaching of Addai* (Missoula, Mont.: Scholars Press, 1981). I will quote from this version.

[3]The story was one that had been known long before the *Teaching of Addai* was written. Papyrus fragments of the Jesus-Abgar correspondence in both Greek and Syriac versions survive from the late third century, and early in the fourth century, Eusebius of Caesarea visited Edessa to see the letters and have them translated into Greek for his monumental *Ecclesiastical History*. Around 384, the Western pilgrim Egeria visited Edessa while on pilgrimage to the Holy Land; while she was there, the bishop showed her the letters, which she noted were a little different than the Latin version of them that she knew at home. For an excellent discussion of the evidence see Sebastian P. Brock, "Eusebius and Syriac Christianity," in *Eusebius, Christianity and Judaism*, ed. H. Attridge and G. Hata (Detroit, Mich.: Wayne State University Press, 1992), 212–34.

[4]Traditionally Addai has been associated with Thaddaeus, one of the seventy apostles whom Jesus sent out in Luke 10: 1–20.

Addai arrives in Edessa, Abgar greets him with rejoicing as the one sent by Christ "for healing and for salvation" (*l'asyutha' w-lhayye'*; 13). After healing Abgar in the presence of his noblemen, Addai performs healings throughout the city. Then King Abgar summons the city to hear Addai preach the gospel. In his preaching Addai announces that the healings prove the truth of the gospel he has been sent to proclaim. Together, the men and women of Edessa convert to Christianity.

It is important that the story does not end there, with the healings of the sick in Edessa. Rather, the *Teaching of Addai* continues to describe the response of the city to those healings: not simply a response of conversion, but one of establishing the church of Edessa in such a way that the city itself is changed in the process. First King Abgar invites Addai to build a church and set up teachers to assist him, offering to provide the expenses for the new building as well as whatever money is needed to enable the clergy to devote themselves full-time to their task of ministry. When Addai has followed these instructions, the nobles and people of the city bring donations of their own, "some things for the house of God and some things for the support of the poor" (73). With ample supplies from the imperial household as well as the wider citizenry, Addai and his priests tend to their ministry, gathering the people daily for services and "making visitations of alms to the sick and to the well according to Addai's teaching." With Edessa as his base, Addai then goes on to build churches and establish the priesthood in other districts as well, "both far and near." Finally Addai falls ill and the people gather to hear his farewell discourse. From his deathbed the apostle exhorts them to follow his example by demonstrating the truth of Christian teaching through active deeds: "Because thus our Lord commanded us, that whatever we preach in words to the people we ourselves should do by deed before all people" (83). And so Addai dies, handing the church of Edessa over to his rightly established successors.

According to the *Teaching of Addai*, the church of Edessa went on to flourish despite vicissitudes because of the faithfulness with which the Edessan Christians followed Addai's final exhortation. Thus the story describes the first-century church of Edessa as a community that displayed in its devotional activities the teachings it preached: "All the men and women were modest, honorable, holy and pure . . . they lived honorably in diligent service, relieving the burdens of the poor, and visiting the sick" (101). Held in the highest honor by all peoples of the city, pagan or

Christian, "the very sight of them spread peace to those who beheld them. . . . For that which they said to others and admonished them to do, they showed by deeds the same thing in their own persons" (103).

Surely the significance of the story lies in this idyllic description of the church of Edessa. The healing miracles acclaimed with such wonder throughout the early part of the story are not, and cannot be, the culmination of Christ's work. As in the gospels, healings of individual problems—among the blind, the deaf, the lame, the sick—are shown in this legend as preludes to the larger healing work of Christ, the healing of the civic community. In that larger task of healing, all followers of the gospel are called to participate. The church is thus shown to be a body itself, "one body of many members" (Rom 12. 4–5), and the health of each member is essential to the health of the whole. Significantly, the *Teaching of Addai* shows this process of healing to be an essentially social one: no individual stands alone. Rather, the Christians of Edessa are known by how they live in relation to others and to the body of which they are part. The establishment of the Edessan church requires not only political tolerance but also considerable economic investment by all members, whether wealthy or not, for the building and proper adornment of church facilities, the financing of clergy and assistants as they are needed, and adequate care for the poor, the sick, and the needy. The Christians there are shown to contribute both of their time and of their goods; moreover, these contributions are identified as necessary for the task of true worship. They are required if the life of true devotion is to be lived properly. Conversion in this story carries an ethical mandate: the healing of one's own body within Christianity endows the believer with the capacity, indeed the moral obligation, to extend that healing beyond one's own self to the body of Christ, the larger community.

The theme of healing as expressed in the *Teaching of Addai* is also found in early Syriac hymnography. The *Odes of Solomon* are a second-century collection of hymns, the earliest Syriac literature that survives to us apart from biblical translations.[5] Beautiful in their simplicity, sometimes enigmatic, they are filled with hauntingly powerful descriptions of the activity of worship as one in which the faithful believer stands wholly in the presence of God. It is a stance that requires the whole of one's being, body and soul. It is a stance in which the believer is brought to wholeness: worship of God is itself a healing activity. Thus the Odist extols the power of singing God's praise:

[5]Edited with English translation by James H. Charlesworth, *The Odes of Solomon*, 2nd ed. (Missoula, Mont.: Sheffield Academic Press, 1977). I follow Charlesworth's translation, with some alterations.

My heart was lifted up and enriched in the love of the
    Most High,
so that I might praise Him with my name.
My limbs were strengthened,
that they might not fall from His power.
Infirmities fled from my body,
And it stood firm for the Lord by His will;
Because His kingdom is firm. (Ode 18.1–3)

The experience of devotion for the Odist is one in which one gains increasing strength from God, so that one's own condition, strengthened and healed, becomes an expression of God's truth. "Thy right hand exalted me, / and caused sickness to pass from me. / And I became mighty in Thy truth, / and holy in Thy righteousness" (Ode 25. 9–10). To sing of God, then, is an act of devotion that changes the self in the process of its doing. One's condition displays one's relationship to the divine.

In the Odes, worship is described as the complete giving of oneself to God. Further, worship is shown as a process in which the giving over of the self brings one into God's presence and there into the experience of being made new. For if God is perfection, all that is near Him or in harmony with Him is affected by His own perfect nature. Thus the Odist expresses his experience:

I lifted up my arms on high [in prayer]
on account of the compassion of the Lord. . . .
And my Helper lifted me up according to His compassion
    and His salvation.
And I put off darkness,
and put on light.
And I myself acquired limbs.
In them there was no sickness,
or affliction or suffering.
And abundantly helpful to me was the thought of the
    Lord,
and His everlasting fellowship. (Ode 21. 1–5)

Repeatedly the Odist extols worship as a state in which the believer is granted tranquility, serenity, and rest in the Lord. The more one gives oneself over to God, the more God pervades one's being. God's healing is shown to be worked on one's disposition no less than one's physical condition.

The *Odes of Solomon* are often thought to be dominated by baptismal imagery.[6] This would account for the emphasis on worship as an experience of being fashioned anew as well as being brought into God's presence. In Ode 6, sacrament (perhaps both baptism and Eucharist) and healing are shown to be foundational for the believing community as a whole, with a description that mirrors the Odist's own account of how worship of God works on him:

> Blessed, therefore, are the ministers of that drink,
> Who have been entrusted with the water.
> They have refreshed the parched lips,
> And have aroused the paralyzed will.
> Even lives that were about to expire,
> They have held back from death.
> And limbs which had collapsed,
> They have restored and set up.
> They gave strength for their coming,
> And light for their eyes.
> And everyone recognized them as the Lord's
> and lived by the living water of eternity. (Ode 6. 13–8)

The *Odes of Solomon* represent something of the devotional experience and activity of earliest Syriac Christianity, when the church was a small minority of believers in a society dominated by other religions of the eastern Mediterranean region. In the course of the fourth century, as Christianity gained ascendancy and grew dramatically in numbers, Syriac writers increasingly show the link between individual and collective healing as one between personal faith and ethical activity: the link stressed in the legendary account of the *Teaching of Addai*.

Aphrahat "the Persian Sage" described faith as like a building, a structure made up of many different pieces: faith, fasting, prayer, love, alms,

[6]A helpful discussion can be found in Michael Pierce, "Themes in the 'Odes of Solomon' and Other Early Christian Writings and their Baptismal Character," *Ephemerides Liturgicae* 98 (1984): 35–59.

meekness, holiness, wisdom, hospitality, simplicity, patience, long-suffering, and purity of heart (Dem. 1, "On Faith").[7] Note that these activities involve not only the Christian's personal disposition in relation to God, but also the expression of that disposition toward others, as in the practice of almsgiving or hospitality.

Elsewhere Aphrahat describes different types of prayer and the activities by which they are offered to God.[8] Care of others is one significant type: "Give rest to the weary, visit the sick, make provision for the poor: this is indeed prayer."[9] In fact, Aphrahat says if you delay such activities because you think you ought to pray first and then act—as if these actions were different in kind from prayer—then you will fail utterly to do the will of God or to offer true prayer. Just as God offers rest to the faithful—an image so powerfully evoked in the *Odes of Solomon*—the Christian, Aphrahat says, must bring about God's rest for others in order to fulfill the action of prayer. If God is to work on the believer—to heal and save the Christian—the believer must work on others, providing the same healing, the same solace and comfort. The body of the individual is part of the larger body of the community.

The greatest of all Syriac theologians and hymnographers was St Ephrem the Syrian (d. 373), and the theme of Christ as the Medicine of Life was a favorite of his.[10] But Ephrem also stresses that healing restores in us the image of our Maker. For Ephrem, as for the *Odes of Solomon*, the bond between Creator and created is an intimate one. As Ephrem explains it, everything made by God is marked by God as by an engraver's stamp; therefore, the whole of the created order demonstrates God's greatness. For humanity, however, the relationship is even more profound. At the incarnation God entered into humanity, becoming what we are; each time we partake of the Eucharist we are filled anew in our very selves, each and every one of us, with Christ. Marked by our Maker, filled with His glory, our only right response can be to portray God throughout our bodies in all that we do:

[7]There is an English translation by J. Gwynn in the *Nicene and Post-Nicene Fathers*, vol. 13 (Oxford: James Parker and Co./New York: The Christian Literature Co., 1898; Repr. Grand Rapids: Wm. Eerdmans, 1988), 345–52. The Syriac text is edited by D. I. Parisot, in *Patrologia Syriaca* I, ed. R. Graffin (Paris: Firmin-Didot, 1894), cols. 5–46.

[8]Demonstration 4, "On Prayer," English translation in Sebastian P. Brock, *The Syriac Fathers on Prayer and the Spiritual Life* (Kalamazoo, Mich.: Cistercian Publications, 1987), 5–25. The Syriac is edited by Parisot, *Patrologia Syriaca* I: cols. 137–82.

[9]Dem. 4.14; Brock, 19.

[10]See Sebastian P. Brock, *The Luminous Eye: The Spiritual World Vision of Saint Ephrem the Syrian* (Kalamazoo, Mich.: Cistercian Publications, 1992), especially ch. 6, "The Medicine of Life," 99–114.

> Let chastity be portrayed in your eyes and in your ears the
> sound of truth.
> Imprint your tongue with the word of life and upon your hands
> [imprint] all alms.
> Stamp your footsteps with visiting the sick,
> and let the image of your Lord be portrayed in your heart.
> Tablets are honored because of the image of kings.
> How much [more will] one [be honored] who portrayed his
> Lord in all his senses.[11]

Once again the Christian, strengthened and healed, is called to ethical action as the fulfillment of that healing.

THE FRAME OF TRADITION

The *Teaching of Addai* was written in the fifth century to draw together stories and pieces of earlier Syriac Christianity. Its purpose was to present a legacy that would articulate how Syriac tradition should be remembered and lived. Its practical counterpart from the same moment in history may be seen in the ecclesiastical reforms initiated by the great bishop of Edessa, Rabbula.[12] Rabbula's legacy in Syrian Orthodox tradition is so great that his name has been associated with a vast range of changes that came about during the fifth century: the triumph in the Syrian churches of Nicene Orthodoxy, the defeat of paganism, revision of the standard Syriac translation of the Bible (producing the Peshitta, the authorized Syriac version), and the regulation of monasticism and of church orders. Above all, Rabbula is remembered for his extensive social welfare programs on behalf of the poor, the sick, the homeless, and the needy.[13] Rabbula's achievements were embellished over time by the accretions of legend, many included in a long, elaborate hagiography, the *Life of Rabbula*, written around 449.[14] But practical

---

[11]Ephrem, *Hymns on Virginity* 2.15; here translated by Kathleen McVey, *Ephrem the Syrian: Hymns* (Mahwah, N.J.: Paulist Press, 1989), 270.

[12]The principal study on Rabbula is Georg G. Blum, *Rabbula von Edessa: Der Christ, der Bischof, der Theologe*, Corpus Scriptorum Christianorum Orientalium (hereafter CSCO) 300/Subsidia 34 (Louvain: Secrétariat du Corpus SCO, 1969).

[13]See the discussion in S. A. Harvey, "The Holy and the Poor: Models from Early Syriac Christianity," in *Through the Eye of a Needle: Judeo-Christian Roots of Social Welfare*, ed. Emily Albu Hanawalt and Carter Lindberg (Kirksville, Miss.: Truman State University Press, 1994), 43–66.

[14]The Syriac text of the *Life of Rabbula* was edited in Paul Bedjan, *Acta Martyrum et Sanctorum* Vol. IV (Paris/Leipzig: Otto Harrassowitz, 1894; repr. Hildesheim: Georg Olms, 1968),

evidence of his reforms survives in two collections of canons for clergy and monks transmitted in Syriac under his name.[15] Large portions of the canons are also quoted or paraphrased in the *Life of Rabbula*, with narrative explication to provide context or interpretation of the rulings.

The *Life of Rabbula* presents the bishop as one who sought to impose order on every part of his church. In fact, the Rabbula canons are notable for addressing each part of the Christian community—the laity, the different ranks of church orders, and monastics—and each is accorded their proper role, conduct, responsibility, and authority. Controls were placed on the laity with regard to marriage, divorce, and sexual relations. The laity were also charged with contributing economic support for the poor, both voluntary (monastics and hermits) and involuntary (victims of calamity, hardship, and tragic circumstance: the sick, destitute, orphaned, or widowed) in their territories; and they were ordered to fast, pray, and seek justice. The effect of these rules in the context of the Rabbula canons is to see the laity as a consecrated group no less than the clergy or monastics.[16]

Still, the laity were distinct from the consecrated offices. The Rabbula canons marked out clergy, consecrated men and women (called the "Sons and Daughters of the Covenant" in Syriac), and monastics by their location of lodging (where and with whom they lived); by clothing, shoes, and tonsure; by restriction on food and drink; by travel restrictions and prohibition from secular jobs.[17] Within these groups, the canons assign separate ministries. The ordained authority of the priesthood was clearly distinguished from the charismatic authority of monk or nun, and each had their different purpose. The canons identify different liturgical responsibilities for each office, safeguarding the complete liturgical cycle of the church. Deacons, deaconesses, and Sons and Daughters of the Covenant assisted

396–450. There is a German translation by G. Bickell, "Sammtliche Prosa-Schriften des Bischofs Rabulas von Edessa," in idem, *Ausgewählte Schriften der syrischen Kirchenväter Aphraates, Rabulas und Isaak v. Ninive, Bibliothek der Kirchenväter* 102–4, 204–5 (Kempten: Rösel, 1874), 155–271. An excellent English translation will soon appear from Cistercian Publications in a volume by Robert Doran entitled "Writings from Fifth Century Edessa: the Man of God, Rabbula and Hiba."

[15]Syriac edition with English translation in Arthur Vööbus, *Syriac and Arabic Documents Regarding Legislation Relative to Syriac Asceticism* (Stockholm: Estonian Theological Society in Exile, 1960), "The Rules of Rabbula for the Monks," 24–33 (hereafter RM), and "The Rules of Rabbula for the Clergy and the Qeiama," 34–50 (hereafter RC).

[16]See, for example, RC 6, 11, 15, 24, 28, 30, 31, 56, and 57.

[17]See RC 2, 3, 6, 10, 18, 19, 22, 23, 24, 25, 26, 29, 37, 38, 41, 42, 45; RM 2, 3, 4, 14, 15, 17, 26. See also the *Life of Rabbula*, Bedjan, *Acta* 14, 405, 406, 412, 415, 420, 421, 422.

in service to the parishes of village, town, and city. The *Life of Rabbula* adds to the canons the information that the Daughters of the Covenant worked in the women's hospital run by the church in Edessa.[18]

The concern with ministries extended into the secular sphere. The canons prohibited monastics from any secular involvement, but the clergy were declared responsible for social justice. The care of widows, orphans, the poor, and sick was specifically their charge. Prohibited from involvement in suspect legal proceedings, they were also prohibited from currying favor with the nobility lest they contribute to the oppression of the poor.[19] This area of concern is elaborated significantly in the *Life of Rabbula*, where the bishop's battles against the existing civil power structures and social hierarchies are treated at length. Doing justice is a major theme of the *Life of Rabbula*, just as it is a recurring theme in the canons. Placing it as a duty on the clergy, rather than on the monastics, protected the primary task of the monastic life as unbroken prayer.

But these canons are also notable for the far-reaching economic consequences of the ecclesiastical situation they prescribe. The Rabbula canons present a specific understanding of holy poverty. Strict financial controls were placed on monasteries to prevent any economic prosperity. Rather, ascetics of all kinds (monastics, solitaries, Sons and Daughters of the Covenant) were counted among the poor and needy charged to the care of the local church. The canons command that if the care of the ascetics should exceed the coffers of village parishes, the situation was to be reported to the bishop so that funding could be sent from Edessa. Further controls were placed on the clergy, who were prohibited by severe penalties from charging fees for services or accepting gifts, from imposing tributes on the laity, and from holding secular jobs. If undo hardship ensued, the bishop was again to be notified for assistance.[20]

The extent of economic control prescribed by the canons receives extensive discussion in the *Life of Rabbula*, where Rabbula's realignment of the economic structure of his see is chronicled in detail. If Rabbula was especially famed for his extensive social welfare programs, he was no less generous in his annual gifts to clergy, monasteries, and ascetics throughout his territory and beyond. While the canons indicate local responsibility

[18]See RC 3, 20, 27, 33, 44; RM 7, 8, 16, 19, 20, 21, 24. *Life of Rabbula*, Bedjan, *Acta* IV, 444.
[19]RC 5, 8, 12, 13, 14, 15, 16, 19, 26, 34, 36, 47.
[20]RC 5, 6, 7, 8, 9, 19, 40, 59.

through the village parishes, Rabbula's system also assumed major centralization through the episcopal seat. Two further points are significant. First,
this system indicates concern for the holy poor, those who voluntarily
chose a life of austerity in the service of the church; placed under the care
of local parishes, these ascetics were free to follow their vocations under the
protective watch of the church. Second, this system sought to ensure that
by the bishop's vigilance each part of the church could follow its professed
and defined function: monasteries were not to be businesses, but places of
prayer; Sons and Daughters of the Covenant were not to be employed in
secular service, but solely in the service of the church; the clergy were to
serve, not to grow rich.

The Rabbula canons gave enormous financial authority into the hands
of the bishop. In the *Life of Rabbula*, we are told that in his concern to allo-
cate church funds for his social welfare programs Rabbula forbid the building of new churches, sold off church treasure, implemented the canons that
gave the church the inheritance of every priest; and sought further funds
from other metropolitan churches and from the imperial court in Constantinople. Rabbula's work strongly parallels that of other bishops of the
patristic period known for their social welfare programs: Basil of Caesarea,
John Chrysostom, and John the Almsgiver are obvious cases. But Rabbula's
activity seems to have been exceptional; his successor, Ibas, lost no time in
reversing his policies.

Like the *Teaching of Addai*, the Rabbula canons provide us with an idealized picture of what the church should be, and what it was understood to
be—or hoped to be—in Syriac tradition. These canons regulate the religious,
social, and economic activity of the Christians of Edessa's see as that of one,
united body. The congregation within that territory was bound together by
structural interdependence (the allocation of different ministries, each necessary to complete liturgical life of the church), and further, bound also by
economic interdependence. According to this system, no part of the
Edessan church could function alone, either structurally or financially.

We might consider further implications of this picture. The Rabbula
canons require that everyone in the congregation be responsible for everyone else. No one is left out; no one can fall by the wayside unattended. The
sick, the needy, the orphaned, the widowed, the stranger, and the poor
(both voluntary and involuntary): all have a place, and all are to be provided sustenance, care, and comfort.

But physical healing was not the only ministry of Edessa under Rabbula's leadership and legacy. The liturgical life of the church was regulated; revised and authorized translations of the Bible were placed in churches; monasteries were established; ministries were defined and designated; the worship activity of the diocese was brought into its full expression. Rabbula's legacy was clearly one that sought to heal Edessa's Christian congregation, body and soul.

However, if such vision was to be implemented—or even attempted—practical resources were needed. The *Life of Rabbula* speaks at length about the various financial strategies Rabbula employed to fund his programs. At the end of the day, what was required was the commitment of every Christian to see themselves, their property, and their resources as inextricably joined to the body of which they were part: to the church, the body of Christ.

Such commitment, such interdependence, such connection would make possible a Christian body—the church—that would truly reflect the salvation promised to every believer, of a body healed and whole. The essential link between individual and collective healing is repeatedly stressed in Syriac tradition. In a mid-fifth century story from Persia, the Christian holy man Pethion is asked to heal a young girl. But before praying for her cure, Pethion admonished her father: "If you want your daughter to be healed, give upright judgment, do not show any favoritism, and do not take bribes. . . . Liberate the needy as far as your means allow."[21] And while the Rabbula canons are notable for their breadth of concern, they accord closely with canons of earlier collections—notably the *Didascalia Apostolorum* and the *Testament of Our Lord*—as well as with subsequent rulings in their insistence on every parish's responsibility for every person in their midst.[22] Ministry is identified time and again as material as well as spiritual in its offering.

There is much evidence from ancient Syriac Christianity that supports and elaborates the vision of the church as the body of Christ in the way

[21]There is an English translation of the story in Sebastian P. Brock and Susan Ashbrook Harvey, *Holy Women of the Syrian Orient*, rev. ed. (Berkeley: University of California Press, 1998) 82–99; here quoted from p. 83.

[22]The Syriac editions of these canonical collections have been published together with English translations as follows: Arthur Vööbus, *The Didascalia Apostolorum in Syriac*, CSCO 401–2, 407–8/ Scr. Syr. 175–6/ 179–80 (Louvain, Belgium: Secrétariat du Corpus SCO, 1979); idem, *The Synodicon in the West Syrian Tradition*, CSCO 367–8/ Scr. Syr. 161–2 (Louvain, Belgium: Secrétariat du Corpus SCO, 1975); idem, *The Canons Ascribed to Maruta of Maipherqat and Related Sources*, CSCO 339–40/ Scr. Syr. 191–2 (Louvain, Belgium: Peeters, 1982).

captured by the story of Addai and the legacy of Rabbula. While both figures were remembered in romanticized and idealized portraits, both present a great deal of practical wisdom and common sense (especially in the case of the Rabbula canons). Only when Christians commit their resources as well as themselves to the church—their goods, their time, their voices, their prayers, their presence, their energy, their activities—can the work of Christ, the healing of soul and body, be done. When we think about stewardship in the church today, we would do well to consider the model from Syriac tradition.

Further Reading

Brock, Sebastian P., *The Luminous Eye: The Spiritual World Vision of Saint Ephrem the Syrian* (Kalamazoo, Mich.: Cistercian Publications, 1992). Excellent introduction to the most important Syriac writer and theologian and also contains lucid discussion of a number of the themes I have discussed in this chapter.

Harvey, Susan Ashbrook, "Embodiment in Time and Eternity: A Syriac Perspective," Tuckahoe, N.Y.: *St. Vladimir's Theological Quarterly* 43 (1999): 105–30. Discusses how in Syriac tradition the theology of embodiment carries an inherent and profound ethical mandate for care of the sick, needy, and poor.

Harvey, Susan Ashbrook, "The Holy and the Poor: Models from Early Syriac Christianity," in *Through the Eye of a Needle: Judeo-Christian Roots of Social Welfare*, ed. Emily Albu Hanawalt and Carter Lindberg (Kirksville, Mo.: Truman State University Press, 1994) 43–66. Provides a treatment of the major paradigms for responses to poverty in ancient Syriac tradition. Simeon the Stylite, Rabbula of Edessa, and the anonymous Man of God of Edessa (the prototype for the story of St Alexius the Man of God) are the main figures discussed.

McLeod, Frederick G., "The Stranger as a Source of Social Change in Early Syriac Christianity," in *Christianity and the Stranger: Historical Essays*, ed. Francis W. Nichols (Atlanta, Ga.: Rowman and Littlefield, 1995) 36–55. Discusses the legend of the anonymous Man of God of Edessa and also the figure of Rabbula to ask how saints' stories in Syriac tradition raise issues about Christianity and social needs.

STEWARDSHIP AS A WAY TOWARD DEIFICATION

Some Moral and Social Issues in St Gregory Nazianzen

——◆——

HILARION ALFEYEV*

"Our philosophy" (ἡ καθ' ἡμᾶς φιλοσοφία), according to Gregory Nazianzen, is divided into two parts: the one that is περὶ λόγους, i.e., that concerns doctrinal matters, and the other which διὰ τῶν ἐθῶν ἔχει τό εὐσεβές, i.e., that concerns moral issues.[1] In other words, dogmatic and moral theology are the two constituents of "Christian philosophy." In this chapter we shall be dealing with the moral side of Christian life and will consider some of Gregory's characteristic moral and social themes related to the issue of stewardship. Gregory turned to these themes throughout the entire period of his ecclesiastical career, but more specifically during the time of his service as a priest in Nazianzus, around A.D. 370 to 380.

THE MEANING OF SUFFERING

In 372, several disasters fell upon Nazianzus: pestilence, drought, and, finally, a storm of rain and hail which devastated the herds and destroyed the year's harvest.[2] For a small Cappadocian city entirely dependent upon agriculture, this was a real catastrophe. People came to church in order to

*Bishop Hilarion (Alfeyev) holds a doctorate from Oxford University and St Sergius Orthodox Theological Institute in Paris. He is head of the Representation of the Russian Orthodox Church to the European Institutions and is the author of many books and articles.

[1]*Disc.* 4, 23, 6–8 (*SC* 309, 116).

[2]P. Gallay, *La vie de S. Grégoire de Nazianze* (Lyon–Paris, 1943), 122.

hear a word of consolation from their bishop, but Gregory Nazianzen the Elder, diminished in health, remained silent. Thereupon, Gregory the Younger was asked to deliver the sermon, and he used this occasion to reflect on the meaning of suffering and on why disasters are sent from God to individuals and nations.

The main idea behind the Discourse 16 is rather simple: Disasters are sent from God as a punishment for sins in order to bring people to repentance. According to the traditional Christian view based on the biblical story before the Fall, nature was obedient to Adam and was in harmony with him, but after he had transgressed the commandment, nature set its face against humans and set itself up against them.[3] Nature is now in an abnormal situation because it is "subjected to futility" and "waits with eager longing" for the liberation "from its bondage to decay."[4] The transfiguration of creation begins with the transfiguration of the human person. But the transfiguration of humans is possible only when they recognize and repent of their sinful deeds, try to liberate themselves from sin, and change for the better. The whole of the Old Testament shows that human sin is the cause of natural disasters: It is enough to remember the Flood,[5] the destruction of Sodom and Gomorrah,[6] and the various punishments sent by God to Egypt.[7] Repentance, on the contrary, can deter God's anger from both individuals and peoples, as confirmed by the prayer of King Hezekiah[8] and the fasting of the people of Nineveh.[9]

According to St Gregory, God's anger and punishment correspond to the measure of people's sinfulness. Natural disasters are caused neither by the imperfection of the universe, nor by the absence of Providence, nor by fate, but only by our sins:

Tell us whence come such blows and scourges, and what account we can give of them? Is it some disordered and irregular motion or some unguided current, some unreason of the universe, as though there were no Ruler of the world, which is therefore borne along by chance, as is the doctrine of the foolishly wise, who are themselves borne along at

[3]Cf. Gen 1.28; 2.19–20; 3.14–18.
[4]Rom 8.19–23.
[5]Gen 6–7.
[6]Gen 18.20–19.28.
[7]Ex 7–12.
[8]Is 38.1–8.
[9]Jon 3.5–10.

random by the disorderly spirit of darkness? Or are the disturbances and changes of the universe . . . directed by reason and order under the guidance of the reins of Providence? Whence come famines and tornadoes and hailstorms, our present warning blow? Whence pestilences, diseases, earthquakes, tidal waves, and fearful things in the heavens? And how is the creation, once ordered for the enjoyment of humans— their common and equal delight, changed for the punishment of the ungodly? . . . What is our calamity, and what its cause? It is either a test of virtue or a touchstone of wickedness.[10]

The reality of devastated land, a destroyed harvest, and farmers grieving over their losses evokes in Gregory a deep feeling of sorrow and compassion. At the same time he does not lose the opportunity to remind his listeners of the moral lessons that can be drawn from what has happened. He calls the citizens of Nazianzus to look at themselves and to remember their sins:

Terrible is an unfruitful season, and the loss of the crops. It could not be otherwise, when men are already rejoicing in their hopes, and counting on their all but harvested stores. Terrible again is an unseasonable harvest, when the farmers labor with heavy hearts, sitting as it were beside the grave of their crops, which the gentle rain nourished, but the wild storm has rooted up. . . . Wretched indeed is the sight of the ground devastated, cleared, and shorn of its ornaments. . . . Why have the crops withered, our storehouses been emptied, the pastures of our flocks failed, the fruits of the earth been withheld, and the plains been filled with shame instead of with fatness: why have valleys lamented and not abounded in corn, the mountains not dropped sweetness, as they shall do hereafter to the righteous, but been stripped and dishonoured. . . . Alas! What a spectacle! Our prolific crops reduced to stubble, the seed we sowed is recognised by scanty remains, and our harvest, the approach of which we reckon from the number of the months, instead of from the ripening corn, scarcely bears the firstfruits for the Lord. . . . Why is this, and what is the cause of the breach? Let us not wait to be convicted by others, let us be our own examiners. . . . One of us has oppressed the poor, and wrested from him his portion of land, and wrongly encroached upon his landmark by fraud or violence, and

---

[10]*Disc.* 16, 4–5 (*PG* 35, 937–941).

joined house to house, and field to field, to rob his neighbor of something, and been eager to have no neighbor, so as to dwell alone on the
earth. Another has defiled the land with usury and interest, both gathering where he had not sowed and reaping where he had not strawed.
. . . Another has robbed God . . . showing himself at once thankless and
senseless, in neither giving thanks for what he has had, nor prudently
providing, at least, for the future. Another has had no pity on the
widow and orphan, and not imparted his bread and meagre nourish-
ment to the needy, or rather to Christ, Who is nourished in the persons
of those who are nourished even in a slight degree.[11]

Reconciliation with God takes place through repentance. All sufferings
and all disasters aspire to this reconciliation. As far as repentance is concerned, it can be both individual and collective. Both can contribute to
changing God's anger into mercy:

Come then, all of you, my brethren, let us worship and fall down, and
weep before the Lord our Maker;[12] let us appoint a public mourning;
in our various ages and families, let us raise the voice of supplication;
and let this, instead of the cry which He hates, enter into the ears of the
Lord of Sabaoth. Let us anticipate His anger by confession; let us desire
to see Him appeased, after He was wroth. *Who knows*, he says, *whether
He will not turn and repent, and leave a blessing behind Him?*[13] This I know
certainly, I the sponsor of the loving-kindness of God. And when He
has laid aside that which is unnatural to Him, His anger, He will betake
Himself to that which is natural, His mercy. To the one He is forced by
us, to the other He is inclined. And if He is forced to strike, surely He
will refrain, according to His nature. Only let us have mercy on ourselves, and open a road for our Father's righteous affections. Let us sow
in tears, that we may reap in joy,[14] let us show ourselves people of Nineveh, not of Sodom. Let us amend our wickedness, lest we be consumed with it; let us listen to the preaching of Jonah, lest we be
overwhelmed by fire and brimstone, and if we have departed from
Sodom let us escape to the mountain, let us flee to Zoar, let us enter it

[11]*Disc.* 16, 6; 17–18 (*PG* 35, 941; 959–960).
[12]Ps 95.6.
[13]Cf. Joel 2.14.
[14]Cf. Ps 126.5.

as the sun rises; let us not stay in all the plain, let us not look around us, lest we be frozen into a pillar of salt, a really immortal pillar, to accuse the soul which returns to wickedness.[15]

That repentance which is here in question is not expressed only in tears; it is also expressed in acts of charity. To distribute bread to the hungry, to offer hospitality to the homeless, to provide clothes for the naked–these are the virtues by which we are reconciled with God, by which the heavens are conciliated, and by which the rain of God's mercy comes upon earth.[16]

The meaning of suffering is also developed in Gregory's Discourse 14, "On Love to the Poor." It was delivered around 373 in Caesarea of Cappadocia and speaks specifically about the lepers. Some scholars believe that Gregory composed this sermon after visiting a hospital for lepers built by St Basil the Great. Others say that Gregory delivered it in order to encourage people to donate money for the building of such a hospital.[17] Whatever its motivation, the discourse constitutes important evidence about Gregory's attitude to people's sufferings. With deep emotion does he describes those who are struck with what he calls "the sacred disease":[18]

> I cannot see their suffering without tears. . . . You are also witnesses of their sufferings. The spectacle which is before your eyes is terrible and piteous, unbelievable for everyone except those who have seen it: people living and at the same time dead. . . . Who they were or where are they from can hardly be recognized. They are rather wretched remains of those who once were humans. In order to be recognized they name their fathers, mothers, brothers, and birthplaces: "I am the son of so-and-so, and my mother is so-and-so, and my name is such-and-such, and you were once my friend and acquaintance." They do this because they have no previous appearance by which they could be recognized. They are people mutilated, deprived of possessions, of family, of

[15]*Disc.* 16, 14 (*PG 35*, 952–953).

[16]*Disc.* 16, 20 (*PG 35*, 961–964).

[17]See Gallay, *Vie*, 87; A. Benoit, *Saint Grégoire de Nazianze, sa vie, ses oeuvres et son époque*, 2ᵉ éd. (Hildesheim, 1971), 272–274.

[18]*Disc.* 14, 6 (*PG 35*, 864–865). Ancient Greek poets and historians usually called epilepsy "a sacred disease." However, from the fourth century onwards this description is applied to leprosy. See H. G. Liddell, R. Scott, *Greek-English Lexicon* (Oxford, 1989), 822; G.W. H. Lampe, *A Patristic Greek Lexicon* (Oxford, 1991), 922; E. Patlagean, *Pauvreté économique et pauvreté sociale à Byzance 4ᵉ–7ᵉ siècles* (Paris, 1977), III.

friends, and even of bodies; the only people of all who pity and at the same time hate themselves; they do not know whether to mourn over those members of the body which they no longer have or those which still remain. . . . Who is closer than a father? Who is more compassionate than a mother? But for these people even the doors of the parents' hearts are sealed. . . .[19] They are expelled from towns, they are expelled from homes, markets, assemblies, roads, festivals, banquets, and—O suffering!—even from water.[20]

The miserable conditions in which the lepers live as well as their social vulnerability compel Gregory to ponder the transience of life and the meaning of suffering. That God allows humans to suffer has always been one of the strongest arguments against faith in God's providence and mercy. On the other hand, some people prefer to fence themselves off by a wall of indifference and hard-heartedness by referring to the will of God: People suffer, they say, because God wants them to suffer. Gregory considers this to be a hypocritical attitude and claims that the ultimate reasons for human suffering are as unknown to us as the rules by which the universe is governed. What seem to us imperfect or deformed may be perfect and beautiful in God's eyes. And if people suffer, this does not necessarily mean that they are punished; sometimes suffering is a test through which people have to pass in order to achieve higher moral qualities. In any event, the ultimate goal of suffering as well as the true meaning of human life will be revealed only in the age to come, where all that seems anomalous will be rectified by God.[21]

So much suffering in the world must provoke in us not accusations against God but a desire to intervene creatively into the situation in order to improve the conditions of people. God calls us to collaboration, synergy: He wants us to share with Him in caring for the needy, the sick, and the suffering. A Christian is called to reveal the face of God and to be "God" for those who have lost their faith and courage, who have fallen into distress, or who are struck by disease:

A healthy and rich person must help him who is sick and the needy; he who has not fallen must assist him who fell and bruised himself; a

[19]Literally, "even nature is sealed."
[20]*Disc.* 14, 9–12 (*PG* 35, 868–872).
[21]*Disc.* 14, 29–31 (*PG* 35, 897–900).

cheerful person, him who is fainthearted; the one who is prosperous, him who suffers from misfortune. Give something to God to thank Him for your being able to become one of those who can do good to others and not one of those who need to be assisted, and that others gaze at your hands[22] and not you at theirs. . . . Be a god for the one who is in misfortune, imitating God's mercy. . . . Every navigator is close to a shipwreck. . . . and everyone who has a body is close to bodily diseases. . . . While you sail free, give hand to the one shipwrecked. . . . If you have nothing to share, shed tears together with an unfortunate wretch: the mercy which comes from your heart is a great medicine for him; and sincere compassion makes mishap easier to be borne.[23]

In summary, Gregory claims that although the ultimate reason for suffering may remain unknown, in some cases it falls upon humans as a punishment from God. Our task, however, is not to speculate about human suffering but to help those who suffer. Every misfortune, disaster, or disease provides us with a chance to help those who have been affected. Any suffering that has befallen our neighbor gives us the possibility to express compassion in concrete deeds. By helping our fellow humans, we assist God and become ourselves "gods" for those who suffer. Thus, the mystery of deification begins in our everyday lives when we imitate God in His compassion and mercy.

SOCIAL INEQUALITY AND CHRISTIAN MORALITY

Gregory was a citizen of a mighty empire in which it was a commonplace for citizens to own slaves. At the head of the social pyramid stood the semidivine emperor, who was supposed to be subject to no one other than God. The slaves formed the bottom of the pyramid. These were to be "submissive to their masters with all respect, not only to the kind and gentle, but also to the overbearing."[24] Slaves were entirely dependent on their masters and without their consent they could neither marry, nor become members of the Christian clergy. In fact, they could not even dispose of their own life.[25] Between these two poles, various social classes were located–from senators, courtiers, governors of provinces and cities, nobles of different

[22]I.e., in the hope of receiving alms.
[23]*Disc.* 14, 26; 28 (*PG* 35, 892–896).
[24]1 Pet 2.18.
[25]Cf. C. Mango, *Byzantium, the Empire of New Rome* (London: Trafalgar Square, 1980), 32–33, 222–223.

ranks, landowners, and army officers to merchants, soldiers, peasants, and libertines. Clergymen could theoretically belong to any social rank; however, from the fourth century it became more and more common to seek candidates for the episcopacy from among the aristocracy; it became less and less feasible for a representative of a lower stratum of the society to become a bishop.

All of society was to be governed by a system of order,[26] one that was inherited from the ancient Roman Empire. The hierarchical structure of Byzantine society corresponded to the underlying notion of a natural inequality of people. At the same time, all were considered to be equal before the law, except the emperor who was above it, and slaves who were below it (for each of whom his or her master was the ultimate authority). Characteristic in this respect is Gregory's remark that, like the beauty of the skies, the light of the sun and the air are a common possession of all people in the same way that "lawgivers and kings" allow "all free people" (i.e., not slaves) to be equally under the protection of law.[27]

Christian loyalty to civil authority has been mandatory in every era in all kinds epochs and under all political regimes, including those hostile to Christianity. St Peter had in mind the pagan Roman state of his time when he wrote: "Be subject for the Lord's sake to every human institution, whether it be the emperor as supreme, or to governors as sent by him. . . . Fear God. Honor the emperor."[28] St Paul called every Christian to be "subject to the governing authorities," since "there is no authority except from God,"[29] and also to make supplications "for kings and all who are in high positions."[30] In the second and third centuries, apologetic works addressed to the Roman emperors repeatedly stressed that Christians are loyal to the civil authorities. The divine origin of the emperor's power was a commonly accepted fact. Even the pagan emperor, according to Tertullian, belongs more to Christians than to the pagans, because God appoints him.[31]

Gregory Nazianzen does not question the divine origin of imperial power even when the issue turns on the person of Julian the Apostate. In Gregory's eyes Julian was not a usurper, nor was his power unlawful: He was

[26]Mango, *Byzantium*, 33.
[27]*Disc.* 4, 96, 16–20 (*SC* 309, 242).
[28]1 Pet 2.13–17.
[29]Rom 13.1–2.
[30]1 Tim 2.2.
[31]Tertullian, *Apology* 33.

a legitimate ruler who did not realize the height of his vocation and who turned himself against God. In his Discourse 19, delivered on the occasion of the population census decreed by Julian, Gregory insists that God acts through the civil authority, even when a pagan such as Octavian Augustus or a criminal like Herod are heads of state. This is confirmed by the Gospel story of Jesus who was born during the time of Herod's population census and who was a loyal citizen of the Roman Empire:

> *In those days a decree went out from Caesar Augustus that all the world should be enrolled.* And the population census began. *And Joseph also went up to Bethlehem to be enrolled with Mary, his betrothed, because he was from the house and lineage of David.*[32] And it is then—O, miraculous thing!—that the Savior, the Creator and Ruler of everything, is born in a squalid and tiny habitation . . . Today Herod rages and slanders the infants, and because of the Liberator he destroys those who were to be liberated. . . . With Christ are you[33] enrolling, with Christ are you measuring, with the Head are you sanctioning, with the Word are you calculating (μετὰ Λόγου λογίζεις). Christ is being born for you, He remains God and becomes man; He associates with humans. What does this word show? It seems to me that it instructs those to whom such things are entrusted that in the most important administrative matters God is always involved. In order to show reverence to those who were conducting the population census He associates with the flesh and humans precisely at that time. And in order to console us in our slavery. . . . He himself pays the tax (τὸ δίδραχμον),[34] and not only for himself but also for Peter, the most venerable among the disciples.[35]

God, therefore, acts through any kind of ruler and any kind of superior, regardless of his attitude toward Christianity. It is for this reason that neither Christ, nor the apostles, nor the apologists of the second and third centuries, nor the later Fathers of the Church saw themselves as social reformers. None called to change the existing social structures. Throughout the many centuries of its existence Christianity did not elaborate its own social doctrine; its moral teaching always addressed individuals rather than

[32]Lk 2.1–5.
[33]These words are addressed to Julian.
[34]Cf. Mt 17.24–27.
[35]*Disc.* 19, 12–13 (*PG* 35, 1057–1060).

the faceless mass or various social structures. By no means did Christians consider this world to be ideal, but they were convinced that as long as humans remained in their fallen state no paradise on earth was possible—hence, the tranquil and conscious obedience of Christians to the authorities, as well as their refusal to be engaged in the struggle for human rights and freedom.[36] For a Christian, a true freedom consists not in being liberated from the power of a superior, lord, or king but in becoming spiritually free, liberated from the chains of sin.

In his Discourse 17, delivered in the presence of the governor (city mayor) of Nazianzus, Gregory speaks of the obligation for Christians to obey the civil authorities and claims that this is a law issued by the Holy Spirit. However, he does not limit himself to this notion. He also addresses the mayor himself and speaks of how he should use his power on behalf of the citizens. For the administrator, the way to deification lies through alms, philanthropy, and a merciful attitude towards his subordinates; for the subordinate, on the other hand, it lies in obedience to God, to the superiors, and to other fellow humans:

> Let us submit to God, to each other, and to earthly authorities: to God because of everything, to each other because of love to our brothers, and to the authorities because of order. . . . There is also the following law among our laws which are praiseworthy and in the most beautiful way decreed by the Holy Spirit . . . that slaves should be obedient to their masters, wives to their husbands, the Church to the Lord, and the students to the shepherds and teachers. In the same way we should submit to every governing authority not only because of wrath[37] but also for the sake of conscience. . . . [38] And what about you, rulers and governors? Now my word will turn to you . . . With Christ are you[39] governing, with Christ are you exercising authority, for from Him have you received the sword—not for action, but for threat. . . .[40] Be with Christ

[36]Both the introduction of a special social doctrine in a number of Christian churches (notably in the Roman Catholic Church) and the involvement of certain representatives of the clergy in the struggle for human rights are essentially modern phenomena. Christian tradition knows many cases of intercession of the Church on behalf of the oppressed, but this was done on a purely philanthropic basis and was not motivated by any political or social doctrine.

[37]I.e., not only in order to avoid God's wrath.

[38]Cf. Rom 1.5.

[39]This and what follows is addressed to the governor of Nazianzus.

[40]I.e., not in order to use the sword but in order to threaten infringers.

and not with an earthly ruler, be with the good Lord and not with a bit-
ter tyrant. . . . Imitate . . . God's love of humans. The most divine in a
human person is precisely this, to do good. You can become god without any labor: do not miss your chance to reach deification. Some
exhaust their possessions, others exhaust their flesh for the sake of the
spirit, still others mortify themselves for Christ and arise and go entirely
away from the world. . . . Nothing of these do we expect from you, only
love of your fellow humans.[41]

In the text quoted, Gregory calls the slaves to obey their masters in the
same way as the Church obeys Christ. In another place he calls the masters
to be merciful to their slaves, remembering that Christ also took upon himself "the form of a servant."[42] For those who are free it is enough that they
have slaves but they must not deal harshly with them.[43] None of these statements imply that Gregory advocated slavery. Though being an aristocrat and
a slave-owner, he understood well that all people were originally created as
free and noble, and it is only as a result of the Fall that inequality existed:

> *From the beginning*, He says, *it was not so*.[44] But *He who made* a human
> person *from the beginning*[45] made him free and self-governed, limited
> only by one law of the commandment,[46] and rich in the delight of par-
> adise. . . . Freedom and richness consisted in keeping the command-
> ment, and true poverty and slavery, in its transgression. However, from
> the time when jealousy, quarrels, and the treacherous tyranny of the
> devil appeared . . . the kinship between humans was broken due to their
> division into ranks, and their natural nobility was destroyed by greedi-
> ness. . . . But you should look at the initial equality of ranks rather than
> at its subsequent division.[47]

Gregory underlines the fact that the division of the human race into
nobles and plebeians is as unnatural as is its division into slaves and

[41]*Disc.* 17, 6–10 (*PG* 35, 972–977).
[42]Cf. Phil 2.7.
[43]*Disc.* 19, 13 (*PG* 35,1060).
[44]Mt 19.8.
[45]Mt 19.4.
[46]Cf. Gen 2.16–17.
[47]*Disc.* 14, 25–26 (*PG* 35, 892).

masters.[48] True nobility and true freedom consist not in one man's noble origins but in his high moral character:

> What is a master? What is a slave? Is it not a false division?
> One is the Creator of all, one law, one judgment.
> See a fellow servant in him who attends upon you . . .
> And what about household slaves, and especially the slaves of God?
> They should not avoid doing good to their masters.
> It is one's way of life (ὁ τρόπος) that makes one either slave or free.
> Christ appeared as a slave but He liberated us.[49]

Elsewhere Gregory speaks more bluntly: "For me every morally perverse person (πᾶς σκαιός) is a slave, and he who is virtuous is free."[50]

Division into rich and poor is also among the consequences of the Fall. Wealth, according to Christian views, is hardly compatible with salvation: Christ himself instructed the rich young man to sell all his possessions and to give to the poor.[51] Gregory, less radical, suggested two possibilities for the rich: either to distribute their possessions to the poor, or to keep it for themselves but to share it with others (he himself chose the latter option). Developing this theme, Gregory criticizes the aristocratic and wealthy people of his time for their squandering and their indifference to the poor:

> We demand that even the floor should exhale the fragrance of flowers
> . . . and the table to be sprinkled with the most aromatic and most
> expensive oils . . . and that adorned boys with exuberant woman-like

[48]In this assertion Gregory is close to Gregory of Nyssa but differs from Basil the Great; the latter regarded the division of humans into free and slaves as instituted by God: see R. Teja, "San Basilio y la esclavitud: teoría y praxis," *Basil of Caesarea: Christian, Humanist, Ascetic. A Sixteen-Hundredth Anniversary Symposium*, J. Fedwick, ed., Part I (Roma, 1981), 396–399; A. Hadjinicolaou-Marava, *Recherches sur la vie des esclaves dans le Monde Byzantin* (Athens, 1950), 15–16; on Gregory of Nyssa's views on slavery see R. Moriarty, *Human Owners, Human Slaves: Gregory of Nyssa*, Hom. Eccl. 4, Studia Patristica 27 (*Papers Presented at the Eleventh International Conference on Patristic Studies held in Oxford 1991*), E. A. Livingstone, ed. (Louvain, Belgium, 1993), 62–69. We should note that the notion of the natural equality of all humans became more and more widespread in Byzantium and by the sixth century was acknowledged even by the civil authorities (it is repeatedly stated in Justinian's *novellae*). This did not lead, however, to the abolition of slavery: See J. Gaudemet, *Institutions de l'antiquité*, 2nd ed. (Paris, 1982), 716–717.

[49]*Carm.* I, 2, 33 (*PG* 37, 938).
[50]*Carm.* I, 2, 26 (*PG* 37, 853).
[51]Mt 19.21.

hair should stand in rows . . . of whom some should hold wine-cups with their finger-tips . . . while others must hold fans above our head and by handmade wafts cool the fullness of our flesh. . . . For the poor even a sufficient amount of water is something great, while we drink glasses of wine until intoxication. . . . What is it, O friends and brothers? . . . Why do we live luxuriously while our brothers are in distress? . . . It is necessary either to reject everything for Christ and sincerely follow Him, having taken the cross. . . .[52] or to share our possessions with Christ in order that our possession of goods—because we possess it in a right way—be sanctified, and that those without may partake of it.[53]

Thus, every social inequality—be it between rich and poor, masters and slaves, nobles and plebeians—is contrary to the original order and is a consequence of the Fall. The same applies to the inequality between men and women.

In Byzantium women, especially those who were married, were considered to be second-rate citizens. Their roles in social life were insignificant; for the most part they remained at home, looked after the children, and occupied themselves with some simple needlework. In Gregory's view, which corresponded to commonly accepted opinions, a woman should not occupy herself with theology or speak on religious matters. Her lot is a loom, yarn, and the reading of pious literature.[54] A woman should neither use cosmetics nor build on her head a tower out of artificial hair; instead she should wear hair-dress and be content with her natural beauty.[55] It is best for a woman is to stay indoors, pray, weave, or spin, speak as little as possible, meet only other pious women, and attend to her own husband.[56] In marriage, the wife is subordinate to her husband, and he must watch her behavior. If cosmetics show on her face, he must wipe them off; if she speaks too much, he should force her to cease; if she laughs, he must stop her; if she spends too much money or drinks too much, he must limit her; if she goes out too often, he must forbid her to do so.[57]

---

[52]Cf. Mt 16.24.

[53]*Disc.* 14, 17–18 (*PG* 35, 877–880).

[54]*Carm.* 1, 2, 3 (*PG* 37, 602–603).

[55]*Carm.* 1, 2, 29 (*PG* 37, 884–885). Cf. A. Knecht, *Gregor von Nazianz Gegen die Putzsucht der Frauen* (Heidelberg, 1972).

[56]*Carm.* 1, 2, 29 (*PG* 37, 903–904).

[57]*Disc.* 37, 8, 15–20 (*SC* 318, 288).

In spite of these views Gregory understood that the primordial equality between woman and man could not be contested. When reasoning as regards the subordinate position of women in ancient Israel, Gregory advances a hypothesis according to which men should be blamed for introducing laws that discriminate against women. In Christianity, on the contrary, every discrimination should be avoided because all are equal before God and in Christ "there is neither male nor female."[58]

For what was the reason they restrained the woman, but indulged the man, and that a woman who practises evil against her husband's bed is an adulteress, and the penalties of the law for this are very severe; but if the husband commits fornication against his wife, he has no account to give? I do not accept this legislation; I do not approve this custom. They who made the Law were men, and therefore their legislation is hard on women, since they have placed children also under the authority of their fathers, while leaving the weaker sex uncared for. God does not so, but He says: *Honor your father and your mother....*[59] See the equality of the legislation. There is one Maker of man and woman; one debt is owed by children to both their parents. . . . If you enquire into the worse—well, the woman sinned, and so did Adam. The serpent deceived them both; and one was not found to be the stronger and the other the weaker. But do you consider the better? Christ saves both by His passion. Was He made flesh for the man? So He was also for the woman. Did He die for the man? The woman also is saved by His death. He is called *descended from David;*[60] and so perhaps you think the man is honored; but He is born of a Virgin,[61] and this is on the woman's side. They two, He says, shall *become one flesh;*[62] so let the one flesh have equal honor. And Paul legislates for chastity by his example. How, and in what way? This mystery is a profound one, and I am saying that it refers to Christ and the Church.[63] It is well for the wife to respect Christ through her husband: and it is well for the husband not to dishonor the Church through his wife. *Let the wife,* he says, *see that she respects her*

58Gal 3.28.
59Ex 20.12.
60Rom 1.3.
61Cf. Mt 1.23.
62Gen 2.24.
63Eph 5.32.

husband,[64] for by doing so she respects Christ; but also he bids the husband cherish his wife, for so Christ does the Church.[65]

In this passage Gregory actually argues against many of the widely held opinions of the average fourth-century Byzantine citizen. He contests a fundamental tenet of Byzantine thinking especially espoused in ascetical and monastic literature, where woman is presented as the "devil's gateway,"[66] a source of everything bad, scandalous, and immoral.[67] Gregory here speaks out in defense of women, in the same way that elsewhere he defends the poor, the suffering, and the discriminated.[68]

Gregory's views on social issues can be summarized in the following three basic concepts: every authority comes from God; every kind of discrimination and inequality is unnatural; and every person, regardless of his or her social rank, can live a virtuous life that leads to deification.

Perhaps the most characteristic feature of Gregory's moral and social teaching is that he considers human life both in the Church and in society as a way towards deification. The observation of God's commandments and living a virtuous life are necessary in order for the human person to be purified and for improving the quality of his life. Virtuous living, through which comes purification, is a person's complete transfiguration, his "second birth,"[69] or birth from above.[70] Life in accordance with Christian moral standards is one's ascent to the heights of the knowledge of God, of theology and of contemplation. Virtuous life is but a means towards this end:

---

[64]Eph 5.33.

[65]*Disc. 37*, 6, 4–7, 20 (*SC* 318, 282–286).

[66]Tertullian, *Women* 1, 1.

[67]Cf. Mango, *Byzantium*, 225–227; J. LaPorte, *The Role of Women in Early Christianity* (New York–Toronto, 1982), 26–27.

[68]In this respect Gregory differs significantly from Basil the Great. As has been noted, the latter's attitude to women in general "did not measure up to modern standards of even those of . . . Gregory Nazianzen"; see F. X. Murphy, *Moral and Ascetical Doctrine in St. Basil,* Studia Patristica 14 (*Papers Presented to the Sixth International Conference on Patristic Studies held in Oxford 1971*, Part III), E. A. Livingstone, ed., *TU* 117 (Berlin, 1976), 325. This is particularly clear from Basil's *Letter 199*, 36–48 (ed. Courtonne, 161–163), where Basil introduces various canonical regulations discriminating against women.

[69]*Carm.* 1, 2, 8 (*PG* 37, 661).

[70]Cf. Jn 3.3.

Ascend through virtuous life. Acquire purity through purification. Do you want one day to become a theologian and worthy of the Divinity? Observe the commandments and progress through keeping His pre-scriptions. For practice is a foothold of contemplation (πρᾶξις γὰρ ἐπίβασις θεωρίας).[71]

---

[71]*Disc.* 20, 12, 4–7 (*SC* 270, 80–82).

THE POWER OF DETACHMENT IN EARLY MONASTIC LITERATURE

John Chryssavgis*

Introduction: The Way of the Desert

One may not immediately or even easily associate the notion of stewardship with the early monastic tradition. Monasticism is normally regarded as a way of giving up, rather than as a way of giving, as a life of sacrifice rather than as a life of sharing. Nevertheless, in their radical renunciation of the world—of worldly principles and possessions—the monastics that fled to the deserts of Egypt and Palestine in fact dealt with and taught about liberation from an attachment to things material as well as about the importance of partnership and stewardship. In this chapter, we shall explore the notion of detachment, as well as its corresponding notion of attachment, particularly as these are reflected in connection with the concepts of charity and community within the monastic literature of the early church. The focus of our attention will be on the *Sayings of the Desert Fathers* (fourth century), the *Ascetic Discourses* of Abba Isaiah of Scetis (fifth century), the *Reflections* of Abba Zosimas (early sixth century), and the *Letters* of Barsanuphius and John (mid-sixth century).[1]

*Dn John Chryssavgis studied theology in Athens and Oxford and taught at St Andrew's Theological College in Sydney and at Holy Cross School of Theology in Boston. His writing has focused on the early ascetic literature of Egypt, Palestine, and Sinai.

[1]On the *Sayings* and the *Reflections*, see J. Chryssavgis, *In the Heart of the Desert* (Bloomington, Ind.: World Wisdom Books, 2003); on Isaiah of Scetis, see J. Chryssavgis and P. R. Penkett, *Abba Isaiah, Ascetic Discourses* (Kalamazoo, Mich.: Cistercian Publications, 2002); on Barsanuphius and John, see forthcoming translation by J. Chryssavgis, *Barsanuphius and John: Questions and Answers* (Kalamazoo, Mich.: Cistercian Publications).

Detachment, or *apotage*, is in fact an ongoing lesson learned over many years in the desert, not an action that occurs once for all. In some ways, it is the first step of monastic renunciation of material possessions or of the flight to the wasteland of the desert.

> Abba Arsenius prayed to God in these words: "Lord, lead me in the way of salvation." And a voice came, saying to him: "Arsenius, flee from people and you will be saved."[2]

Yet, detachment is always far more than merely spatial or material.

> Abba Zosimas always liked to say: "It is not possessing something that is harmful, but being attached to it."[3]

This kind of detachment is not primarily the inability to focus on things, material or other; it is the spiritual capacity to focus on all things, material and other, without attachment. It is something profoundly spiritual; it is an attitude of life. And in this respect, detachment is ongoing, requiring continual refinement in the life of every monastic, as in the life of every Christian.

In this light, perhaps it would even be inappropriate to speak of renunciation as merely the first stage—albeit essential—of detachment. Rather, there are many stages in the way of detachment, just as there are a number of steps in the ladder of spiritual life. Indeed, we might refer to a series of *stages of refinement*. There are, it seems, a number of successive detachments that one undergoes in the desert, where detachment resembles the shedding of coats of skin, until our senses are sharpened, or until "our inner vision becomes [more] keen."[4] After all, when we learn to let go of something, we also learn what is truly worth holding on to. Detachment is, therefore, the beginning of humility, just as stewardship is a way of submitting to the needs of neighbor and to the priority of grace.

> Abba Zosimas said: "In time, through neglect, we lose even the little fervor that we suppose that we have in our ascetic renunciation. We become attached to useless, insignificant and entirely worthless matters,

[2]Arsenius 1.
[3]*Reflections* I, b and XV, d.
[4]Doulas 1.

substituting these for the love of God and neighbor, appropriating material things as if they were our own or as if we had not received them from God. 'What do you have that you did not receive? And if you received it, then why do you boast as if it were not a gift?'" (I Cor 4.7)[5]

DETACHMENT FROM THE BODY AND THE WORLD: THE *Sayings of the Desert Fathers*

For many of us, the early monastics seemed to discipline the body in cruel ways. Indeed, many of the *Sayings of the Desert Fathers* appear to treat the body very harshly. In fact, however, the emphasis is always on shedding the excess layers, on getting rid of the dead layers, which this literature defines as "flesh." It is another aspect of offering, even sacrificing oneself to the world and to God. In the desert, detachment is precisely a way of renouncing excess baggage and of traveling light. And the truth is that we can always manage with less than we have; indeed, we can often manage with a lot less than we would dare to imagine. Even while claiming that the entire world belongs to God, the desert elders would strive no longer to depend on material possessions. Their context is a struggle to become less centered on the world; it is an effort to establish another order and focus, where the entire world is in fact centered on God.

Refocusing our vision

Nonetheless, the ascetic's treatment of the body appears negative to contemporary readers and practitioners because we have overloaded the body with far too much. The change, therefore, as we move from our own lifestyle to that espoused by Antony or Arsenius, seems so overwhelming and so enormous that it creates a sense of vertigo within us. Our bodies literally go through "withdrawal symptoms" when confronted with the radical withdrawal of Antony into the desert. After all, our culture teaches us that the more we have, the better we are; Antony's context taught him that the less he had, the more he was! We appear to be carrying so much baggage, so many preoccupations and concerns, and such great loads that walking freely with God truly appears frightening, unfamiliar, and perhaps painful. Our natural response, then, is to resist such change, to defy the divine vocation to give, and to refuse the opportunity of stewardship. It simply makes no sense to us.

[5] *Reflections* X, c.

Abba Antony said: "A time is coming when people will go insane. And when they see someone who is not insane, they will attack that person saying: 'You are crazy; you are not like us.' "[6]

Thus, in the fourth century, detachment meant that the desert Fathers and Mothers became as nothing, much like the sand of the desert that surrounded them. Moreover, detachment further implied a sense of becoming *one with the environment.* Their holiness was part and parcel of a sense of wholeness. Just as "at-one-ment" with one's neighbor was of the essence of desert spirituality, so too was "at-tune-ment" to one's environment, to the world, and to God.

Abba John the Eunuch said: "My children, let us not pollute this place, since our Fathers have previously cleansed it from demons."[7]

If the purpose of fleeing to the desert was to re-establish a lost order, then reconciliation with creation and reconnection with God was critical. These elders may sometimes appear eccentric, but *eccentricity literally means moving the center, re-centering the world on God.* The world becomes a wasteland unless it, too, comes alive in an authentic human being, who in turn becomes the eyes and conscience of the world.

We might think of it in this way: it is simply not possible to share something precious, or even to hold a lover's hand, when we keep our fists clenched, or if we are holding onto something so tightly. The genuine purpose of monastic detachment is not to live apart from society, but ultimately to learn how to live as a part of society.

One day Abba Longinus . . . said to Abba Lucius: "I wish to flee from people." The old man replied: "If you have not first of all lived rightly with people, then you will not be able to live properly in solitude either."[8]

The aim, then, is to be neither dependent nor detached from people. Instead, it is to be more transparent, allowing for sincerity in personal relationships and sensitivity in material possessions.

[6]Antony 25.
[7]John the Eunuch 5.
[8]Longinus 1.

> Abba Agathon said: "Under no circumstances should a monk let his conscience accuse him of anything."

> He also said: "I have never gone to sleep with a grievance against anyone. And, as far as I could, I have never let anyone go to sleep with a grievance against me."[9]

Detachment implies a corresponding sincerity and sensitivity in actions, words, and even gestures.

> Abba Isaiah said: "When someone wishes to render evil for evil, that person can cause harm to another's soul even by means of a single nod of the head."[10]

This attitude also extends beyond one's connection with other people to one's relationship to material things.

> Abba Agathon was walking with his disciples. One of them, on finding a small green pea on the road, said to the old man: "Father, may I take it?" The old man, looking at him with astonishment, replied: "Was it you that put it there?" "No," said the brother. "How then," continued the old man, "can you take up something, which you did not put down?"[11]

Work and prayer; words and silence

The detachment that is recommended here is actually a form of letting go. We are to let go of our actions, of our statements, and finally of our very existence. The aim of letting go of our actions is in fact the first step in the learning of prayer, which in itself is the starting-point and ending-point of all authentic action, of any action that stems from the heart.

> Abba Nilus said: "Everything that you do in revenge against a brother who has harmed you will come back to your mind at the time of prayer."

> He also said: "Whatever you have endured out of love of wisdom will bear fruit for you at the time of prayer."[12]

[9]Agathon 2 and 4.
[10]Isaiah 8.
[11]Agathon 11.
[12]Nilus 1 and 5.

In prayer, we are literally letting go: renouncing and refining so many images and so much information that tend to veil our relationship to God and heavily weigh down on the soul. By letting go, we also learn to pray more spontaneously–a gift that children seem to have innately but which takes a lifetime for us to recover as adults.

When we are detached from material things, then the way of silence and the way of service coincide.

> Abba Poemen said: "If three people meet, of whom the first fully pre-serves interior peace, and the second gives thanks to God in illness, and the third serves with a pure mind, these three are doing the same work."[13]

Furthermore, through detachment, work is never separated from prayer.

> It was said of Abba Apollo, that he had a disciple named Isaac, perfectly trained in all good works and in the gift of ceaseless prayer. . . . He used to say that all things are good in their proper time, "for there is a time for everything."[14] (cf. Eccl 3.1–8)

Just as prayer conditions our works, silence too conditions our words. Such silence is yet another form of freedom and detachment.

> Abba Poemen said: "If you are silent, you will have peace wherever you live."[15]

Such prayer in silence frees us for carefree service of others, where we are no longer conditioned by the burden of necessity but always prepared for the novelty of grace's surprise.

DETACHMENT IN PERSONAL RELATIONS: THE *Discourses* OF ABBA ISAIAH OF SCETIS

A later emigrant from Egypt, Abba Isaiah had spent many years in a monastery as well as actually residing in the desert of Scetis. He moved to Palestine–fleeing fame, as we are informed–between 431 and 451. He first

---

[13]Poemen 29.
[14]Isaac the Theban 2.
[15]Poemen 84.

settled near Eleftheropolis, moving finally to Beit Daltha near Gaza, some four miles from Thavatha, where Barsanuphius and John would later establish their reputation. There, Isaiah stayed for several decades, serving for his contemporaries and visitors as a living example of the old Scetiote ascetic life, until his death in 489. Abba Isaiah inserted numerous *Sayings*, both identifiable and original, in his *Ascetic Discourses*, possibly regarding himself as responsible for preserving and even promoting the words of the elders that he had either personally heard or heard about in Egypt.

An asceticism of sensitivity

Drawing on a rich monastic tradition that defines regulations for those living in a religious community, as well as on the basic evangelical precepts of charitable conduct (cf. Mt 7.12 and Lk 6.31), Abba Isaiah is careful to delineate clearly the boundaries of respect in regard to personal and interpersonal relations. The *Ascetic Discourses* [hereafter *A.D.*] clearly emphasize the primacy of charity:

> Without charity, virtue is only an illusion. (*A.D.* 21)

For Isaiah, such sensitivity in brotherly relations is part and parcel of monastic detachment. The ultimate aim of renunciation is learning not simply to give up, but in fact to give freely of one's own possessions and one's self. The desert ascetic in Egypt—so Isaiah would have recalled from his own sojourn there—was called to let go of all control—material, verbal, and even spiritual:

> Our fathers of old said that the flight is one from one's own self. (*A.D.* 26)

"Letting go of oneself before God," "letting go of other people," and "letting be of things in general" are phrases frequently repeated in Isaiah's ascetic writings (cf. esp. *A.D.* 4). Such is "the power of renunciation" that is discovered in "the power of the cell" (*A.D.* 4). Indeed, without such surrender, the act of worldly renunciation is worthless (*A.D.* 26).

Asceticism and community

In this regard, Abba Isaiah appreciates how an untold number of variables interact upon and influence the dance that we call life. More than we often realize or perhaps care to admit, our lives hinge on little things: on a word, a gesture, a nod, a smile, and a glance. This gentle approach extends to "the slight and trivial" (*A.D.* 15) details of daily routine:[16] from how one greets another to how one holds a vessel given by another; from how one stands in prayer to how one behaves in the privacy of the cell; from how one notices a person of the opposite sex to how one walks with a friend of the same sex; from how one carries out the shopping to how one converses in public; from discussions about Scripture to disputes about theology (cf. *A.D.* 3–5).

These details are personal, and yet so general; they are particular, and at the same time so universal. Our words (or our silence) and our deeds (or our indifference) have a profound impact on our neighbor and on our world. Even minor actions have significant spiritual consequences. Abba Isaiah is convinced that it is not life in ascetic isolation, but life in shared participation that renders the monk a genuine disciple of Christ.

The grace of love

This is why we are called not only to "*love praying* ceaselessly," but–as Abba Isaiah observes–"we are to *love to love*" (*A.D.* 16). Love is the only purpose [*telos*: cf. *A.D.* 16), the climax [*oros*] of all virtue, while "the end of all passion is self-justification" (*A.D.* 7). Nothing is more detestable and dangerous in the spiritual life than insensitivity toward the pain of others and toward the presence of God (*A.D.* 5, 16, 26, and 18). When we are not sensitive to others, when we do not love, "then our prayer, too, is unacceptable" (*A.D.* 16). Love is identified with life (cf. *A.D.* 21; see also I Jn 3.13–14); "detachment" is the other side of the same coin known as "dispassion" (*A.D.* 21 and 26). Indeed, such loving detachment is "the very seal of the soul" (*A.D.* 7), "the actual image of Christ within us" (*A.D.* 25).

Often we reduce the concept of love or stewardship merely to outward actions. Yet love involves the "visible" dimensions of charity as well as the "invisible" aspects of support and silence. Conversely, being silent when we are supposed to speak "can be the cause of our spiritual death;" at the same time, a word out of place "can also be the death of our soul" (*A.D.* 5). The context within which Abba Isaiah perceives the virtue of love is the Pauline image of the body, wherein the least significant members deserve the greatest attention, the most vulnerable are indispensable, ultimately invaluable (I Cor 12.12):

[16]Cf. also Abba Isaiah, *Saying* 8.

Every one of the body's stronger limbs takes care of the weaker members in order to attend and care for them until the latter are healed; and they say: "I am the weak one." But the cruel person busies himself, asking: "What have I to do with the weak? I am not weak." (*A.D.* 26).

We have learned this way of love—so Isaiah believes—directly from the incarnate Son of God, in whom we have been nurtured from the vulnerability of childhood to the maturity of sainthood. In his 25th *Ascetic Discourse*, Abba Isaiah analyses this image of the providential and maternal love of God:

> While the young infant is still in its mother's bosom, she guards it at all times from every evil. When it cries, she offers it her breast. Gradually, she gives it breath with all her strength, helping it to learn fear . . . in order that its heart is not filled with boldness. But when it cries, she is moved to pity, for it is born of her entrails. She consoles, embraces, and comforts it again, by giving it her breast. If it is greedy for gold, silver, or precious stones, nevertheless it overlooks these while being in the mother's bosom. It scorns everything in order to take the breast.

We are raised on this milk of love, which comprises the "great mystery" revealing us as being "members of Christ's body, of His flesh and of His bones" (here, Abba Isaiah is paraphrasing St Paul in Ephesians 5.30), as well as "members one of another."

DETACHMENT FROM MATERIAL THINGS: THE *Reflections* OF ABBA ZOSIMAS

One of the most likely places that the *Sayings of the Desert Fathers* were first recollected and then collected was in Palestine, partly due to its geographical proximity to Egypt, but also due to the steady progression of Egyptian monks to the southern parts of Judaea. *The Sayings of the Desert Fathers*, in both their alphabetical, and anonymous or systematic collections, are already found in seminal texts of the early period. Such texts include, among others, the *Ascetic Discourses* of Abba Isaiah of Scetis in the late fifth century and the *Reflections* of Zosimas, who founded a community in the first half of the sixth century. In particular, the monastery of Seridos in the Gaza region played an important and influential role, which is reflected in the *Correspondence* of Barsanuphius and John.[17] It is to these latter two texts that we now turn our attention.

Abba Zosimas' *Reflections* make numerous citations of the *Sayings*, implying perhaps that Zosimas borrowed these from existing written texts. Abba Zosimas even reveals having heard various *Apophthegmata* from others, which attests to the fact that these were widely known and, possibly, even accessible more or less everywhere in monastic circles of lower Palestine by the middle of the sixth century. Indeed, Zosimas' reference to "the sayings of the holy elders"[18] is perhaps the earliest such characterization of the sayings with this specific title. In a quaint passage, we are told that:

> The blessed Zosimas always loved to read these *Sayings* all the time; they were almost like the air that he breathed.[19]

Like *The Sayings of the Desert Fathers* themselves, these "reflections" were related but not actually recorded by Zosimas. In content and style, they very much resemble the *Ascetic Discourses* of Abba Isaiah of Scetis. Zosimas flourished between 475 and 525, namely from the period just after the fourth Ecumenical Council (in 451) until around the time of the great Gaza elders Barsanuphius, John, and their disciple Dorotheus. He is mentioned several times by Dorotheus of Gaza, who knew him personally and visited him as a younger contemporary and compatriot. Dorotheus may in fact be the compiler of the *Reflections* of Abba Zosimas. In this section, we shall simply quote excerpts from some key passages from the *Reflections*, which speak clearly about attachment to and detachment from material possessions.

Chapter I: On Detachment

Whoever so desires is able to regard the whole world as being nothing.

Abba Zosimas would take whatever he could find—whether a nail or some thread, or anything else of insignificant value—and say: "Who would ever fight or argue over this; or else, who would keep a grudge or be afflicted over this? Unless it be someone who has truly lost his

---

[17]Cf. L. Regnault, "Les *Apophtegmes des Pères* en Palestine aux Ve et VIe siècles," *Irénikon* 54 (1981): 320–330.

[18]Cf. *Reflections* XII.

[19]See *Reflections* XII, b.

mind. Any godly person, who is progressing and advancing, should consider the whole world as this nail, even if that person actually possesses the entire world. As I always like to say: 'It is not possessing something that is harmful, but being attached to it.'"

[Zosimas] remembered the brother who owned some vegetables, and used to say: "Did he not sow the seed, or toil in labor, or plant and nurture their growth? Did he perhaps uproot them or throw them away? No. Yet, he possessed these vegetables as if he did not in fact own them (I Cor 7.30–31). He was not therefore worried when his elder, wishing to test him, began to destroy them. This appeared as nothing to him; instead, he concealed his feelings. Moreover, when one root remained, he said to his elder: 'Father, if you wish, you may leave it, so that we may share a meal.' Then, that holy elder understood that his disciple was genuinely a servant of God and not of the vegetables."

Abba Zosimas also used to say that if the demons notice someone not being attached to things, because they are neither afflicted nor troubled by them, then they know that such a person may walk on this earth but does not in fact have an earthly mentality.

Chapter XV: On Perfect Detachment

Once, Abba Zosimas remembered the saying about the Old Man, who was robbed by his neighboring brother. Instead of ever rebuking his brother, that Old Man began to work harder, thinking that the brother had need of these. Abba Zosimas also told the following story.

"There was an Old Man, who lived near our monastery and who had a very good soul. There was another brother, who also lived nearby. When the Old Man was absent one day, that brother was tempted to open the Old Man's cell, enter inside, and take his vessels and books. So when the Old Man returned, he opened the door and, not finding his vessels, he went to announce this to the brother. However, he found his vessels still lying in the middle of the brother's cell; for, the brother had not yet put them away. Not wishing to put the brother to shame or to rebuke him, he pretended that he had a stomachache and went to the toilet for enough time so as to allow the brother to put away the vessels. Then, the Old Man returned and began to speak with the brother on another subject. He did not rebuke the brother at all. After a few days, however, the Old Man's vessels were recognized, and the brother was taken to prison without the Old Man knowing anything about it. When he heard about the brother, namely that he was in prison, he was still unaware of the reason for which the brother was imprisoned. So he came to me, said the Abbot, for he would frequently visit us, and said: 'Please, be so kind as to give me some eggs and some church bread.' I asked him: 'Do you have visitors coming today?' He said: 'Yes.' However, the Old Man wanted these in order to visit the prison and bring some consolation to the brother. Now, when he entered the prison, the brother fell to his feet and said: 'I am here on account of you, Abba. For, I am the one who stole your vessels. Nevertheless, here, take your book; it is here. And take this clothing; it is yours.' The Old Man told him: 'Child, may your heart be assured, that this is not the reason I came here. I did not know at all that you are here because of me. Nevertheless, on hearing that you are here, I was saddened. Therefore, I have come to bring you some consolation. Look, here are some eggs and some church bread. Now, then, I shall do all that I can in order to have you removed from prison.' Indeed, the Old Man went off and begged certain dignitaries—for, he was well known among them because of his virtue—and they arranged for the brother to come out of prison."

"Again, they also used to say the following about the same Old Man. Once he went to the market place in order to purchase some clothing for himself. And he bought it. Having given a piece of gold, he still had to pay some small change. So he took the clothing and placed it beneath him. While he was counting out the coins on the counter, someone came along and wanted to steal the clothing. The Old Man perceived this and understood what was happening. Yet, since he had a merciful and compassionate heart, he lifted himself up gradually, supposedly pretending to reach out over the counter in order to pay the coins. In this way, the other person was able to steal the clothing, and departed. The Old Man, however, did not rebuke him."

And the blessed Abba Zosimas would conclude: "How expensive were the clothing and the vessels, which the Old Man had lost? Yet, his great will power revealed that he possessed these material things without any attachment to them. He neglected the fact that they had been stolen, and simply remained the same person; he was neither saddened nor troubled. For, as I always like to say: 'It is not possessing something that is harmful, but being attached to it.' Even if this Old Man possessed the whole world, he would have done so without being attached to it. From his actions, he proved that he was free from everything."

Extreme lessons in giving up and in giving freely!

DETACHMENT OF THE WILL:
THE *Letters* OF BARSANUPHIUS AND JOHN

The geographical region of Gaza became indelibly marked in the following century by the presence of two remarkable elders, Barsanuphius and John, as well as by their most intimate disciple, Dorotheus. We do not know exactly when Barsanuphius, himself an Egyptian monk, entered the region of Thavatha and chose to be enclosed as a recluse in a nearby cell. From this position, he offered counsel to a number of ascetics who were gradually attracted around the Old Man as he developed a reputation for discernment and compassion. One of these monks, Abba Seridos, who also attended to Barsanuphius, was appointed abbot of a monastic community, probably established in order to organize the increasing number of monks that looked to Barsanuphius as their elder. Seridos was the only person permitted to communicate with Barsanuphius, acting as a mediator for those who sought counsel.

Some time between 525 and 527, another hermit, named John, came to live beside Barsanuphius, also known as "the holy Old Man" or "the Great Old Man." John was simply called "the Other Old Man." These two shared the same life-style and supported one another's ministry. Around eight hundred and fifty letters survive from these two Old Men. Monks in communities, hermits in isolation, spouses in families, professionals in society, and laypersons of every vocation submitted questions in writing to the wise elders and received a response through their scribes.

The responses are spontaneous and balanced, wise and witty, reminiscent of their predecessors in the Egyptian desert. The *Letters* of Barsanuphius and John in fact reveal another element that gradually disappeared from the *Sayings*, as these began to be collated and edited. For, during the stage of transition from an oral culture to a written text, the *Sayings* became more static, losing some of the personal and spontaneous element that originally sparked them; more significantly, the actual process and critical struggle that shaped these words was also concealed. What was recorded, instead, was the intense drop of wisdom, yet without the long and arduous stages that led to the final product of the experience. What is missing is the ongoing process—all of the contentions, hesitations, and limitations of the spiritual aspirant. The *Sayings* present the spiritual reality in *the way that it should be*, rather than in *the way that it is*—together with all the denials, doubts, and temptations. Yet, in the *Letters* of Barsanuphius and John, we witness each of the painful stages unfolding in slow motion before our very eyes, like a film consisting of many, gradually changing pictures.

There are two concepts developed in the *Letters* of Barsanuphius and John that are of particular interest to our study about stewardship and sharing.

Το αψηφιστον (the *apsepheston,* or not reckoning oneself as anything)

Be carefree from all things; then, you will have time for God. Die unto all people; this is true exile. Moreover, retain the virtue of not reckoning yourself as anything; then, you will find your thought to be undisturbed. And do not consider yourself as having done anything good; thus, your reward will be kept whole. (*Letter 259*)

Indeed, Barsanuphius is specifically asked to explain this complicated notion, which is so central to his teaching.

Father, what does it mean not to reckon oneself as anything?[20]

Brother, not reckoning oneself as anything means not equating oneself with anyone and not saying anything in regard to any good deed that you may also have achieved. (*Letter 227*)

Barsanuphius knows that he is not innovative in this aspect of his teaching, which he actually attributes to his predecessors in the desert of Egypt.

---

[20]See also *Letters* 123 and 157.

We are called to strive for these things, for which our Fathers also strove, namely those around Abba Poemen and the others who have struggled in this way. This struggle includes reckoning oneself as nothing, not measuring oneself at all, and regarding oneself as earth and ashes (cf. Gen 18.27). Whereas, the struggle of those in the world involves regarding oneself as knowledgeable, bringing oneself to puffing up, and reckoning oneself as being someone, measuring oneself in everything. All this keeps us away from humility. (*Letter* 604)

Το δικαιωμα *(the dikaioma, or pretense to rights)*

Elsewhere, the Great Old Man explains another complex virtue, namely the pretense to rights, and describes its origin.

The notion of pretense to rights is something that does not contain arrogance, but rather contains the denial of fault, in the manner of Adam and Eve and Cain and others who sinned, but who later denied their sin in order to justify themselves. (*Letter* 477)

Barsanuphius is drawing on his own long experience and spiritual appropriation of the desert tradition, where the monk was never evasively to blame other people or situations but always directly to assume the burden of personal responsibility.

Abba Antony said to Abba Poemen: "This is the great work of a person: always to take the blame for one's own sins before God and to expect temptation to the last breath."[21]

Bearing One Another's Burdens

The clearest evidence that one is laboring for such responsibility or commitment in love lies in the fulfillment of the Apostolic commandment to "bear one another's burdens" (Gal 6.2), which is nothing less than an imitation of the example set—ultimately, a commandment ordained—by Christ Himself:

Come to me, all you that are weary and are carrying heavy burdens, and I will give you rest. Take my yoke upon you, and learn from me; for, I

[21]Cf. Antony, *Saying* 4.

am gentle and humble in heart, and you will find rest for your souls. For, my yoke is easy, and my burden is light. (Mt 11.28–30)

These texts from Paul and Matthew are quoted in numerous *Letters*,[22] while the Old Men themselves explicitly bear the burdens of their own disciples— sometimes only half the burden,[23] at other times two-thirds of the bur- den,[24] while on other occasions even the entire burden![25]

> I admire your love, brother, but you do not understand the affairs of love that is according to God. . . . Yet, if I say something to someone beyond my measure, or beyond my power, I speak moved by the love of Christ, knowing—as I said—that I am nothing but a worthless slave. Since then you did not understand what I told you, namely that I bear half your sins, I have made you a partner with me. For, I did not say to you: "I bear one-third," leaving you to bear more and be burdened more than I. And again, I said what I have said in order to banish self- love; this is why I did not speak to you of bearing two-thirds, showing myself to be stronger than you; for, such conduct would be vainglory. And I did not say: "I bear the whole." This belongs to the perfect, to those who have become brothers of Christ, who laid down His own life for our sake, and who loved those who have loved us with perfect love in order to do this. . . . However, if you wish to cast on me the whole burden, then for the sake of obedience I accept this too. Forgive me that great love leads me to talking nonsense. (*Letter 73*)

Conclusion: Detachment as Humble Stewardship

As we have seen, in the early monastic literature, the concept of detach- ment signifies a letting go of our valued possessions and of our very being. It is, ultimately, a sign of humility, which in the desert is clearly treasured "above all virtues."[26]

> Amma Theodora said that neither asceticism, nor vigils, nor any kind of suffering are able to save. Only true humility can do that. There was

[22]See, for instance, *Letters* 94, 96, 104, 108, 123, 239, 243, 483, 575a, 579, and 604.
[23]See *Letters* 70 and 72.
[24]See *Letter* 73.
[25]See *Letters* 73, 553, and 833.
[26]John the Dwarf 22.

a hermit who was able to banish the demons. And he asked them: "What makes you go away? Is it fasting?" They replied: "We do not eat or drink." "Is it vigils?" They said: "We do not sleep." "Then what power sends you away?" They replied: "Nothing can overcome us except humility alone." Amma Theodora said: "Do you see how humility is victorious over the demons?"[27]

In the final analysis, humility looks to shift the focus of oneself as the center of the world and to place oneself in the service of others.

Abba Or gave this advice: "Whenever you want to subdue your high and proud thoughts, examine your conscience carefully: Have you loved your enemies and been kind to them in their misfortunes?"[28]

It is humility that makes sense of all giving:

If I give away all my possessions, and even if I hand over my body so that I may be burned but do not have love, I gain nothing. (I Cor. 12.3)

The humble person is always satisfied, always shares, always gives, and always gives thanks. Therefore, the humble person "is patient, kind, not envious, . . . bears all things, believes all things, hopes all things, endures all things" (I Cor 12.4–7). In fact, the humble person learns to assume responsibility for the misfortune of others and even learns to give thanks for one's own misfortunes.

Abba Zosimas said: "It is true that one ought to give thanks for all circumstances and . . . to regard such people [who bring us misfortune] as doctors who heal the wounds of the soul; indeed, one should regard them as benefactors who procure for us the heavenly kingdom."[29]

Such a sense of genuine gratitude (*eucharistia*) is the vessel that contains God's grace (*charis*); it is the human expression of a divine experience defined as learning to give and to share.

[27]Theodora 6.
[28]Or 11.
[29]Abba Zosimas, *Reflections* XII, a.

SOME ASPECTS OF STEWARDSHIP OF THE CHURCH OF CONSTANTINOPLE[1] UNDER OTTOMAN TURKISH RULE (1453–1800)

DEMETRIOS J. CONSTANTELOS*

I n his *monodia* on the capture of Constantinople by the Ottoman Turks in 1453, Andronikos Kallistos, an eyewitness and one of the last writers of the Byzantine era, lamented the fall of Constantinople and cried out:

Where are the hospitals (*nosokomeia*), the hospices (*xenones*), the homes for the poor (*ptochokomeia*), the homes for the aged (*gerokomeia*), the

---

*The Very Rev Demetrios J. Constantelos is the Charles Cooper Townsend Sr Distinguished Professor of History and Religious Studies *Emeritus* at Richard Stockton College in New Jersey and a specialist in the history of Byzantine philanthropy.

[1]For the history of the Ecumenical Patriarchate see Maximos, Metropolitan of Sardis, *To Oikoumenikon Patriarcheion* (Thessaloniki: Patriarchikon Idryma Paterikon Meleton, 1972); Gennadios, Metropolitan of Heliopolis, *Historia tou Oikoumenikou Patriarcheiou*, vol. 1 (Athens, 1953); Vasil Istavrides (Stavrides), *Historia tou Oikoumenikou Patriarcheiou–1453 eos simeron* (Thessaloniki, 1987); Steven Runciman, *The Great Church in Captivity* (Cambridge: Cambridge University Press, 1986); and *International Relations*, No. 7–8 (Dec. 1964–April 1965) where several authoritative studies examine various aspects of the Ecumenical Patriarchate's history, importance, and status.

houses for poor girls (*semneia*), and the convents (*parthenones)* for which the city was very proud? With the sack of Constantinople all lost–the elderly lost those who looked after them; the poor lost a city which fed them; the prisoners of war lost their emancipator; the destitute lost a city which provided for them; the farmers lost their distributor of justice; the orphans were deprived of a mother and the widows lost their protector.[2]

Andronikos Kallistos did not exaggerate and his *monodia* was not a rhetorical eulogy. Primary sources such as historical accounts and patriarchal documents, legal enactments and epigraphical evidence, seals and inscriptions, *typika* of monasteries, and last wills confirm beyond any doubt that Constantinople had many philanthropic institutions.

For nearly one thousand years (A.D. 330–1453), church and state, episcopal headquarters and monastic communities, and churchmen and laypersons of the Byzantine Empire had established and maintained numerous philanthropic institutions–hospitals, orphanages, hospices, (*xenones*), homes for the elderly (*gerokomeia*), reformatory establishments, and more. Philanthropy was practiced extensively in the form of daily charities and distributions to the poor and needy, and as institutionalized agencies and foundations.[3] But how many of those institutions survived the desolation of the city? We do not really know. We assume that some were confiscated and turned into Islamic *Awqaf* (pious foundations). It is believed that Byzantine philanthropic institutions became models for emulation by the Ottoman Turks.[4] Others were burned and destroyed as Kallistos indicates.

It is well known that for three days the captors of Constantinople engaged in unrestricted pillage and plunder. "They slew everyone that they met in the streets, even women and children without discrimination. The blood ran in rivers down the steep streets . . . toward the Golden Horn. . . . Many of the lovelier maidens and youth and many of the richer-clad nobles were almost torn to death as their captors quarreled over them. . . . Women were distributed among the captors [while] some of the younger nuns

[2]Andronikos Kallistos, "Monodia," *Patrologia Graeca*, ed. J. P. Migne, vol. 161, col 1135A.

[3]See Demetrios J. Constantelos, *Byzantine Philanthropy and Social Welfare* (New Brunswick, N.J.: Rutgers University Press, 1968); 2nd revised and enlarged ed., New Rochelle, N.Y.: Melissa Publishing Co., 1990); idem, *Poverty, Society and Philanthropy in the Late Medieval Greek World* (New Rochelle, N.Y.: Melissa Publishing Co., 1991)

[4]Cf. John Robert Barnes, *An Introduction to Religious Foundations in the Ottoman Empire* (Leiden, The Netherlands: Brill Academic Publishers, 1986), 12–13.

preferred martyrdom to dishonor. . . . When the three days ended "there was little left to plunder." Nearly all the churches had been thoroughly sacked and desecrated. Treasures were snatched from churches and institutions and most of the books in monastic and private libraries, both secular and religious were burned. . . . "The city was desolate, lying dead, naked, soundless, having neither form nor beauty."[5]

Special privileges given to the Church through Patriarch Gennadios by the "generosity" of the conqueror, Mehmet II, were soon forgotten. Mehmet ordered the elimination of all the leading officials of the Byzantine Empire who had survived the three-day onslaught and one by one the old Christian churches were taken from them to be converted into mosques. Since philanthropic institutions in Byzantium were next to churches, it is reasonable to think that when Turks seized Christian churches, they seized along with them the adjacent charitable institutions, transforming them into Islamic pious foundations.

The relevant "generosity" promised by Mehmet to Patriarch Gennadios changed dramatically after 1464 when the conquest of the Kingdom of Trapezond was completed. A few years after the fall, Patriarch Gennadios wrote, "We have neither a country nor a free church." He indicates that there was anything but toleration on the part of the conquerors. Because of the prevailing conditions, including much poverty, Christians lost heart, compromised and surrendered beliefs and traditions for the sake of survival. Poverty was so great that many walked around in rugs.[6] Poverty remained a standard feature of the Church under Islamic Ottoman Turkish rule.

A synodic tome issued by the Holy Synod of the Ecumenical Patriarchate on October 10, 1474, confirms that the church of Constantinople was in great poverty. No sooner had Mehmet II completed his conquest of the last Byzantine province, he forgot his pledges and imposed upon the Patri-

---

[5]Michael Doukas, Historia Byzantina, Ch. XLI 40. For an English translation see *Decline and Fall of Byzantium to the Ottoman Turks*, by Doukas, Harry J. Magoulias, tr. (Detroit, Mich.: Wayne State University Press, 1975), 235; *History of Mehmed the Conqueror by Kritovoulos*, Charles T. Riggs, tr. (Westport, Conn.: Greenwood Press: 1970), 72–74; Georgios Frantzes, Chronikon, Bk III, ch. 8. English translation by Marios Philippides, *The Fall of the Byzantine Empire* (Amherst, Mass.: The University of Massachusetts Press, 1980), 130–133 [This part of Frantzes or Sphrantzes is attributed to Makarios Melissenos. For a modern account of the capture of Constantinople and its consequences see Steven Runciman, *The Fall of Constantinople* (Cambridge: Cambridge University Press, 1965), 145–159.]

[6]L. Petit, X. A. Siderides, M. Jugie, *Oeuvres Complétes de Georges Scholarios*, vols. 1–8 (Paris-Athens, 1928–1936), 1:285–293.

archate an annual tax (*kharadj*) of two thousand gold *nomismata*. The tax
was a heavy burden for a church that was still mourning its losses in terms
of both manpower and wealth. How is it possible "for the Church of Christ
to sustain such a heavy burden" finding itself "in such a poverty?"[7] As the
years passed, the financial burden increased to the extent that by 1621 the
tax to the Sultan was six thousand gold *nomismata*, and another amount of
some four thousand given to different Ottoman officials. It was for this reason that the Ecumenical Patriarchate was always in debt. Nevertheless, it is
fair to say that, in general, Ottoman policies toward the Church varied
according to circumstances, time, and space.

The revenues of the Patriarchate, the source of its stewardship,
depended on the generosity of merchants and traders, on laymen who
entered the administrative machinery of the Patriarchate, on contributions
of metropolitans and eparchial bishops, on gifts of priests upon their ordi-
nations, and on a form of tax that the Patriarchate could impose upon its
flock. Ultimately the Patriarchate came to rely greatly on the generosity of
adelphata, brotherhoods or guilds of various trades, including merchant
marine owners and sailors.[8] Thus it should not surprise us that the earliest
indications of the Patriarchate's stewardship are mentioned in the sources
of the first quarter of the sixteenth century. The theoretical foundations,
the theology about philanthropy and *agapitic* stewardship, were never
absent from the life of the Church, but it was the lack of funds that delayed
its application.

The question is: Who looked after the physical needs of the Greek
Orthodox under Ottoman rule? Pious fellow Christians and the organized
church as a whole is the answer. The Orthodox Patriarchate became not
only the spokesman, the guardian, the administrator, and the spiritual
guide but also the dispenser of charities and the founder of philanthropic
institutions. Whether through the humble parish priest, the anonymous
working monk, the wealthy merchant or ordinary artisan, the bishop's res-
idence or the monastery, the church continued its philanthropic social
work. "The grand achievement of the Patriarchate was that in spite of
humiliation and poverty and disdain, the Church endured . . . as a great

---

[7]Demetres G. Apostolopoulos, *O Ieros Kodix tou Patriarcheiou Konstantinoupoleos sto miso
tou 15ou Aiona* (Athens: Ethnikon Idryma Ereunon, 1992), 91.

[8]See A. E. Vakalopoulos, *Istoria tou Neou Ellenismou*, vol. B, part 1 (Thessalonike, 1964),
134–175; also Chrysostomos A. Papadopoulos, *E Orthodoxos Anatolike Ekklesia* (Athens: Apos-
tolike Diakonia Press, 1954), 174–175.

spiritual force" in the words of Sir Steven Runciman, one of the most authoritative scholars of the subject.[9] Its spiritual obligations were dispensed not only through sacramental services, the liturgy in particular, but also through the daily practice of philanthropy. Under adverse circumstances, the Patriarchate proved itself a spiritual power in *diakonia*.

During the early four hundred years of Ottoman rule the church assumed the role of the protector, the apologist, and the defender of its people. Patriarchs, bishops, and priests became the guardians of social justice and the advocates of a more humane treatment of the poor, the persecuted, the orphans, the prisoners, and others in need. Philanthropic concern was both the Patriarchate's policy and a local communal responsibility. The Greek nation under the Ottoman Empire included both wealthy and poor, but there was no sharp division between social classes, for all were second-class citizens under Turkish law and Islamic custom. The more affluent among the Orthodox Christians had consideration for the less fortunate among their brethren while the latter had accepted willingly the paternalism of the former. Under the circumstances, Greek Orthodox Christians, whether wealthy or poor or masters or servants, were forced to develop bonds of unity and mutual assistance. Law did not enforce the philanthropic spirit, but it was a manifestation of a long-standing benevolent tradition. It was this spirit that sustained the Greek people, united under a foreign and hostile system. The role of the community and the contributions of the individual parish in promoting a sense of unity with reciprocal rights and responsibilities are increasingly appreciated by modern scholars of the Ottoman centuries.

As a rule, the social philanthropy of the Church in this period was not manifested on a systematic or organized basis; it was not a social or well-constructed establishment as we know it today, but an everyday activity, the result of mutual concern, mercy, and compassion; a conscious participation in the sufferings and the needs of all. The Church had understood its social mission as one of religious *philanthropia* rather than as social welfare, i.e., an expression of Christian *agape*. Following a long-standing tradition inherited from the Byzantine experience of philanthropy, the Church fostered social justice and perpetuated the Christian vision of the human being as an image and likeness of God.

[9]Runciman, op. cit., 412; see also Timothy Ware, *Eustratios Argenti: A Study of the Greek Church under Turkish Rule* (Oxford: Clarendon Press, 1964), 1–5, 41–42.

Though we find several organized philanthropic institutions, of which
we shall speak shortly, the Church emphasized individual virtue and goodwill, a practice that expressed its theological and ethical philosophy. The
philanthropic activity of the Church as a community of believers and as
individuals was done as a rule not on the basis of a planned program or as
a predetermined effort, but as an obligation of a believer to a fellow
believer. The philanthropist clergyman or layman gave higher value to the
needy as an individual, as a person. Thus, altruistic love was much of the
background of the Church's charitable work. The clergy treated their sub-
jects as children of God who had been entrusted to them, while the wealthy
believers were urged to consider the poor and needy as their brethren. The
sermons of leading men of this period, such as Elias Meniates (1669–1714),
Nicephoros Theotokes (1731–1800), and Kosmas Aitolos (1714–1806), reveal
that the rich were advised against a self-centered wealth and were urged to
see themselves as stewards of possessions belonging to God for the service
of men everywhere.[10]

It was the task of the clergy to awaken in their flocks a love and compassion, and activity and involvement for the improvement of the lot of
the less fortunate. Bishops in particular made numerous appeals on ethical
but also eschatological grounds for orphans, widows, the sick, and the
release of prisoners. Contributions for dowries of poor or orphaned girls,
donations for the release of people imprisoned because of debts to a tyran-
nical state, and other humane measures which were encouraged by the
Church, indicating that in the practice of philanthropy, the Church was
motivated more by religious and humanitarian principles than by sociological considerations.

While social justice is subject to laws, *philanthropia* in its Graeco-
Christian connotation is a free manifestation of love, a spontaneous and
natural overflow of concern for the welfare of one's fellow human being,
perceived as the ideal, harmonious development of all human values and
potentialities—grounded upon faith in God as the Supreme Being, the
source and creator of all, and upon faith in the human being as the crown
of creation and the spiritual likeness of the Creator. Thus emphasis was

---

[10]See Nicephoros Theotokes, *Kyriakodromion*, 9th ed. (Athens: Ekdotikos Oikos "Zoe,"
1930), 49–53, 134–139, 307–312; N. M. Vaporis, *Father Kosmas, the Apostle of the Poor* (Brookline,
Mass.: Holy Cross Orthodox Press, 1977); Constantine Cavarnos, "St. Cosmas Aitolos,"
Tuckahoe, N.Y.: *St Vladimir's Seminary Quarterly* 4.4 (1966).

placed on a *philanthropia* that would embrace the totality of the person—framed in miseries and glories and strength and weaknesses.

The underlying concepts of the Church as well as the political circumstances during the Ottoman subjugation made philanthropy a movement, an everyday awareness and activity. It was practiced for purely religious reasons, because without applied charity there is no salvation. The clergy viewed philanthropy as an obligation toward one's fellow human being, accompanied by almsgiving, guidance, sympathy, altruism, and selfless concern. St Kosmas the Aitolian, an eighteenth-century champion of the poor, writes: "I have a loaf of bread to eat, while you do not; love tells me: do not eat it alone, but give some to your brethren and you eat the rest. I have clothes; love tells me: give one to your brother and you wear the other one." St Kosmas upbraided those who exploited the weak and poor and advised repentance and philanthropic action.[11] The early and medieval Christian view, that philanthropy must be exercised in order to please God and receive forgiveness of sins and achieve eternal life, was repeated like a refrain by church fathers. Philanthropy is not only contributions of money to needy individuals but also a response to spiritual or psychological hunger, to the human being's thirst for love, guidance, certainty, and restoration of personal dignity. Churchmen made exhortations on the basis of the Scriptures but also of Greek and Roman classical authors, of Byzantine emperors and Jewish kings.

Prayers, fasting, and spiritual exercises must find an outlet in good works, while memorials for the deceased must be accompanied by charities. Such a combination on the part of the faithful is so powerful that even pagans can be saved. St Thecla succeeded in freeing from hell the pagan and unbaptized Phalkonila. St Gregory Dialogus saved the soul of the pagan emperor Trajan.[12] Patriarchs and bishops appealed for support to wealthy constituents but also to princes and friends in foreign lands. For example, Meletios Pegas, Patriarch of Alexandria († 1601), in several letters to Theodore Ivanovitch (d. 1584–1598) the "king of Moscow and emperor of all Russia," solicited assistance for the poor of his jurisdiction. His arguments are very much like those of Byzantine times. He writes: "Imitate God the merciful, who desires mercy and not sacrifices." The Russian emperor responded, sending him help for which the Patriarch acknowledged the

[11]Cavarnos, op. cit., 192.

[12]Theophilos of Ioannina, *Tameion Orthodoxias*, 5th ed. (Athens: Typografeion I. Nikolaidou, 1980), 146.

king's generosity. Theodore had helped the Patriarchate of Antioch and the Patriarchate of Jerusalem. Other Russian tsars had assisted the Greek churches to free themselves from debts and continue their philanthropic work.[13]

There were several forms of philanthropy. Wealthy laymen took initiatives and conducted drives for public works such as bridges and schools in their villages or provinces. A certain pious man named Photos conducted *eleemosynary* drives and built the bridge of Kremmenitza in Epiros. Bessarion of Larissa (sixteenth century) became renowned for his efforts to emancipate prisoners, to feed the hungry, and to assist the poor. He was honored as a great benefactor of the province of Thessaly. Through his efforts several bridges were built in Thessaly and other parts of Greece:[14] specific mention is made of two bridges at Leukopotamos and at Acheloos Rivers. Anastasios Argyris of Ioannina had made a sizable fortune through trade with Western Europeans. He used much of his wealth for the welfare of his compatriots. Among his philanthropic contributions were the establishment of a hospital, the distribution of funds to poor prisoners (in addition to money, he sent a hot dinner to every prisoner each Sunday), widows, and orphans. Furthermore, he built roads and bridges. But his wealth and his generosity caused the jealousy and envy of Ali Pasha of Ioannina. Upon Argyris' death, the Pasha took advantage of the weakness of Argyris' son, Nicholas, and through perfidies and various pretexts, Argyris' wealth was decimated. Ali Pasha's policy and legacy were renowned: "When any rich citizen died, Ali's hands itched to take hold of the dead man's estate."[15]

There were numerous Orthodox Greeks in the diaspora who supported their fellow countrymen living under the Ottoman Turks. They erected churches, schools, and libraries and redeemed prisoners and proved themselves pillars of the Orthodox Church and the Greek nation. An orphanage that existed in the city of Moschopolis in the eighteenth century might have been the work of the great family of benefactors who were descendents of the priest George Sina. It might have been the first such institution in the Christian East of modern times. The orphanage was known as *Orphanodioiketerion*.[16]

[13]Meletios Pegas, *Epistles*, No. 2, ed. by W. Regel, *Analecta Byzantino-Russica* (St Petersburg, 1898), 95.

[14]Spyridon Lambros, *Neos Hellenomnemon*, vol. 13 (Athens, 1916), 135; for other philanthropists see vol. 5 (Athens, 1908), 293.

[15]William Plomer, *The Diamond of Jannina* (London: Jonathan Cape, 1970), 72.

[16]Constantine I. Amantos, *Mikra Meletemata* (Athens, 1940), 42–43.

Ordinary clergymen and lay people became instrumental for benevolent institutions in provincial towns and islands. Theophilos Kaires (b. 1784) erected an orphanage on the island of Andros; Philothee Benizelou built outside of her monastery in Athens a hospital and a hospice for poor visitors. Her community became renown for philanthropic services to the poor and the persecuted. Her religious commitment and philanthropic principles led her to extend protection to four persecuted women sought by the Turks. They had been apostates to Islam, but later on they repented and returned to their ancestral Christian faith. Apostasy from Islam carried the penalty of death. Thus they sought protection in Philothee's monastery. Philothee paid for her act of philanthropy with her own life.[17]

We know of several hospitals during this period in cities other than Constantinople. A hospital was erected in Adrianople around 1752 through the generosity of Demetrios Ioseph. Nicholas Karayiannes, past president of the Greek community in Venice (1727–1733), established a hospital in Jerusalem around the year 1714. The hospital was opened to clergymen, monks, and laymen alike. The Church maintained a hospital in Smyrna and perhaps other institutions in other major cities. It also maintained a hospital in Mytilene, built in the year 1691, known as *xenodocheio* and located across from the Church of St Therapon (i.e., "Healer"). A church hospital existed in Heracleion (c. 1800), Crete, which was transformed into a teacher's college and later into a grammar school.[18]

Thus, the Ecumenical Patriarchate had developed an extensive program of philanthropic activity in Constantinople, including the establishment of hospitals, old age homes, orphanages, asylums, and reformatory homes. However, it is not known whether any of Constantinople's many philanthropic institutions survived the onslaught of May 29, 1453. Andronikos Kallistos, who witnessed the sack of Constantinople, implies that many of the capital's philanthropic institutions were destroyed by the conquerors. Pierre Gilles, a Frenchman, indicates that two major institutions of the Byzantine era, the hospitals of Sampson and Eubolos, were not in existence when he visited Constantinople in 1544.[19]

What about philanthropia and institutionalized philanthropy of the Ecumenical Patriarchate in Constantinople proper? The theoretical principle

[17]Zoe Genakos, *E Epanastase mias gynaikas, Philothee Benizelou* (Athens, 1985).

[18]"To Bostaneion Nosokomeion kata to 1966," *O Poimen* 32.1 (Mytilene, 1967), 30.

[19]Pierre Gilles, *The Antiquities of Constantinople*, 2nd ed., Ronald G. Musto ed. (New York: Italica Press, 1988), 73–74.

for the application of philanthropic stewardship remained the same: "God is love and love is from God. . . . If God so loved us, we in turn are bound to love one another" (1 Jn 7–11). The gospel pericope read on the third Sunday of the *Triodion* had a telling effect on the faithful everywhere.

A common feature of sermons and admonitions of the church was an analysis of the words of Christ concerning the Last Judgment. He will save those who when he was hungry they gave him food; when thirsty, they gave him drink; when he was a stranger, they took him into their home; when naked, they clothed him; when he was ill they came to his help; when in prison they visited him. Those who fail to serve the needs of the hungry, the thirsty, the naked, the sick, and the poor strangers will be eternally damned (Mt 25.31–43). Personal charity was widely practiced. The same ethical principles led some wealthy individuals, including clergymen, to found or endow philanthropic institutions.

Established in Constantinople through the generosity of a certain Petros Sophianos, the earliest church hospital appears to have been erected in 1517 in the district of Galata. Sophianos requested in his last will and testament that Orthodox and non-Orthodox Christians who happened to fall sick while in Constantinople could be treated in his institution. The establishment was endowed with sufficient funds for distribution among the patients, a nurse, a priest, an undertaker, and for the maintenance or replacement of furniture and utensils.[20] A monk named Joseph was the founder of a *xenon* (hospital) in Constantinople during the patriarchal tenure of Jeremiah II Tranos (1572–1579; 1580–1584), but we know nothing else about it.

By the close of the eighteenth century, around 1794, the Greek community of Constantinople supported three hospitals. All three were under the aegis of the Ecumenical Patriarchate but received the support of the whole Greek community. The first hospital was established in 1753. Some years later it was destroyed by an unknown cause and rebuilt by the patriarch Neophytos the Seventh in 1793. The hospital included a chapel in honor of the physician-saints Cosmas and Damian, "the unmercinaries," and it was located not far from the Seven Towers of the Great Walls. This hospital ultimately evolved into a major philanthropic complex, and at one time, it included the largest hospital in the Balkans. It survives to the present day

[20]M. Gedeon, "Peri Philoptochon kai Philantropon diataxeon . . . ," *Hellenikos Philologikos Syllogos* 21 (Constantinople, 1891): 80, col. 2.

as the hospital of Baluokle. The union of the Greek grocers of Constantinople built the original hospital.

The second hospital was built ca. 1762, and it was located in the district of Galata. It was also known as the *Nautikon Nosokomeion* because it was for sailors and sea merchants. This hospital, too, had been burned down before 1814, and it was rebuilt through contributions of the Greek community under the Patriarchate of Patriarch Kyrillos the Sixth.

The third hospital was built ca. 1780 and located in the district of Staurodromion-Beyoglou. Each hospital had its own constitution and administration but all three were under the supervision of one board of trustees whose members were appointed by the Ecumenical Patriarch.[21]

In addition to these three hospitals, the Greek community supported an old age home for men, another old age home for women, an asylum for insane men and another asylum for insane women, a reformatory institution for girls, and an orphanage. All were under the supervision of the Church, and they became known collectively as *Ethnika Philanthropika Katastemata*–National Philanthropic Establishments.[22]

As to hospitals, every one of them had a major philanthropist whose name appears on inscribed plaques. Hospital archives and records reveal that the Greek hospitals were open to all and offered their services to patients of various religious beliefs and ethnic origins: Greek Orthodox, Roman Catholics, Protestants, Oriental Christians of the Armenian and Coptic Churches, and Muslims and Jews; Greeks and Bulgarians, Albanians, Romanians (Vlachs), Russians, Austrians, Illyrians (Serbians or Albanians), Arabs, Persians, English, Germans, and Dutch. The Greeks are named on the basis of the city's or the province's name from which they came. Greeks were from Constantinople, Thrace, Macedonia, Epiros, Thessaly, Anatolia, the Aegean Islands, and Greece proper (Central Greece-Attica-Boeotea-Acarnania) and Peloponnesos.[23]

---

[21]The hospitals of the Greek community in Constantinople under the aegis of the Ecumenical Patriarchate are conveniently discussed by Eugenios, *E Zoodochos Pege kai ta hierea autes proskynemata* (Athens, 1886), 139–183 and more fully in Aristoteles K. Stavropoulos, *Ta Nosokomeia kai e Noseleutike politike tes Ellenikes Ethnotetas sten Konstantinoupole* (Athens, 1984), esp. 92–95.

[22]Ibid., 154; T. Siofis, "Ethnika Philantropika Katastemata," *Hemerologion* 1906 (Constantinople, 1905), 83–94.

[23]Information on the ethnic and religious background, the number of patients treated, the nature of illnesses, and salaries of physicians and staff is provided by the annual reports of the philanthropic institutions. Cf. also Stavropoulos, op. cit., 135–173.

Hospital records also indicate that there were twelve sources of revenue, including individual donations and private charities; donations from bishops, who were obligated to contribute to the hospitals upon their ordination to the episcopal office; the product of the special collection boxes stationed in every parish church; special gifts from the Greeks of the diaspora, especially the Greek communities in Romania, Austria, and Hungary; from rentals of houses which had been donated to the hospitals by wealthy individuals; and the interest from endowments.

In order to systematize its philanthropic policies, maintain a just distribution of its charities, and have all parish churches and provincial dioceses contribute their share, in 1791 the Patriarchate established a common treasury. All churches were expected to maintain "sacred boxes" known as *hiera kouteia*, or *kivotia eleous*. The collections were used to support local needs but also the philanthropic obligations of the mother church in Constantinople.[24] Ioannes Kallimaches served as the first supervisor of this program. Nevertheless, much of the responsibility was left in the hands of each local community: each congregation was responsible for support of local orphans, deserted children, and for the procurement of dowries for poor girls. Often, the local parish was called upon to contribute toward the redemption of prisoners of war and to use the income of the "poor boxes" for medical expenses of the poverty-stricken. It was not uncommon that the annual income of a certain church or shrine was set aside exclusively for the benevolent program of the Patriarchate.

Certain community churches had been charged with the responsibility of looking after the needs of insane people, such as the church of *Panagia tou Kyrou* in Egrikapio.[25] In the year 1780, the Ecumenical Patriarchate imposed new financial obligations upon the churches of Constantinople in order to support the hospital at Stavrodromion. This hospital had been designated for a time to receive victims of plagues. The income of the prosperous Zoodochos Pege shrine after 1794 was set aside for the maintenance of all three hospitals.[26]

The Patriarchate dispensed annual contributions for the relief of prisoners. Local churches took special offerings several times during the year for those who were in prison because of debt or for some other reason. Several

[24]A. Papadopoulos-Kerameus, *Analecta*, vol. 2 (Brussels, 1963), 326, 346–347.

[25]R. Janin, *Constantinople Byzantine* (Paris: Institut Francais D'Etudes Byzantines, 1950), 351; Eugenios, *E. Zoodoches Pege*, op. cit.

[26]Eugenios, op. cit.

committees were established, and each one was in charge of some philanthropic project. On the other hand, all trade unions of Orthodox Christians in Constantinople—tailors, grocers, moneychangers, and others—had their own funds for charitable purposes.[27]

The philanthropy of the Church was extended to include education and educational institutions. Through the generosity of individuals, the Church maintained schools for poor children. For example, a certain George Kastoriotes had undertaken all the expenses for the establishment of a school at Kastoria where education was free of charge and available to all. Kastoriotes endowed sufficient funds for the salaries of two teachers. The Patriarchate of Jerusalem maintained a representative in Constantinople whose responsibility was to collect funds for schools in Palestine. Kastoriotes paid the wages of two laymen and several clergy in Palestine for the instruction of Greek and Arabic to children of Orthodox Christians. But philanthropy and education is a major subject that cannot be treated extensively here.[28]

The Christian commandment about "diakonia" (servanthood) was taken seriously by the Church whether in Constantinople or elsewhere. The Church was close to its people, and the people remained faithful to their Church amidst persecutions, pressures of proselytism, and other tragedies. In essence, the Church was where life was: in the capital and in provinces; in cities and villages; on the mountains and in the valleys; at the bedside of the sick at home and in the hospitals; in prison with the fallen or the hard pressed; and close to individuals unjustly persecuted—present where even the needs of the faithful called.

There were several other considerations that contributed to philanthropic stewardship in major cities. For example, in Constantinople the Greeks settled in certain specific districts such as Galata, Psamathia, and Fanar, the latter of which became the nucleus for the Greek community at large. The compactness of these districts encouraged intensive socialization and facilitated personal relationships and extensive cooperative networks. No person in need went unnoticed, and frequent church services enhanced the Church's knowledge of people in need—whether material or moral. Loyalty to the Church and constant contact with priests and bishops fostered philanthropic concern and activity. Cooperative activities, economic independence, and self-respect through economic achievement always

[27]Ibid.
[28]*Ekklesiastike Aletheia*, vol. 1 (1880), 175–176, 205–207, 209; Papadopoulos-Kerameus, op. cit., 323, 326.

have been encouraged in the Greek community which, however, acknowledges that not everyone can become self-sufficient and financially independent. Thus the need to put to practice the biblical injunctions: help the sick, protect the orphan and the widow, assist the elderly, and clothe the poor. The priest of the community had an obligation and even a personal economic interest in addressing the well-being of his poor parishioners and the generosity of the well-to-do families.

This neighborhood, or *enoria*, philanthropic stewardship was an individualized, spontaneous, and generally very caring phenomenon. A common heritage, the use of a common language, theological teachings and religious traditions, and social cohesiveness and humanitarian instinct became binding factors, reinforcing and strengthening the Greek community-at-large under Ottoman Turkish rule.

SELECTED BIBLIOGRAPHY

Apostolopoulos, D. G. *O Ieros Kodix tou Patriarcheiou Konstantinoupoleos sto miso tou 15ou Aiona*. Athens: Ethnikon Idryma Ereunon, 1992.

Arampatzoglou, Gennadios M. (Metropolitan of Heliopolis). *Fotieios Bibliotheke*, part 2. Constantinople, 1935.

Arnakis, George G. "The Greek Church of Constantinople and the Ottoman Empire." *Journal of Modern History* 24 (1952): 235–250.

Istavridis, Vasil. *Istoria tou Oikoumenikou Patriarcheiou*. Athens, 1967.

———. *Synoptike Istoria tou Oikoumenikou Patriarcheiou*. Thessalonike, 1991.

Maximos, Metropolitan of Sardis. *To Oikoumenikon Patriarcheion en te Orthodoxo Ekklesia*. Thessaloniki, 1972.

Papadopoullos, Theodore H. *Studies and Documents Relating to the History of the Greek Church and People under Turkish Dominion*. Hampshire: Variorum, 1990.

Ricaut, Paul. *The Present State of the Greek and Armenian Churches*. London, 1679; Reprinted New York, 1970.

Runciman, Steven. *The Great Church in Captivity*. Cambridge: Cambridge University Press, 1968.

———. *The Fall of Constantinople 1453*. Cambridge: Cambridge University Press, 1965.

Stavropoulos, Aristoteles K. *Ta Nosokomeia kai e Noseleutike Politike tes ellenikes Ethnotetas sten Konstantinoupole (1453–1838)*. Athens, 1984.

Vakalopoulos, A. *Istoria tou Neou Ellenismou*, Vol. 2. Thessalonike, 1964: 134–220.

Ware, Timothy [Kallistos of Diocleia]. *Eustratios Argenti: A Study of the Greek Church under Turkish Rule*. Oxford: Clarendon Press, 1964.

Ye'or, Bat. *The Decline of Eastern Christianity under Islam: From Jihad to Dhimmitude*, trs. by Miriam Kochan and David Littman. Madison-Teaneck, N.J.: Fairleigh Dickinson University Press, 1996.

GENEROSITY, ACCOUNTABILITY, VISION

Historical Perspectives on Orthodox Stewardship in America

———◆———

JOHN H. ERICKSON[*]

In 1915, shortly after arriving to head the Russian Orthodox Church's North American archdiocese, Archbishop Evdokim Meshchersky wrote an impassioned essay on "Religious Life in America." In it he tried to refute the misconception widely held in Russia that Americans were indifferent to religion and interested only in business. After providing a detailed statistical report on the various Christian denominations in America, noting in particular their work with youth, their missionary efforts at home and abroad, and the amount of private donations given for religious causes, the archbishop concluded:

> Have you encountered the same labor in your country? Have you seen the same rivers of gold, which are poured out here by the private people and not by the government or state institutions? Have you seen such intense service rendered to those who suffer? Have you seen such multitudes of self-denying workers who voluntarily, without any pay, toil in Christ's vineyard?[1]

[*]John H. Erickson is Dean of St Vladimir's Orthodox Theological Seminary in Crestwood, NY and the Peter N. Gramowich Professor of Church History at the seminary.

[1](Sergiev Posad: 1915), cited in *Orthodox America 1794–1976* (Syosset, N.Y.: Orthodox Church in America, 1975) 128–29.

The archbishop here calls attention to one of the most striking features of the American religious scene. In contrast to the prevailing situation in the Old World, whether in Russia and other traditionally Orthodox lands or in Western Europe, funding for churches and other worthy causes in America depends largely on the generosity of private individuals, in many cases very humble individuals, and not on the state or other public agencies. The archbishop also alludes in passing to another feature of the American religious scene. Religious association, and with it support for churches and their activities, is a voluntary matter. In America it cannot be taken for granted that every citizen belongs to the church and therefore is obliged to support it through taxes and other public funds. Americans are free to contribute to their churches and other worthy causes, but they are also free not to contribute. In practice they are most generous when they themselves have embraced the mission of the church or agency in question. Their generosity thus depends in large part on the vision offered to them. And they are less likely to be generous when they do not trust the church or agency in question. Their generosity therefore also depends on accountability. They like to know that the "rivers of gold" which they voluntarily pour out in fact are being spent for their intended purpose.

Some of the practical implications of Archbishop Evdokim's assessment of American religious life can be seen in the early history of what was to become Holy Trinity Orthodox Church in New Britain, Connecticut. In 1899, Mr John J. Hamilla, a Carpatho-Russian immigrant from the Austro-Hungarian Empire, joined with fourteen of his countrymen to form the Sts Cyril and Methodius Brotherhood. Their goal was to establish a church, and to raise funds for this endeavor, they circulated through the public gathering places of the city to listen for people speaking their language. The potential contributors whom they encountered sometimes were suspicious. One of them exclaimed, "It's not possible to build [Orthodox] churches in America. In Russia, only the tsar builds churches. How can you build a church in America?" He then added: "All you want to do is collect a few dollars and then, skip town!" The brotherhood members devised a plan in order to convince the man of their good faith. First, each of them placed five dollars on a table and asked him to do the same. Then the new man was allowed to select one of his own friends as treasurer for the money, holding it in trust until it was needed.[2]

[2]Recounted in *Orthodox America*, 122.

Several points should be noted in this account. The first, though perhaps the least obvious, is the generosity of these new Americans. Five dollars may not seem like much today, but for a recent immigrant in 1899, working in a factory or mill for ten cents an hour, it amounted to a week's wages. Parishes like Holy Trinity in New Britain were not built by the tsar or even by large contributions from a handful of wealthy patrons. They were built by ordinary men and women who contributed generously from their own often meager resources. But even these ordinary men and women had to be asked to contribute. Members of the Sts Cyril and Methodius Brotherhood had to seek out potential contributors wherever they might be, not limiting themselves to their immediate circle of friends and acquaintances. And they had to ask for their support.

The brotherhood also had to demonstrate their good faith to potential contributors. Without accountability on their part, their appeals very likely would have fallen on deaf ears. The new man whom they approached was generous but also prudent. He had the capacity for responsible stewardship. In return, the brotherhood demonstrated their own capacity for responsible stewardship by allowing a trustworthy independent agent to serve as treasurer, so that the finances of their project would be fully transparent to the new contributor.

This concern for accountability may strike us as very American. In fact it also is very much in line with the canonical tradition of the Orthodox Church. As is often pointed out, the ancient canons do not deal in detail with the administrative structures of the local church, or diocese. In general they presuppose the full authority of the bishop within his own church. He is its *episkopos* (overseer); he is ultimately responsible for the *oikonomia* (management, stewardship) of all aspects of its material and spiritual life. But the canons also recognize the possibilities for financial abuse within the diocese or any other ecclesiastical entity. Note, for example, Apostolic Canon 38:

> Let the bishop have the care of all the goods of the church, and let him administer them as under the authority of God. But he must not alienate any of them or give the things which belong to God to his own relations. If they be poor let him relieve them as poor; but let him not, under that pretense, sell the goods of the church.[3]

[3]Trans. "The Seven Ecumenical Councils of the Undivided Church," ed. Henry R. Percival (*A Select Library of Nicene and Post-Nicene Fathers*, series 2, vol. 14) 596, slightly modified.

Such concern for financial integrity led the Council of Chalcedon (Fourth Ecumenical Council, 451 A.D.) to require each diocese to have an *oikonomos* (treasurer, steward) to "administer the church's goods with the advice of his own bishop," so that "the administration of the church will not be without checks and balances, the goods of the church will not be dissipated, and the priesthood will be free from all suspicion" (canon 25).[4] The same concern is evident in the elaborate enforcement mechanisms prescribed by the Second Council of Nicea (Seventh Ecumenical Council, 787 A.D., canon 11):

> Since we are under obligation to guard all the divine canons, we ought by all means to maintain in its integrity that one which says that there are to be *oikonomoi* [treasurers, stewards] in every church. If the metropolitan appoints an *oikonomos* in his church, he does well; but if he does not, it is permitted to the bishop of Constantinople by his own authority to choose an *oikonomos* for the metropolitan's church. A like authority belongs to the metropolitans, if the bishops who are subject to them do not wish to appoint *oikonomoi* in their churches. The same rule is also to be observed with respect to monasteries.[5]

Here the Church's usual insistence on the full and exclusive authority of the bishop within his own diocese, of the metropolitan within his own province, of the abbot within his own monastery, and so forth, is superseded by its concern for financial integrity and accountability at all levels of church life.

But even the most elaborate mechanisms for maintaining responsible stewardship can break down, and even when they are in place, they offer no guarantee against financial disaster. When something does go wrong, most of us tend to be like the potential contributor in New Britain, Connecticut. We suspect willful malfeasance on the part of those in charge. In fact other factors—inexperienced leadership or extraordinary circumstances, unforeseen and unforeseeable—may be more decisive. But when, for whatever reason, something does go awry in church finances, trust breaks down, and trust once lost is very difficult to regain. This was to be

[4]Trans. Abp. Peter L'Huillier, *The Church of the Ancient Councils: The Disciplinary Work of the First Four Ecumenical Councils* (Crestwood, N.Y.: St Vladimir's Seminary Press, 1996) 264.

[5]Trans. "The Seven Ecumenical Councils," 562–63, slightly modified.

the sad experience of the North American archdiocese of the Russian Orthodox Church in the decades following the Communist revolution in Russia (1917).[6]

At the time when Archbishop Evdokim was extolling the generosity of private philanthropy in America, his archdiocese could boast not only of over three hundred parishes but also of a seminary, an orphanage, a monastery, a "women's college," and a national center and savings bank intended to serve the needs of recent immigrants. But much of the funding for these enterprises—even including a significant portion of clergy salaries and pensions—came not from "rivers of gold" poured out by private individuals within the North American archdiocese—for indeed the immigrant flock was hardly in a position to pour out "rivers of gold"!—but rather from an annual subsidy from the state church in Russia. By Archbishop Evdokim's day, this subsidy—not raised for nearly two decades—was woefully inadequate to meet the growing needs of the archdiocese and its many charitable activities. The archdiocesan newspaper was filled with articles and letters suggesting ways that the archdiocese could become more nearly self-supporting. But in fact the archdiocese still depended on support from the mother church in Russia. In what was to be his final report to the Holy Synod in Russia, Archbishop Evdokim proposed raising the annual subsidy from 89,300 rubles to 1,000,000. Since the exchange rate at the time was two rubles per U.S. dollar, and the dollar had approximately five times its present purchasing power, the archbishop was asking for roughly $2,500,000 in today's terms. But "rivers of gold" were not forthcoming from the government and state institutions of Russia either. The Holy Synod initially agreed to a subsidy of 550,000 rubles ($275,000, or roughly $1,375,000 in today's terms), but almost none of this money ever arrived. Russia was in the midst of revolutionary chaos. The financial support that the tsarist government provided had not always been adequate for the church's needs—state support seldom is! Nor was it motivated simply by the Russian government's disinterested love for the church's religious mission. The church in North America among other things was expected to promote Russian "public relations." But hitherto the link between church and state had been advantageous for the North American archdiocese. With the coming of the

[6]For what follows about the fate of the North American archdiocese, a somewhat more detailed account is provided in John H. Erickson, *Orthodox Christians in America* (Oxford and New York: Oxford University Press, 1999) 78–80.

Communist revolution in Russia and the establishment of a militantly athe-
istic regime, that link became an overwhelming liability.

Archbishop Evdokim was not on hand to witness the resulting crisis in
North America. In 1917, he had left for Russia for what everyone believed
would be a brief absence, leaving his auxiliary, Bishop Alexander
Nemolovsky, in charge of the archdiocese. At the time the archdiocese had
a debt of over $100,000, and by 1919, this amount would nearly double.
Meanwhile revenues plummeted. Receipts for 1922 would total only $2,557.
The inexperienced Bishop Alexander proved utterly incapable of dealing
with this mounting crisis. Like many in America and abroad, he believed
that the revolutionary tumult in Russia would be short-lived. As a stop-gap
measure he resorted to more loans and to mortgaging parish property–a
move that proved to be as unpopular as it was unwise from a financial perspective. Meanwhile his opponents challenged the legitimacy of his
appointment and brought lawsuits against him, accusing him of flagrantly
misspending the church's money.

It is unnecessary to give a detailed account here of the subsequent tribu-
lations of Bishop Alexander, of his successor Metropolitan Platon, and of
the troubled North American archdiocese. Suffice it to say that the sense
of trust and mutual accountability fostered by earlier ruling hierarchs was
effectively destroyed. Ordinary parishioners in places like New Britain,
Connecticut, wished to remain loyal to the church as they knew it and
loved it. They showed little desire to ally themselves with the Communist-
backed "Living Church," which, claiming to be the legitimate Russian
Orthodox Church, sought to gain control of church assets in America. But
neither did they want to leave their parish properties vulnerable to lawsuits
or to ill-advised financial moves on the part of the central church administration. Motivated by what at the time could only have been regarded as
prudent stewardship, they sought to save the church they knew and loved
by effectively severing the administrative and financial life of the parish
from the wider concerns of Orthodoxy in America. For example, many
parishes introduced "protective clauses" into their by-laws, such as:

> The Russian Orthodox Greek Catholic Church [name], of [city and
> state], hereinafter referred to as the "Church" or as the "Corporation,"
> as an ecclesiastical corporation organized and existing under and by
> virtue of the laws of the state of [state], hereby recognizes and will

honor the canons of the Russian Orthodox Greek Catholic Church of North America for spiritual guidance and, accordingly acknowledges its authority in all matters of a purely religious or spiritual nature as distinguished from all matters of an administrative, or temporal, or secular nature, which have been, are, and will be governed and administered in accordance with the charter, the by-laws, and the rules and regulations of the Corporation.

No patriarch, archbishop, metropolitan or bishop, or any ecclesiastical authority of the North American diocese or any other diocese shall have any authority, claim or right to manage, or in any way to control or affect, the real or personal property of the Corporation.

No unincorporated or incorporated diocese, sobor, diocesan convention, diocese council, or any ecclesiastical authority of the Russian Orthodox Church, or any other church, shall administer and/or dispose of the real or personal estate of the Corporation for the benefit of any church, corporation, society, or institution. . . .

No bishop of the Orthodox Church or any convention, or any sobor of the Orthodox Church, or any other church, shall have the right to assess the Corporation or its members without the permission of the Corporation membership.[7]

Such clauses may have helped save parish properties, but in the process, they set up a false dichotomy between the spiritual and the material, between religious matters and financial matters—a dichotomy alien not only to the Orthodox canonical tradition but also to the most basic principles of Orthodox theology. They also fostered a faulty understanding of Christian stewardship by implying that, in financial matters at least, the parishioners' first and foremost responsibility was to the Corporation. Forgotten was the ancient canonical understanding according to which "the goods of the church . . . belong to God" and are to be administered "as under the authority of God."

The crisis that arose in the North American archdiocese of the Russian Orthodox Church in the wake of the Communist revolution is remarkable

[7]Virtually the same paragraphs can be found in now-superseded by-laws of at least six New England parishes.

only for its magnitude and for the extraordinary circumstances that gave rise to it. Other Orthodox jurisdictions have experienced similar crises, some great and some small. This was not a crisis of generosity. Notwithstanding low-paying employment and then the hardships of the Great Depression, Orthodox immigrants and children of immigrants continued to contribute to their churches in amounts disproportionate to their income. Neither was this simply a crisis of accountability, as though better bookkeeping and reporting mechanisms might have remedied such a truly desperate situation. Ultimately this was a crisis of vision, a crisis in how Orthodox Christians in America understood—and sometimes still understand—the Church and its mission.

Like so many other Orthodox immigrants to America, the members of the Sts Cyril and Methodius Brotherhood of New Britain, Connecticut, wanted to establish a church. They and those whom they approached for support took for granted that this was a worthy cause. But what was their understanding of the Church? In their Old World villages, the Church had been a self-evident and organic part of life. Its daily and annual cycles of worship determined the patterns for work and leisure, fasting and feasting. Its moral teaching provided a common point of reference for behavior. Its sacraments and other rites gave the faithful tangible experience of the Holy. Immigrants to America—whether Greeks or Slavs, Arabs or Armenians—wanted such a Church for themselves and for their children. But they wanted something more as well. They wanted a place where they could be with their compatriots from the Old World, where their very particular social, cultural, linguistic, and spiritual heritage could be affirmed, where they could find some shelter from the pressures of New World life, where some semblance of the community they had left behind could be recreated. As a result, the relationship between Church and community underwent a subtle change. In the Old World, it was the Church that determined the shape and tone of community life. In America, this relationship came to be reversed. Now it is the community that determines the shape and tone of church life. The interests and concerns of a particular natural community—of this or that nationality, of this or that village—take precedence over the wider demands of the Church understood as a community of faith, a community open in principle to all nations and all peoples.

The process of parish formation in America offers many examples of this tendency. One example must suffice. Around 1892 a group of Greek

Orthodox immigrants in Chicago, hailing for the most part from Sparta, organized a parish and obtained a priest from that region. But the parish also included a growing number of Greek Orthodox immigrants from the rival region of Arcadia. In 1897 some of these Arcadians went off to fight in the Greco-Turkish war. They arrived too late for the war, but while in the old country, they met a priest from their own region who was eager to visit his children in Chicago. With a congenial priest so conveniently at hand, the Chicago Arcadians quickly established a parish of their own.[8]

In America, immigrant Orthodox almost inevitably tended to identify loyalty to the Church with loyalty to the ethnic community—or even, as in the example just given, with loyalty to the Old World village. Distrustful of bishops and other "outsiders," particularly when financial matters were involved, they also tended to identify loyalty to the Church with loyalty to the parish corporation. To be a good Orthodox Christian, to be a good member of the Church, meant to be a good member of the community, a member in good standing in the parish. The horizon of responsible Christian stewardship narrowed correspondingly. Orthodox Christians continued to be generous with both time and money. They continued to support the Church they knew and loved. But this meant, first and foremost, the local parish. Anniversary books, parish records, and similar sources tell of one fund-raising activity after another, generally culminating in the burning of a mortgage. But these sources show relatively little evidence of concern, much less of generosity, extending beyond the parish level. Even after the hardships of the Great Depression gave way to the relative affluence of the post-World War II era, as many parishes accumulated substantial reserve funds and embarked on grand building programs, money raised in the parish seldom went beyond the parish. To be sure, an occasional "special collection" might be earmarked for some wider purpose, usually in response to a "special appeal" from the central church administration. On the whole, however, parish financial records show little sustained and planned support for the kinds of social, educational, and missionary programs that Archbishop Evdokim and other early hierarchs had promoted.

The parish became introverted, turned in upon itself, with virtually no sense of mission and outreach and with only a minimal sense of responsibility toward anyone outside its own immediate membership.

[8]This episode is recounted at somewhat greater length in Erickson, *Orthodox Christians in America*, 72.

Older parish by-laws illustrate this point very vividly. A member in good standing, i.e., one who has paid his annual church dues and other assessments in full, "is entitled to all Church Rites and ministrations which the Priest of said Parish administers"—at least at a very reasonable price! "Baptism $5.00, Matrimony $20.00, Funerals (Adults) $20.00, Funerals (Children) $10.00, Requiem Divine Liturgy $5.00," and so forth. On the other hand, a member who is suspended because of non-payment of dues "loses all rights to church services such as Baptisms, Wedding and Funerals." "Any non-member who desires the services of the Church for Baptism [his own? his child's?] must declare his intentions of becoming a member of this Parish, [and] shall be assessed the sum of Fifty ($50.00) dollars plus cost of services." "Any nonmember who desires the services of the Church for a Wedding must declare his intentions of becoming a member of this Parish, [and] shall be assessed the sum of Fifty ($50.00) dollars plus cost of services." "Any expelled or non-member desiring the services of the Church for funerals shall be required to donate the sum of Two Hundred and Fifty ($250.00) dollars in addition to the cost of such services performed."[9] Such provisions in effect reduce the sacramental life of the Church to a series of commercial transactions intended, among other things, to ensure the financial stability and material well being of the parish. Absent is any sense that the Church has a responsibility in and for the world—or even for Orthodox Christians who happen not to be dues-paying members of the parish in question.

Fortunately the parish has not been the only outlet for the generosity of Orthodox Christians in America. Working on local, regional, and national levels, Greek-American, Russian-American, Serbian-American, and diverse other hyphenated-American Orthodox men and women have established a number of organizations devoted wholly or partially to philanthropic purposes. For the most part these organizations have been lay-initiated and lay-led. Though usually church-related, possibly with a bishop enrolled as honorary "patron" and priests more or less actively involved as "spiritual advisors," they have not always been closely tied to church structures. For example, the Federated Russian Orthodox Clubs (FROC), established in 1927, for much of its history declined any formal ecclesiastical affiliation in order to remain "above" the jurisdictional divisions that

[9]The parish by-laws quoted here were first ratified in 1959 and amended in 1967; they reflect a common and long-standing pattern especially for Slavic parish life in America.

plagued the Russian-American community in the wake of the Communist revolution in Russia. [10]

Of these philanthropic organizations, arguably the most significant, in terms both of scope of activities and size of budget, has been the Greek Orthodox Ladies Philoptochos Society. (The Greek word *philoptochos* means "friend of the poor.") Its history shows both the strengths and the inherent limitations that have characterized these organizations. Greek Orthodox women of Holy Trinity Church in New York City formed the first Philoptochos chapter in 1902, in order to provide social services for the many Greek immigrants who at the time were beginning to stream into America. Other local chapters helped to extend the society's activities to meet the expanding needs of the Greek community, and in 1931, its president, Mrs. Eriphili Vrachnos, turned over its charter to Archbishop Athenagoras, then newly assigned to America and later patriarch of Constantinople, thus marking the society's transition from a largely parochial organization to one of national importance. The range and scale of the Philoptochos Society's activities has been truly extraordinary. For example, in 1937, the society assisted in the establishment of Holy Cross Seminary (originally in Pomfret, Connecticut, later in Brookline, Massachusetts). In 1944, it helped to purchase what was to become St. Basil's Academy, a home for orphaned and semi-orphaned children. In the wake of World War II it mobilized relief efforts for war-torn Greece. In 1974, it instituted national support for the Greek Children's Cardiac Program, which flies children to the United States for heart surgery unavailable in Greece. In the wake of the Cyprus tragedy, from 1974 onward, it provided care for over five thousand displaced Cypriot children and contributed well over $100,000 in other relief assistance.[11]

The litany of Philoptochos accomplishments could go on and on— volunteer work of Philoptochos women in hospitals and nursing homes, support for research on Cooley's Anemia (a type of anemia common in Mediterranean countries), participation in arthritis and Easter Seals

[10]The FROC voted to become an official organization of the Orthodox Church in America (formerly the Russian Orthodox Greek Catholic Church in America, or "Metropolia") only in 1994, when it also changed its name to the more inclusive Fellowship of Orthodox Christians in America, or FOCA.

[11]For further details see Stella Coumantaros, "The Greek Orthodox Ladies Philoptochos Society and the Greek American Community," in *The Greek American Community in Transition*, ed. Harry J. Psomiades and Alice Scourby (New York: Pella Publishing, 1982) 191–96.

telethons, and so on. But certainly the Philoptochos Society's largest and most conspicuous projects have focused on the Greek community, whether at home or abroad. And in this respect, as in so many others, the Philoptochos is just typical of the philanthropic organizations that Orthodox Christians in America have established over the decades. Emphasis has been on the ethnic community, and this has been true even when the ethnic community itself has not been the immediate beneficiary of the organization's philanthropic activity. Press releases invariably call attention not only to the noble cause that is being supported but also to the noble generosity of the ethnic group that is providing the support. All this may seem perfectly natural, but it also serves to limit the horizon of Orthodox stewardship. Like the parish corporation, the ethnic community can become an end in itself. Here again, the problem is one not simply of generosity or even of accountability. The problem is one of vision. What is our vision of the Church and of its mission? What is our understanding of our own role in this mission?

Often we Orthodox Christians in America have tended to identify the Church with our particular ethnic communities or with the Church's most tangible institutional expressions—the parish, the jurisdiction, the patriarchate. Ultimately, however, the Church is more encompassing than this. It embraces men and women of all ages and peoples who have been called— and are still being called—to a new life of communion with God and with each other. This new life of communion seeks visible expression in institutional forms, but these forms in themselves must not become a substitute for other expressions of communion, such as the sharing of resources. Fortunately in recent years our vision of the Church—and with it our understanding of responsible stewardship—has been expanding. Agencies such as International Orthodox Christian Charities (IOCC) and the Orthodox Christian Missions Center (OCMC) have reminded us that the mission and witness of the Church go beyond our own particular ethnic institutional interests.

How can God's call to reconciliation and communion, expressed in and through the Church, become truly credible and effective in the world today? In its Old World setting, the Church very often took for granted the moral, political, and financial support of the state in advancing its mission, but this support, even when generous, often as not served to obscure the Church's mission and compromise its witness by identifying the Church with the powers of this world. In America, in any case, it is now "private people" and not "the government or state institutions" that bear primary responsibility for advancing the Church's mission and witness, through the "rivers of gold" that they are invited to pour out. In America we are all invited to exercise responsible stewardship, to share our resources in a generous but also disciplined and accountable way. But if this is to be truly Christian stewardship, we also need a vision. We need to make God's *oikonomia,* God's plan of salvation for humankind, the model for our own human *oikonomia,* for our stewardship of God's many gifts to us.

Further Reading

Efthimiou, Miltiades B., and George A. Christopoulos, eds. *History of the Greek Orthodox Church in America.* New York: Greek Orthodox Archdiocese of North and South America, 1984. Includes a chapter on the history of the charters of the archdiocese.

Erickson, John H. *Orthodox Christians in America.* New York and Oxford: Oxford University Press, 1999. Popular-level illustrated survey of the history of Orthodoxy in America, emphasizing how ordinary Orthodox Christians in America have experienced their Church.

Fitzgerald, Thomas E. *The Orthodox Church. Denominations in America,* no. 7. Westport, Conn.: Greenwood Press, 1995. Detailed account particularly of institutional developments.

Gaustad, Edwin. *Church and State in America.* New York and Oxford: Oxford University Press, 1999. Popular-level illustrated survey of church–state relations in the United States, among other things clearly explaining implications of the First Amendment's establishment clause.

———. *Religious History of America.* Rev. ed. San Francisco: Harper & Row, 1990. Readable general introduction to the place of religion in American life, including the ways in churches are financed.

Psomiades, Harry J., and Alice Scourby, eds. *The Greek American Community in Transition.* New York: Pella Publishing, 1982. Valuable sociological essays with extensive bibliography.

Schmemann, Alexander. *Church, World, Mission: Reflections on Orthodoxy in the West.* Crestwood, N.Y.: St. Vladimir's Seminary Press, 1979. A collection of essays, many of which offer stimulating, observations on differences between Old World and New World experiences of Orthodoxy.

———. *Clergy and Laity in the Orthodox Church.* Orthodox Life pamphlet series no. 1. New York: St. Vladimir's Seminary, ca. 1957. Includes pungent observations concerning parish by-laws as well as theological reflection.

Stokoe, Mark, with Leonid Kishkovsky. *Orthodox Christians in North America 1794–1994.* Syosset, N.Y.: Orthodox Christian Publications Center, 1995.

Highly readable illustrated history written to mark the bicentennial of Orthodoxy in America.

Tarasar, Constance J., and John H. Erickson, eds. *Orthodox America 1794–1976: Development of the Orthodox Church in America.* Syosset, N.Y.: Orthodox Church in America, Department of History and Archives, 1975. Includes many historic photographs, extensive excerpts from primary sources, biographical sketches of key leaders, and summaries of parish development.

ON STEWARDSHIP AND PHILANTHROPY

Forty Sentences

━━━◆━━━

Thomas Hopko*

W hen we contemplate God's Word in the Old and New Testaments and see how the Christian saints understood and applied the Scriptures, a vision of stewardship and philanthropy emerges that may be summarized in forty sentences.

1. **Giving belongs to God's very being.** The biblical God is by nature the perfect giver. God gives not only in creating the universe. God gives in an exclusively divine manner within His divinity. Christian Scriptures reveal God begetting His Son Jesus and breathing forth His Holy Spirit from all eternity as essential actions of His divine being and life. Perfectly good and loving, God is constrained by His divinity, so to speak, to share all that He is and has in a strictly divine manner, without reference to creation. Being what God is, God cannot *not* fully share the fullness of His divine being and life in an exclusively divine way. God's goodness requires Him, as it were, to "reproduce Himself" in another divine person. It requires Him to have a perfectly divine Son who is all that He is, not being Himself. It requires that He always have with Himself, as essential to His very nature, His Son Jesus Christ.[1]

*The Very Rev Thomas Hopko is Dean *Emeritus* of St Vladimir's Orthodox Theological Seminary in Crestwood, NY and taught Dogmatic Theology at the seminary from 1972 to 1992. He served as a parish priest for many years and is a world-renowned lecturer.

[1]Some church fathers claim that even the Hellenist philosophers saw that the Good cannot but be self-diffusive and self-sharing. The logic here is that if a being is, it is good; and if it is good, it must give according to its power to do so. If it fails to give, it is not good, but

2. Jesus Christ is the perfect expression of God's goodness and love.
Christians believe that God eternally gives all that He is to His Son Jesus in
the Holy Spirit. God the Father begets His Son before the foundation of the
world in a manner beyond human comprehension, which same Son is born
on earth as a man of the Virgin Mary. As God's theanthropic Son, Wisdom,
Word and Image, Jesus Christ is and has everything that God His Father is
and has. He is eternally "light from light, true God from true God." And He
is fully human from the moment of His conception in time. He is "of one
essence" *(homoousios)* with God the Father according to His divinity, and "of
one essence" *(homoousios)* with all people according to His humanity. There
never was when God's Son was not. The eternal existence of Jesus Christ the
Lord is the supreme example of God the Father as the perfect giver.[2]

3. God creates all things through, in, and for Jesus Christ. Jesus
Christ is the personal agent by whom God creates all things by the Holy
Spirit. Being God's Son, Word, Wisdom and Power, the agent of God's creative activity, all things in heaven and on earth, visible and invisible, exist
by and for Jesus in whom they consist and are held together (Col 1.15–17).
Israel's Messiah is He by whom all things are made, the one through whom
all things come to be. He is also the ever-existing divine pattern of all that
exists in the order of creation.[3]

4. All things belong to God and Christ as their creator. "I am God,

becomes evil. This, the saints argue, is why God must have a Son and Spirit according to the
demands of divinity, and why, therefore, the one God must necessarily be Father by nature
and extend His being in a strictly eternal and divine manner by begetting the Son and breathing forth the Spirit. In this view, God the Father is the principle *(arche)*, source *(pēgē)* and cause
(aitia) of His Logos/Son and Holy Spirit according to nature *(kat' ousian)*, but is the creator
of all things, through His Logos/Son and Spirit, according to His good will *(kat' eudokian)*.
Thus, against the Arians, there never was when the Son and Holy Spirit were not, but there
surely was (without entering into the issue of the created character of time) when there was
no creation.

[2]Cf. Ps 110.1 [Psalm numbers are from the English Bible, though texts quoted or referred
to may be at times from the Septuagint.]; Mt 16.16, 22.41–46; Jn 1.1–18, 20–28; 1 Cor 24; Col
1.15–20; Heb 1.1–4, et al. See also the dogmatic definitions of the seven ecumenical councils.

[3]It is a common patristic teaching that all that exists in creation somehow exists beyond
human comprehension and imagination in a divine manner within the Godhead, and that
the divine Logos, incarnate as Jesus, is the divine hypostasis in whom all creatures find their
divine pattern and ground. This is to say, in other words, that all creatures exist in God's mind
and that God brings them into being according to His divine ideas *(logoi)*, united in the one
divine Logos, incarnate as Jesus. These ideas *(logoi)* are themselves actualized in a divine way
within the Godhead in the countless divine energies flowing necessarily from God's divine
nature (or supranature) from the Father through the Son in the Holy Spirit, which ideas *(logoi)*
then are concretely realized in created form as actually existing things in this world.

your God . . . the world and all that is in it is mine" (Ps 50.7–10). Being God's creatures, human beings have nothing that we can claim as our own. We are nothing and have nothing that we have not received from God. We belong to God, together with every created thing, because God made us by His divine will and action, through His Son and Word, Jesus Christ, and the Holy Spirit. Because all things belong to God the Father, they belong also to His Son Jesus Christ by, in, and for whom they have come to be by the Spirit's power.[4]

5. **Everything that God made is good.** "And God saw everything that He had made, and behold, it was very good" (Gen 1.31). This line from the first creation story in Genesis is to be read with the "not good" of the second story when God sees the earth creature Adam all by himself and says that "it is not good that man should be alone" (Gen 2.18). God fashions Woman from Man's side, and all becomes very good as it should be. Nothing is bad by nature. Each and every creature, from the greatest spiritual power to the smallest material particle is blessed by God as a created expression of that which exists in God's uncreated, supradivine being beyond human comprehension and imagination. Indeed, it is a Christian *theologoumenon* (i.e., a theological opinion) that God will ultimately bring into being everything that can possibly exist. For if God is good and wise and powerful, why would He deny existence to anything that He could bring from nothingness into being? It seems that He cannot, and will not. It seems that God will give being to all that can possibly be.[5]

6. **Human beings are made in God's image and likeness to participate in God's divine being and life.** "Let us make man in our image, after our likeness . . . so God created man in His own image, in the image of God He created him; male and female He created them" (Gen 1.26–27). God created and continues to create human beings, male and female, to be by grace all that God Himself is by nature. We humans are creatures with the commandment not merely to imitate God, but to become divine by God's

[4]See note 2. Also Jn 16.14–15.

[5]Seven times in Genesis, at each stage of creation's unfolding in greater multiplicity and variety, it is written, "God saw that it was good" (Gen 1.3, 10, 12, 18,21,25,31). The *theologoumenon* that God will make everything that can be made parallels the dogmatic assertion that God does not wish anything in creation to be lost, but nevertheless gives existence even to those beings who in their self-destructive madness choose to be lost. Thus, ironically, the unending corruption of the blasphemers of the Holy Spirit who hate reality and attempt to defy the way things are may serve as the crowning argument for God's goodness and love, as well as for the hypothesis that God will create everyone and everything that can possibly exist.

grace. We are made to be "partakers of the divine nature" (2 Pet 1.3) ever more perfectly participating in God's supraessential divinity through God's actions in creation by agency of Christ and the Holy Spirit. Indeed, we are made to become ever more fully what God's unique Son, Word, and Image, Jesus Christ, is, in whom dwells "the whole fullness of divinity bodily" (Col 1.19, 2.9). We are made and saved and empowered by Christ and the Holy Spirit to be "filled with all the fullness of God" (Eph 3.14–19).[6]

7. **To be made in God's image means to have dominion over all that God has made in and with Jesus Christ.** Humans are made personal, spiritual beings with minds, souls, and bodies, possessing intelligence, will, and power to guide and govern ourselves, each other, and the whole of creation, by the grace and power of God. "Then God said . . . 'let them have dominion over the fish of the sea, and over the birds of the air, and over the cattle, and over all the earth, and over every creeping thing that creeps upon the earth'" (Gen 1.27). Our human being and life as persons in communion with other persons caring for creation with knowledge, goodness, wisdom, and love is what it means for us to be made in God's image and likeness. Only Jesus has fulfilled God's will for humans to be and act according to God's image and likeness. Indeed, Christ Himself is the image of the invisible God according to which all humans are made (Col 1.15, 2 Cor 4.4). He alone among the "sons of men" has dominion over all things in heaven and on earth, which are brought into perfect unity in Him (Eph 1. 9 ff; Rev 4.9–5.13; Dan 7.13–14).

8. **God made humans to be prophets, priests, and pastors of creation in and with Jesus Christ.** Human beings are commanded by God to govern the earth and all that is in it. We may even be called in ages to come to govern the billions of galaxies, each with its billions of planets and stars. We are to do so as *prophets* who know God's word and will by the direct inspiration of God's Holy Spirit; as *priests* who consecrate all things by God's Word and Spirit and intercede on behalf of all through a continual sacrifice of praise and thanksgiving to God; and as *pastors* who govern all things in God's name through a constant sacrificial service of love to those entrusted to our care. Humans fail in this magnificent calling through sin

---

[6]See Jn 1.16, 10.10; Eph 1.22–23, 3.14–19; Col 1.19, 2.9; and other New Testament Scriptures that deal with fullness of grace, truth, life, and divinity. The letter to the Ephesians (5.1) exhorts Christians, by faith and grace, to "become imitators of God *(ginesthe mimētai tou theou)*." Many church fathers go further in exhorting believers by the gracious divine energies flowing from the Father through the Son in the Holy Spirit simply to "become god *(ginesthe theon)*."

and rebellion. God sends His Son Jesus, the new and final Adam, to be and to do what humans have all failed to be and do from their very beginnings on earth.[7]

9. All things are God's not only as their creator, but also as their redeemer. Everything belongs to God, first of all humans beings, not only because God made all things by and for His Son Jesus Christ, but because God also redeemed and saved all things by and for the same Lord Jesus. When creatures rebelled and sinned against God, being fools who refuse to give glory and gratitude to God, and who desecrate, pollute, and corrupt God's good creation, thereby becoming enslaved to its destructive powers by rejecting their calling to rule in God's name, God sends His Son to save them. God owns us, therefore, because He has redeemed us in His Son Jesus when we destroyed ourselves, each other, and our world through our rebellion and sin. We belong to God, and most specifically to His Son Jesus, because God buys us back by Christ's blood when we became captivated by the devil and subjected to sin, suffering, and death. God sets us free when we are enslaved to our madness through the devil's deceit. He gives us life when we commit suicide through our sins. He pays our debt of love when we refuse to give the love that we owe to God and our neighbor. We are not our own. God's Son to whom we belong as our creator and redeemer has purchased us.[8]

10. The only thing that creatures can claim as their own is evil. God has created only good. Sin is a perversion, distortion, and destruction of the good things God gives us. It is a pollution and corruption of what is holy and blessed. It is a misuse and abuse of what is entrusted to creatures for their unending delight. It is even inaccurate, strictly speaking, to say that evil is our own, because evil has no existence of its own. It is always and necessarily a parasite on something good, a negation and perversion of something blessed by God. It is a futile attempt to destroy the good things that can alone be said, strictly speaking, to have being and life.[9]

---

[7]Acts 2.14–21, 3.22–26; Rom 5.14; 1 Cor 15.45–49; 1 Pet 2.9; Rev 1.5–6.

[8]Mt 20.28; Cor 6.20, 7.23; Eph 1.7; Col 1.14; 1 Tim 2.5–6.

[9]The word *sin* means literally to "miss the mark." Thus the "mark" is presupposed in the very conception of sin. The same is true about all concepts, symbols, and words for evil and wickedness. Fall presupposes a condition from which one falls. Transgression and lawlessness presuppose the law. Stain, pollution, and impurity presuppose cleanliness. Alienation and estrangement presuppose the homeland. Deviation presupposes the way. Perversion, distortion, and corruption presuppose wholeness and integrity. Thus our very language affirms the "parasitic" character of evil.

11. Sin is a destructive act born of the lie that we are free to do what we will with what is our own. Sin is not a wrong or bad use of human freedom and choice. It is rather an act born of the falsehood that we are free in the first place to be and to do what we choose. If we are God's creatures, and most certainly if we are Christians, we have no choice but to obey God and to do God's will in all things. Sin, therefore, is not a matter of making wrong and bad choices. It is rather, more subtly, the foolish and self-destructive act of thinking that one has choices at all. It is the refusal to accept oneself as a creature whose only real and rational choice is to obey God freely with love and gratitude, and so to choose God, and life with God, in obedience to God's benevolent will which alone constitutes for creatures perfect freedom and life. In this sense, sin is the foolish madness of creatures attempting to be gods without God. It is the insanity of creatures acting as if all things, including themselves, are their own.[10]

12. Humans become God's sons, the heirs of all things, in Christ Jesus. God sent His Son into the world as its redeemer, the new and last Adam, to restore all things in Him. As redeemed sinners purchased by Christ's blood and baptized into Christ in the name of the Father, Son, and Holy Spirit, human beings become "sons of God" in Christ, and co-heirs (*synklēronomoi*) with Him who is the heir of all things (*kleronomos pantōn*).[11] Only when a person confesses before God that he or she is unworthy to be a son, and wishes only to be a slave, does that person become by God's grace a truly adopted first-born son possessing everything that belongs to God alone. People who have never heard of Jesus, or who refuse faith in Him because of misunderstanding or perverse teaching, or who have been scandalized by the behavior of people claiming to be Christians, may in fact be participating in Christ's divine sonship and inheritance without knowing it. If so, they, too, will ultimately possess all things in the Savior.[12]

---

[10]The first chapter of St Paul's letter to the Romans is the classical scriptural description of this tragic truth. See also Deut 11.26–32, 30.15–20, referred to also in the early Christian *Didache*.

[11]See Rom 8.17; Gal 4.1–7; Heb 1.2, 14; et al.

[12]Women as well as men are called God's "sons" in Christian Scripture and liturgy, and not simply God's children or daughters, because they have received and become everything that Jesus Christ is and has as God's only-begotten (*monogēnes*) firstborn (*protōtokos*) Son. Thus all in Christ enjoy all the fullness of God in the Spirit, having become sons by faith and grace (Gal 4.4–6). All who are baptized into Christ have put on Christ and have God as Abba/Father in the Holy Spirit. In the new covenant in the Messiah all the faithful are full members; not only free Jewish men, but enslaved Gentile women. This is God's gospel in Jesus. Cf. Jer 31.31–34; Joel 2.28–32; Acts 2.17–21; Gal 3.27–4.7; Eph 2; Col 2.9–3.17. About servanthood and

13. Humans become God's sons and heirs by being God's servants and slaves in and with Jesus Christ. Jesus Christ, the unique Son of God, makes us to be God's sons by grace by being obedient in love to God His Father even unto death on the cross. Being God's Son, Christ becomes God's suffering servant and slave in order that we, through Him, may possess every grace and blessing for eternal life in and through Him as we were intended to do from the beginning of creation. Jesus makes us to be God's sons with Himself. Through our suffering and death in obedient service and servitude to God in and with Jesus, we are given everything that God Himself is and has. Truly, in Christ, God has given all things unto us, beginning with His own supra-abundant fullness of divinity.[13]

14. A steward is a bonded slave who manages his master's affairs. A steward (*oikonomos*) in the ancient world was a superior slave in a household who acted in the master's name, accounted for the master's possessions, distributed the master's goods, and often governed the master's other servants. But the steward was not the master himself.[14] Human beings who have become sons of God in Christ continue to act as stewards, knowing that their sonship is God's gift of which they are not worthy. Paradoxically, therefore, it may be said that Christians understand themselves as stewarding their divine sonship in Jesus as their most precious gift and possession from God. In this sense, they imitate the "Son of God's love" who is sent into the world "not to be served, but to serve, and to give His life as a ransom for many" (Col 1.13, Mt 20.28).[15]

sonship see Is 53; Rom 6–8; Gal 3.26–29; Phil 2. It is also God's gospel that Christ is the savior of the whole world and all human beings, not only (however especially) those who believe. See 1 Tim 4.10; 1 Jn 2.2. The saints also speak of the "baptism of desire" and the "baptism of fire" for those who do not have sacramental baptism in the Church but who live lives of love and justice, sometimes even unto their sacrificial death. The saints also add the ominous warning to the baptized that without living such lives, sacramental baptism is not for salvation but unto condemnation and judgment, as it is an unworthy participation in sacramental communion.

[13]Jn 1.16; Col 1.19–20; Eph 1.22–23, 3.14–19.The great anaphora prayer of the Liturgy of St Basil the Great which sums up all of God's saving and redeeming acts from the first moment of creation to the final coming of Christ ends with these words: "Receive us all into your kingdom, showing us to be sons of the light and sons of the day. Grant us your peace and your love, O Lord our God, for you have given all things unto us."

[14]Lk 12.41, 16.1ff; 1 Cor 4.1–2 where Jesus is called the "son of His [God's] love" 1 Pet 4.10. The term "bishop" (*episkopos*)–"God's steward (*theou oikonomos*)" in apostolic Scripture (Tit 1.7) and employed as a title for Christ Himself (2 Pet 2.25)–was the title of the chief managerial slave in a large ancient household. For this reason bishops came to be known as "servants of the servants of God."

[15]"The many" in Scripture means "the multitude," or simply "all."

15. Christians see themselves as stewards, servants, and slaves in all things with Jesus Christ. Faithful Christians have come in Christ to know themselves as God's stewards, servants, and slaves who have become by grace in Jesus God's children and sons. We realize that all that we are and have comes from God and belongs to Him and His Son. We know that we deal with our powers, properties and possessions as well as our infirmities, pains and sufferings, and even our very deaths, as not our own, but as God's and Christ's. We see ourselves, and everything with which we have to deal, including our sicknesses, sufferings, and deaths, as belonging to our Master and Lord. "None of us lives to himself and none of us dies to himself. If we live, we live to the Lord and if we die, we die to the Lord; so whether we live or whether we die, we are the Lord's" (Rom 14.7–8).[16]

16. Stewardship extends to every aspect of our life and work in the world. Care for what is entrusted to us by God is not limited to any particular aspect of our life and work, but covers all things. Humans are to be stewards of all that they are and have which comes from their divine Master. They are to care first for their own souls and bodies, then for those of their family members and others immediately given to their care, then for all people, as it is given them to do. They are to care also for the earth, the plants and the animals, the fish of the sea and the birds of the air. Finally they are to steward their time and energies, their talents and gifts, their properties and possessions, and even their sufferings and pains, using all that God gives them for His glory and the good of all His creatures, first of all one's fellow human beings.[17]

17. God's main characteristic as Love is His mercy. Virtually every book of the Old Testament, and every genre of biblical literature (law, history, prophets, psalms, wisdom, and apocalypse), proclaims "the Lord is compassionate (*oiktirmōn*) and merciful (*eleēmōn*), long-suffering (*makrothymos*) and full of mercy (*polyeleos*).[18] He is the Lord who does mercy (*eleos*) and executes merciful deeds (*poiōn eleēmosynas ho kyrios*)."[19] New Testament Scriptures state simply "God is love (*ho Theos agapē estin*)" (1 Jn 4.8, 16). He is the lover of man (*philanthrōpos*) who exercises philanthropy

[16]Stewardship of one's infirmities and sicknesses in and with Jesus is the most glorious of Christian callings. Victims of sudden death are spared this service for reasons known to God alone.

[17]Gen 1.28–31, 2.15–25, 3.1–20; Ps 8, 24, 33, and 37,104,115,148. Song of the Three Young Men.

[18]Ex 34.6; 2 Chr 30.9; Ps 103.8; Jon 4.2.

[19]Ps 103.6.

(*philanthrōpia*).[20] To be merciful and do mercy, to perform acts of mercy and philanthropy, is to love through concrete acts of generosity and kindness. It is to give, to share, and to act unconditionally for the good of others. According to the Scriptures of the Old and New Testaments, these are the quintessential expressions of God's divine perfection as Love.

18. **Mercy in Scripture means steadfast love, generosity, kindness, and goodness.** In the Bible the word *mercy* (Heb *hesed,* Grk *eleos*) is not the antonym of legal justice. It does not mean to be granted pardon or let off easily when strict justice is deserved in a legal situation. It is not primarily a legal term at all. It is rather the biblical word for God's goodness, kindness, generosity, tenderheartedness, and loving kindness, which in more contemporary biblical translations is rendered in English as steadfast love, or simply as love.[21]

19. **Humans can imitate God and fulfill God's intention for us only by doing good works and acts of mercy with love.** The way for human beings to be, and ever more perfectly to become, "gods by grace" is to become givers of good things just as God is. It is for us to share all we have, and indeed all we are, with others, for their good. To be "perfect as our heavenly Father is perfect," as Jesus commands in the gospel, is to be "merciful as God our Father is merciful."[22]

20. **To give alms means literally to do merciful acts.** In His Sermon on the Mount in Matthew's Gospel, the Lord commands His disciples how to behave when they fast and pray and give alms. Christ's words normally rendered in English as "when you give alms" literally say "when you do acts of mercy" (*hotan ouv poiēs eleēmosynēn*) (Mt 6.2). This is the exact expression used for the Lord Himself in the Psalms when it says, "the Lord executes mercy (*poiōn eleēmosynas ho kyrios*)" (Ps 103.6). Thus we see in a striking

---

[20]God is called *philanthrōpos* (usually rendered "Lover of Mankind") countless times in Orthodox liturgical hymns and prayers but seems never to have been referred to with this term in the Bible. Only once does New Testament Scripture speak of the Lord's *philanthrōpia* as our Savior (Tit 3.4).

[21]*Kyrie eleēson,* the most repeated of Christian prayers, is not in the first instance a plea to God to pardon our sins, or to let us off when we deserve just punishment for our offenses. It is rather a prayer to God to be as He has revealed Himself to be: merciful, gracious, long-suffering, and full of steadfast love and kindness. It is a prayer, in a word, asking God to love us, as He does in any case without our asking. See Mt 5.44–48.

[22]The parallel text in Luke's Gospel to Christ's commandment to His disciples in Matthew that they "must be perfect, as your heavenly Father is perfect" (Mt 5.48) is that they must "be merciful, even as your Father is merciful" (Lk 6.36).

manner how God commands His people to imitate Him in the activity which is most divinely characteristic of all, the primary expression of God's divine nature: the commandment to do concrete acts of mercy in love.

21. Christ's new commandment for believers in God is to love one another as He has loved us. "A new commandment I give to you, that you love one another; even as I have loved you, that you love one another. By this all people will know that you are my disciples, if you have love for one another" (Jn 13.34–35). "This is my commandment, that you love one another as I have loved you" (Jn 15.12). Human beings, according to Jesus, are to love one another, including their worst enemies, with the very love that God is, for God is Love (1 Jn 4.8, 16). We are to love with the very love with which God in Christ has loved us all. We are to love one another as God has loved us in Jesus, His only Son. We are to love as Christ loved: fully, completely, unconditionally, unto death. This divine love, which is always empowered in human beings (whether they know it or not) by God's Holy Spirit (Rom 5.5), is expressed exclusively through concrete acts of mercy, through giving and sharing in concrete acts of kindness.

22. The first and great commandment in the law—to love God with all one's heart, soul, mind, and strength—can be fulfilled only by loving others. It is clearly taught in Scripture that if we say that we love God, and do not love our fellow creatures, beginning with our families and friends and ending with our most hated enemies, through concrete acts of mercy, we are liars, and the truth of God is not in us, "for he who does not love his brother whom he has seen, cannot love God whom he has not seen. And this commandment we have from Him, that he who loves God should love his brother also" (1 Jn 4.20–21).

23. To love God with all one's strength is to love God with all one's possessions. Loving with all one's strength means loving with all that one has and controls. It is to love with all one's wealth, riches, property, and power, beginning with one's money. This is literally what God's law prescribes when God commands His people to love Him with all their *strength* (RSV) or *might* (KJV) (Deut 6.4).

24. God commands His people to express their faith and love in active works of mercy. Jesus teaches that His disciples are to love as He has loved. He also teaches that a person's faith will be expressed in acts of love, since the one who believes in Christ will do the works that He does, and even greater works than He does, because He goes to the Father (Jn 14.12).

Scriptures attributed to James and John emphasize Christ's affirmation of the old commandment that belief in God must be expressed in philanthropic deeds, i.e., in loving God with all one's strength by sharing one's goods with others. The Lord's brother asks the question, "What does it profit, my brethren, if a man says he has faith but has not works? If a brother or sister is ill-clad and in lack of daily food, and one of you says to them, 'Go in peace, be warmed and filled,' without giving them the things needed for the body, what does it profit? So faith, by itself, if it has no works, is dead" (Jas 2.15–17). And the beloved disciple puts the question, "But if any one has the world's goods, and sees his brother in need, yet closes his heart against him, how does God's love abide in him?" He then exhorts the faithful saying, "Little children, let us not love in word or speech, but in deed and in truth" (1 Jn 3.17–18).

25. Spiritual acts of mercy are a necessity for everyone. If we are unable to do material acts of mercy because of our lack of means and our physical weakness, we can still show mercy and give for alms our spiritual support. We can give our prayers and intercessions. We can inspire, edify, encourage, and comfort by our words and example (1 Cor 14.3). We can show goodwill and offer tears of compassion and blessed mourning. Not all can give money or goods. Not all can work and assist. But all can pray, all can weep, and all can express co-suffering love with mercy for all, without discrimination or condition.[23]

26. Love for fellow creatures, and especially for fellow human beings, begins with one's family. Those who fail to do acts of mercy in loving care for their family members are despised in God's eyes above all others. "If any one does not provide for his relatives, and especially his own family," says the Apostle, "he has disowned the faith and is worse than an unbeliever" (1 Tim 5.8). The prophet Isaiah also, when describing a fast well pleasing to God, condemns those who hide from their relatives who ask for their aid and assistance (Is 58.6–9).

---

[23]The saints teach that three things are for everyone, regardless of their earthly circumstances or conditions: prayers, tears, and love. Monastics who are theoretically exempt from offering material acts of mercy because of their poverty are nevertheless seen to be offering aid and assistance to the poor and needy in more than spiritual ways. The lives of the monastic saints are filled with examples of stewardship over creation and philanthropic activity expressed without discrimination or condition to human beings and beasts down to the last shred of one's clothing, the last crust of one's bread, the last ounce of one's strength, and the last breath of one's life.

27. Merciful acts performed in love extend beyond the family to those of the household of faith. The greatest sign in the early church that Gentiles were saved by God's grace through faith in Christ was that they sent money to the poor Jewish-Christians in Jerusalem, which, it is written, they were very pleased to do, affirming God's love for the "cheerful giver" (2 Cor 9.7; Phil 4.15–19; Acts 24.17). This teaches us that within the church there can be no discrimination in regard to philanthropy on the basis of race, ethnicity, or nationality. Indeed there can be no discrimination for any reason whatsoever. If persons or community of persons are brothers and sisters in Christ, they deserve our philanthropic activity as an essential element of our common faith. Christians do not give only to "our own people" humanly speaking. We give to all people, without discrimination or condition, since, in Christ, every person is "our own" and we are "theirs."[24]

28. The first Christians held all things in common. The scriptural image of the first Christian community in Jerusalem shows that all who believed were together and had all things in common. They sold their possessions and goods and distributed them to all, as any had need. This was not, as some have alleged, a primitive form of communism. It was rather the expression of the Christian conviction that one's biological and physical family according to human flesh and blood, which remains fully intact until Christ's second coming, is sanctified and superceded by one's ecclesial and spiritual family according to Christ's flesh and blood, with all believer's having the same God and Father in the Holy Spirit.[25]

29. Christian philanthropy is not limited to members of the household of faith. While the Church's sacraments are reserved exclusively for believing Orthodox Christians who take full responsibility for the faith and life of the Church, who identify fully with the Orthodox Church in history, and who are fully at peace with all people, having heartfelt sorrow and repentance for their sins, the Church's philanthropy excludes no one. Christians must perform acts of mercy, both material and spiritual, for all human beings, whoever they may be. This fulfils the Lord's teaching to love our neighbors, including our enemies, as our very selves. This is the point of Christ's parable of the Good Samaritan, which the Lord Himself demonstrated in His own earthly life and work (Lk 10.25–37). It is the teaching and practice of the holy apostles (Rom 12.20–21).[26]

[24]See Acts 10.1–11.18, 17.22–31; Eph 2.11–22.
[25]See Acts 2.43–47, 4.32–5.11, 10.1–11.18; 2 Cor 8–9.
[26]Samaritans for Jews were heretics who did not accept the whole of inspired Scripture.

30. Christians must do good deeds and merciful acts for all human beings without condition or discrimination. As Christ died on the cross not only for His own people, or for believers, or for good people, but also for all people and the whole world, so merciful acts of Christians must embrace everyone, everywhere, without boundaries or conditions.[27] This, as the saints testify in their words and deeds, includes even atheists, heretics, peoples of other faiths and convictions, and persecutors of the Church.[28] As Christians are called to do good to their enemies, so they are called to pray for them and weep for them as well. The Christians' all-inclusive prayers include supplications, intercessions, and thanksgivings performed at Church services. Christians always offer the eucharistic Divine Liturgy on behalf of all and for all, including those excluded from sacramental communion because of their separation from the faith and life of the Church.

31. Acts of mercy with love are performed by Christians without desire for thanks, honor, or praise. Good deeds, such as working for justice and peace and aiding those who suffer from sickness or want, even including miracles, may be done without love. They may be performed out of pride, vanity, arrogance, and love of praise. They may be done with ungodly anger in one's heart and judgment of others. When such is the case, such acts are not pleasing to God. They profit nothing. And even worse, they are performed unto self-condemnation and judgment since they are enacted in an unworthy manner.[29] Jesus commands us to pray, fast,

They were not to be greeted or spoken to. They were to be treated as dogs. This is crucial for understanding Jesus' parable of the Merciful Samaritan (as the story is called in Greek and Slavonic), as well as Jesus' conversation with the Samaritan woman in St John's Gospel.

[27] 1 Tim 4.10; 1 Jn 2.2.

[28] See, for example, the writings of St John Chrysostom (e.g., his homilies referring to Mt 18.15–17 and 1 Tim 2.1–20) and the lives and teachings of Basil the Great, John the Merciful, and Simeon the New Theologian, and, nearer to our times, the acts of Russian saints like John of Cronstadt, Grand Duchess Elizabeth the New Martyr, and Patriarch Tikhon the Confessor. These saints prayed for everyone, including the non-Orthodox and non-Christian, both in their personal prayers and during church services at the altar. They performed acts of mercy for them in regard to food, drink, shelter, and clothing and healed them of illnesses of soul and body, even performing miracles on their behalf. Some historians tell us that the Roman emperor Constantine was forced to give freedom to Christianity after the last great persecution of Christians by Diocletian because of pressures brought to bear by the many non-Christians who had received mercy and philanthropy from persecuted Christians during times of sickness and famine.

[29] Mt 8.21–23; 1Cor 13.1–8. When asked why acts of mercy and even miracles may not save those who do them without love, the saints tell us that it is the love that counts in God's eyes and not the acts in themselves. The saints also explain that God may empower good deeds,

and do merciful acts in secret, hidden even from ourselves. We are to do these acts without showing off, lording it over others, judging others, or drawing attention to ourselves. This is what Jesus means when He says that when we give money and do other acts of mercy, we should not blow the trumpet or stand on street corners, but should cover our acts, not even letting our left hand know what our right hand is doing. Jesus speaks here about our attitude toward what we are doing, and how and why we are to do what we do (Mt 6.1–6).

32. Acts of mercy are a grave spiritual danger and risk. Acts of mercy almost always become known to others. This is inevitable, and somehow even necessary, if Christians are to be examples to others and to fulfill Christ's command to "let your light so shine before men, that they may see your good works and give glory to your Father who is in heaven" (Mt 5.16). It is particularly important for Christians to inspire and encourage family members and others entrusted to our care, as well as our fellow Christians and other people of good will, to do good deeds and merciful acts. To bear people's honor and praise, which will surely come from doing good things, as well as their envy and scorn, is no small achievement. To let one's good deeds be known for the sake of encouraging others, without seeking personal glory, and without being adversely affected either by praise or vilification, is the greatest of all graces. Bearing glory, according to the saints, is incomparably more difficult than bearing scorn. Freedom and detachment from earthly honor and praise, while being publicly acknowledged for good things, belongs only to the holy ones who are especially covered by God's grace and protection. Only the holy can remain unscathed in such spiritual danger.

33. Money, according to the Scriptures and God's gospel in Jesus Christ, is not evil in itself. Wealth and riches are goods to be used in good ways. Jesus' teaching recorded in the Gospels, as well as His behavior and that of His disciples, demonstrates this clearly. Judas Iscariot was charged with carrying the money for the use of Christ and His apostles for such necessary duties as paying taxes and celebrating feasts and, most of all, for caring for the poor and needy.

34. Some Christian saints, including some of Jesus' disciples, were wealthy. Tradition tells us that Joachim and Anna, the parents of Christ's

prophetic words, and even miracles in order to bring glory to His name and blessings to those who receive them, even when these acts bring judgment on those through whom God works because of their lack of love.

mother Mary, were a very wealthy couple who surpassed the Mosaic rule of tithing by distributing a third of their possessions to the temple and a third to the poor. The apostles Peter, Andrew, James, and John were partners in a prosperous fishing business who left everything to follow Christ. Paul, the tent-maker, was learned and not poor. Cornelius the centurion and the Ethiopian eunuch were certainly well off. Those who supported Paul's ministry, such as Aquila and Priscilla, Lydia, and Apollos were people of means. The rich man with the Lord's suffering servant at His death, prophesied by Isaiah, was the noble councilor of Jerusalem, Joseph of Arimathea, who buried Christ's body with linen and spices in His own new tomb.[30] Some saints gave up all they had to preach the gospel, while others supported them in this blessed work with their wealth. Through the centuries, especially after the establishment of Christianity as the official religion of the Roman Empire, the richest members of society supported the church in building houses of worship, monasteries, schools, hospitals, orphanages, and other eleemosynary institutions. The rule of contemporary philanthropy, that 80 percent of good works are made possible by the gifts of 20 percent of the donors, and that major projects cannot succeed without major gifts from wealthy givers, is hardly something new in human and Christian affairs.

35. Christian saints performed good deeds and merciful acts through their public and institutional strength. After the legitimization and establishment of Christianity in the Roman Empire, Christians gained great political, social, and economic power. This was especially so in the Byzantine and Russian empires as well as the Christian nation-states such as those of the Bulgarians, Romanians, and Serbians. Christian emperors and rulers, such as Saints Constantine and Helen, Justinian and Theodora, Vladimir and Olga, following the examples of the stewardship and philanthropy of Israel's faithful kings and judges, used their God-given secular powers and positions to do good works and merciful deeds. The Christian bishops also did so when they became public figures. This tells us that Christians in all times and places, whatever the form of government and socio-economic system in which they find themselves, are obliged by their faith to use their legitimate public authority and power for doing good. This is so even when they cannot do so openly and overtly in Christ's name, for even then their acts of stewardship and philanthropy will be to

[30]Cf. Is 53.9; Mk 15.43–46, et al.

God's glory for the good of God's creatures including those who do not believe in God or acknowledge Christ's lordship over creation.[31]

36. No passion is more treacherous and more difficult to conquer than the passion for possessions, property, and wealth. Scripture teaches that the love of money (*philargyria*) is the root of all evil (1 Tim 6.10). Covetousness (*pleonexia*) is idolatry (Col 3.5). Covetousness, possessiveness, greed, acquisitiveness, and envy are, according to the gospel, the greatest temptations for human beings. In affirming that with God all things are possible, Jesus points to the possibility of a rich man entering God's kingdom (Lk 18.18–27).[32] The cause of Jesus' betrayal by Judas, a scriptural testimony endlessly repeated in Orthodox Holy Week services, is the apostle's love for money, which goes together with love for carnal pleasure, secular power, and earthly glory.[33]

37. A "good answer" at Christ's judgment belongs only to those who do good deeds according to their ability. Each person, believer and unbeliever, Jew and Gentile, Orthodox and non-Orthodox, will answer to God for what they have done in their life (Rom 2.5–16). According to Scripture, the Lord will test each person's works as with fire (1 Cor 13–15) and will render to everyone according to their works (Ps 62.12; Prov 24.12; Rom 2.6). Revelation states that all people will be judged by what they have done (Rev 22.12). We can add here, without fear of error, that all will be judged by what they have specifically done with their money, possessions, property, and wealth. In His parable of the final judgment Jesus lists the acts of mercy for which human beings will answer: feeding the hungry, giving drink to the thirsty, clothing the naked, sheltering the homeless, and caring for the sick, the imprisoned, the poor, and the needy. The absence of such acts in our lives, when they are within our means to accomplish, proves that faith and love for God are not in us (Mt 25.31–46).

---

[31]Christians believe that all power, including the secular power of governments, whatever their origin or form, comes from God and Christ. Christians also hold that all secular rulers and civil authorities, especially those claiming to be Christians, will answer before God for how they used the strength and authority given to them. For this reason, among others, prayers and intercessions are offered at the Church's liturgical services for those in civil authority, whatever their policies and religious convictions. For this reason also prayers are made for the military.

[32]St Luke's Gospel especially warns of the danger and treachery of riches, as do the Letter of James and the Old Testament book of Proverbs and the writings of the Prophets.

[33]See especially the Orthodox liturgical services for Great and Holy Wednesday, Thursday, and Friday.

38. Christians are themselves "the poor." Several uses of the term *poor* are at work in the Scriptures. The Lord is with the materially poor and identifies Himself with them. This was a teaching of God's word already in the Old Testament.[34] It is not unique to Christians. Unique to Christians is the conviction that God's Son Jesus identifies with the poor and ultimately becomes poor Himself in the most literal way. Extreme nonacquisitiveness, though not destitution, and spiritual poverty, i.e., knowing that we have nothing of our own, is a calling for all Christians. The "poor" (in Hebrew, *anawim*) was actually a title for God's People in the Bible and particularly for the first followers of Jesus as Israel's messiah.[35] Poverty of spirit and body was a sign of a person's divine calling and perfection in and with Jesus. "Blessed are the poor in spirit, for theirs in the kingdom of heaven" (Mt 5.3). "Blessed are you poor, for yours in the kingdom of God" (Lk 6.20).[36] "If you would be perfect, go, sell what you possess and give to the poor, and you will have treasure in heaven; and come, follow me" (Mt 19.21).

39. Spiritual poverty is for all Christians. Wealthy Christians must be poor in spirit. They must know that their wealth is from God even when they have earned it through hard work and not simply by good fortune or inheritance. The opportunity to work, the intelligence and diligence to succeed, and the good fortune to be successful are all gifts of God's providence. When riches increase, the righteous do not set their heart on them or trust in them. They know, with St Paul, how to abound and how to want (Phil 4.11–13).[37] They do not allow their possessions to choke the word of God in their lives (Mt 13.22; Lk 8.14). And most important of all, they use their wealth for the growth of the gospel, the edification of the Church, the enlightening of the ignorant, the healing and comfort of the sick and suffering, the care of the poor and needy, and the salvation of souls.

40. Detachment and moderation in regard to possessions is the rule for Christians. The norm for nonmonastic Christians is to be moderate in our possessions, to have only what is absolutely necessary, to give away more than we need in concrete acts of mercy, and thereby to be godly and

[34]Cf. Prov 14.31, 19.17 and all the prophetic writings.

[35]E.g., see the canticle of Jesus' mother Mary patterned after the song of Samuel's mother Hannah (1 Sam 2.1–10 and Lk 1.46–55). See also Jesus' use of Isaiah in Lk 4.18–19. Cf. Ps 70.5; 72.2, 12; 74.19–23; and 82.4, 86.1; et al.

[36]St Luke's Gospel especially stresses the need for material poverty and the danger of riches and possessions.

[37]Ps 49.5–12; 52.7; 62.10. The apostle Paul also invokes God's law (Ex 16.18) saying, "He who gathered much had nothing over, and he who gathered little had no want" (cf. 2 Cor 8.8–15).

spiritually free.[38] The question, of course, is about what and how much are truly necessary. What do we really need? How much is enough? Each of us will have to decide for ourselves and our families, as well as our churches and nations. We can do this only by the Holy Spirit's power, with the guidance of Scripture, participation in the Church's liturgical and sacramental life, the reading of the lives of saints, and the counsel of wise and loving pastors and elders in the faith.

A fitting epilogue to these sentences on stewardship and philanthropy is found in St Paul's first letter to Timothy.

> There is great gain in godliness with contentment; for we brought nothing into the world, and we cannot take anything out of the world; but if we have food and clothing, with these we shall be content. But those who desire to be rich fall into temptation, into a snare, into many senseless and hurtful desires that plunge people into ruin and destruction. For the love of money is the root of all evils; it is through this craving that some have wandered away from the faith and pierced their hearts with many pangs.
>
> But as for you, man of God, shun all this; aim at righteousness, godliness, faith, love, steadfastness, gentleness. Fight the good fight of faith; take hold of the eternal life to which you were called when you made the good confession in the presence of many witnesses.[39]
>
> In the presence of God who gives life to all things; and of Christ Jesus who in His testimony before Pontius Pilate made the good confession, I charge you to keep the commandment unstained and free

[38]This is the point of the wonderful word found among the sayings of St Anthony the Great. "It was revealed to Abba Anthony in his desert that there was one who was his equal in the city. He was a doctor (presumably married) by profession and whatever he had beyond his needs he gave to the poor, and everyday he sang the *trisagion* with the angels" (*Sayings of the Desert Fathers*, Anthony, 24).

[39]The "confessing of the good confession (*hōmologēsas tēn kalēn homologian*)" here almost surely refers to the person's baptism and entrance into the eucharistic communion of the Church. The expression "many witnesses (*pollōn martyrōn*)" may be a play on words meaning both the many faithful who witnessed the "good confession" at baptism and the many martyrs who witnessed by their suffering and death their "good confession" of the gospel before the persecuting Romans. In both instances, the reference made to Christ at His passion "witnessing His good confession before Pontius Pilate (*martyrēsantos epi Pantiou Pilatou tēn kalēn homologian*)" is strikingly relevant.

from reproach until the appearing of our Lord Jesus Christ; and this will be made manifest at the proper time by the blessed and only Sovereign, the King of kings and the Lord of lords, who alone has immortality and dwells in unapproachable light, whom no person has ever seen or can see. To Him be honor and eternal dominion. Amen.

As for the rich in this world, charge them not to be haughty, nor to set their hope on uncertain riches, but on God who richly furnishes us with everything to enjoy. They are to do good, to be rich in good deeds, liberal and generous, thus treasuring up for themselves a good foundation for the future, so that they may take hold of the life which is life indeed. (1 Tim 6.6–19)

OFFERING YOU "YOUR OWN OF YOUR OWN"

Stewardship in the Liturgy

———◆———

Paul Meyendorff[*]

Τὰ σὰ ἐκ τῶν σῶν σοὶ προσφέροντες—κατὰ πάντα καὶ διὰ πάντα—σὲ ὑμνοῦμεν, σὲ εὐλογοῦμεν, σοὶ εὐχαριστοῦμεν, Κύριε, καὶ δεόμεθά σου, ὁ Θεὸς ἡμῶν.

Offering you your own of your own—in all things and for all things— we praise you, we bless you, we give thanks to you, O Lord, and we pray to you, our God.[1]

E ach Sunday, Orthodox Christians gather together to celebrate the Eucharist. At this assembly the Church (*ekklesia*, means "church" or "assembly") is realized as the "body of Christ," and individual Christians affirm their membership in this body.[2] It is no accident that from its earliest days, the Church would gather together "on the first day of the week" to "break bread."[3] At this gathering, Scripture was proclaimed and expounded, collections were taken, and bread and wine were prayed over and distributed to the faithful. So central were these

---

*Dr Paul Meyendorff is the Alexander Schmemann Professor of Liturgical Theology and the Associate Dean for Academic Affairs at St Vladimir's Orthodox Theological Seminary in Crestwood, NY.

[1]English translation from *The Divine Liturgy of Our Father Among the Saints John Chrysostom* (Oxford: Oxford University Press, 1995), 32–33. Hereafter cited as *The Divine Liturgy*.

[2]This is the essential teaching we see emphasized in much contemporary Orthodox thought, particularly in the writings of N. Afanasiev, A. Schmemann, J. Zizioulas, and J. Meyendorff.

[3]Acts 2.46; 20.7.

liturgical gatherings to the early Church that, even during the age of persecutions, Christians continued to meet in secret, each time putting their
lives at risk. So central has the liturgy remained for Orthodox Christians
that among the Slavic churches, in particular, the very word "Orthodoxy"
(in Slavonic, *pravoslavie*) has come to be understood not just as "right
faith," but as "right worship." The liturgy, then, has from the beginning
been a privileged locus for the encounter between God and humanity.

The liturgy is central to our formation as Christians. Every important
event in our lives is marked liturgically. When we are born, we are churched
and then baptized into the local community of the faithful. Significant
events, particularly marriage and death, are accompanied by elaborate liturgical rituals. And even ordinary, everyday life takes on a liturgical dimension as we live from morning to evening (the daily cycle of worship,
including matins and vespers), from week to week (with each Sunday com-
memorating Christ's resurrection), from year to year (with the annual cycle
of feasts and fasts, culminating each year on Pascha). In ages long before
Sunday schools or seminaries, Christians lived in and through these liturgical cycles, whose aim was to transform each and all into conformity with
the risen Lord through active participation in His body, the Church.

The liturgical life of the Church, in short, is a primary bearer of tradition. Scripture is read in a liturgical context. Scripture readings, at least at
the eucharistic liturgy, are normally followed by a sermon, whose primary
aim is to make the words of Scripture speak to the gathered assembly. The
gathered assembly in turn offers its prayers to God, led by the bishop or
presbyter who stands at the head of the local congregation. The faith of the
Church is taught through the creed, as well as through a rich body of
hymnography. The church building, typically covered by a large dome, the
abundance of icons on the iconostasis and the walls, all remind the faithful that the Church is cosmic, transcending both time and space. The
liturgy, in the words Fr Alexander Schmemann, is thus a primary source of
theology, the very condition of doing theology.[4] It is in the here that we
encounter God, and that God speaks to us.

----

[4]See his posthumously published collection of articles, *Liturgy and Tradition*, T. Fisch, ed.
(Crestwood, N.Y.: St Vladimir's Seminary Press, 1990). This notion is picked up in much con-
temporary liturgical theology: see, for example, A. Kavanagh, *On Liturgical Theology* (New
York: Pueblo, 1984), 89, 96, 109, 110, 124, 146, 151 (the volume is dedicated in memory of
Alexander Schmemann); as well as D.W. Fagerberg, *What Is Liturgical Theology? A Study in
Methodology* (Collegeville, Minn.: Liturgical Press, 1992).

From the early days of the Church, therefore, liturgical life, and the Eucharist in particular, were absolutely central to Christian life. Thus it was quite natural for the authors of Scripture to use the Eucharist as a paradigm for Christian living. St Paul, for example, whose writings are among the earliest in the New Testament corpus, criticizes the Corinthians for their failure to be united: "When you meet together, it is not the Lord's supper that you eat. For in eating, each one goes ahead with his own meal, and one is hungry and another is drunk" (1 Cor 11.20). In discussing idolatry and the consumption of meat offered to idols, Paul again uses a eucharistic image:

> Therefore, my beloved, shun the worship of idols. . . . The cup of blessing which we bless, is it not a participation [*koinonia* = "communion"] in the blood of Christ? The bread which we break, is it not a participation [*koinonia*] in the blood of Christ? Because there is one bread, we who are many are one body, for we all partake of the one bread. (1 Cor 10.14–17)

So, whether one eats meat offered to idols, neglects the poor, or splits into factions, one breaks the unity of the Church which is expressed in the eucharistic assembly.

What, then, does the liturgy say to us regarding stewardship? At first glance, not very much! If one considers stewardship primarily in financial terms, no prayers in the eucharistic liturgy speak directly to the subject, and the rubrics typically do not even mention when the collection should be taken up. If one considers stewardship in a broader sense, as the offering up of one's talents, as the various ministries performed by members of the liturgical assembly, one finds a little more—but all too often in contemporary Orthodoxy the people in the pews are simply reduced to passive spectators. Indeed, liturgical developments in recent centuries have led to increased clericalism on the one hand, and a marginalization of the laity on the other. At the same time, due primarily to the encroachment of secularism, financial issues have all too often been relegated to the purely secular sphere. It is as though our spiritual and liturgical lives would somehow be tainted by concern with money; and this is particularly so in the Eucharist, at which we are told to "lay aside all earthly cares."[5]

Yet both liturgical history and the deeper sense of liturgical texts paint

---

[5]In the Cherubikon, sung at nearly every eucharistic liturgy in the Byzantine tradition.

a vastly different picture. Stewardship has always been an integral part of the liturgical life of the Church. Some form of collection has found a place in the assembly from the very beginning, and the Church, at least in theory, requires all Christians to offer up their talents to God. All Christians, and not just the clergy, are responsible and accountable for maintaining the Church and its faith. In this chapter, however, we will focus primarily on the material aspects of stewardship—realizing, however, that this will hardly exhaust the full meaning of this important concept.

In the early days of the Church, persons coming to church on Sunday would bring offerings with them. Typically, these would include bread and wine, as well as wheat, oil, and other basic staples, which they would leave with the deacons upon entering. From these gifts, the deacons would select a suitable amount of bread and wine for the Eucharist, and the remainder was used to support the clergy, as well as to feed the poor, the widows, and others for whom the Church provided.

In the pre-Constantinian era, when Christians met primarily in private homes, this was a simple matter. With the massive increase in numbers after the legalization of Christianity and the building of large new churches, the process became more complex. It became too cumbersome for the deacons to collect the gifts at the entrances of the church. To accommodate the larger numbers, special buildings, called *skeuophylakia*,[6] were built near the main church. Before the liturgy began, the faithful would drop off their gifts at the *skeuophylakion* and would then wait in the courtyard for the bishop. Upon the arrival of the bishop, everyone, clergy and people, would enter the church. It is this entrance which in the Byzantine tradition subsequently comes to be known as the Little Entrance.[7]

A special case presented itself when the emperor was present. Rather than dropping off his gifts in the *skeuophylakion*, he entered the church together with the bishop and placed his gift directly on the altar table. Many are familiar with the famous sixth-century mosaics in the basilica of San Vitale in Ravenna, Italy. Emperor Justinian is represented carrying a

[6]On the *skeuophylakion* at Hagia Sophia, see T. Mathews, *The Early Churches of Constantinople: Architecture and Liturgy* (University Park & London: Pennsylvania State University Press, 1971), 13, 14, 38, 89, and figs. 2–3, pl. 1b.

[7]J. Mateos, *La célébration de la parole dans la liturgie byzantine* (Orientalia Christiana Analecta, 191) (Pont. Institutum Studiorum Orientalium, 1971), 71–90. Cf. also R. Taft, *The Great Entrance: A History of the Transfer of Gifts and Other Preanaphoral Rites in the Liturgy of St John Chrysostom* (Orientalia Christiana Analecta, 200) (Rome: Pont. Institutum Studiorum Orientalium, 1978). On the offering of the gifts by the faithful before the liturgy, see esp. 12–32.

paten or shallow golden bowl, while Empress Theodora carries a chalice. The scene depicts the royal retinue entering the nave of the church in a procession that scholars once thought to have been the Great Entrance. Thomas Mathews, however, has demonstrated convincingly that these mosaics in fact represent the Little, or First, Entrance, and that even in later centuries the emperor would always bring his gift into the church at this point, typically a purse filled with gold, but occasionally a chalice and paten as well.[8] Thus, even emperors, who in Byzantine tradition are often understood to represent the whole laity, graphically demonstrate the ancient custom of bringing gifts to the liturgical assembly.

At the appropriate moment in the liturgy, the deacons would go out to the *skeuophylakion* to get the necessary bread and wine and bring them to the altar. At first, this procession was done in silence and without pomp, but eventually this became the Great Entrance.[9] And the preparation of the gifts, at first performed very simply by the deacons alone, also developed into an elaborate rite known as the *prothesis*, or *proskomide*, and began to be carried out by priests.[10]

In contemporary practice, this bringing of gifts to the liturgy survives only in vestigial form. The bread used for the Eucharist is still referred to as *prosphora* (lit: "offering"), and in many communities this bread is still prepared by individual parishioners. The Russian practice of bringing *prosphora* in commemoration of the living and the dead is another remnant of these ancient offerings.

It is an interesting fact that neither liturgical books nor commentaries, whether ancient or modern, mention a collection taken up during the liturgy. This can partly be explained by the fact that during the era of the imperial Church, whether in the Byzantine Empire from the Peace of Constantine to the fall of Constantinople in 1453, or in Russia until 1917, the Church was supported primarily by the state. For rank and file faithful, this meant that they supported the Church not directly, but through the taxes

[8]T. Mathews, *Early Churches*, 146–47, and *pl. 91, 92*.

[9]On the development of the Great Entrance, see R. Taft, *The Great Entrance*. In this exhaustively documented study, Taft demonstrates that the Great Entrance is not the offertory procession (as in the West), but simply a highly elaborated transfer of gifts—originally from the *skeuophylakion*, but later from the *prothesis*, to the altar. The actual offering of gifts, he maintains, takes place *before* the liturgy, when people bring their gifts to the church and hand them over to the deacons.

[10]On the *proskomide*, see M. Mandalà, *La protesi della liturgia nel rito bizantino-greco* (Grottaferrata, 1935).

they paid to the emperor. And the social work of the Church after the fourth century often fell to the rapidly expanding monastic movement.[11] Few are aware, for example, that the hospital originated in Byzantine monasticism.[12]

The historical evidence for financial stewardship, therefore, is ambiguous. For much of the Church's history, the state took over much of the responsibility of supporting the Church. This does not mean, of course, that individual stewardship was entirely forgotten. Individuals continued to build churches, monasteries, and other institutions.[13] Almsgiving remained one of the cardinal virtues and was strongly encouraged, particular during the penitential season of Lent. The message of 1 Corinthians 16, which describes the collection for the church in Jerusalem at the Sunday assembly, was never entirely forgotten.

"YOUR OWN OF YOUR OWN"

These words, proclaimed aloud by the presiding bishop or presbyter at each eucharistic liturgy, affirm that what is offered already belongs to God. At this moment, the deacon elevates the bread and wine in a gesture of offering. Of course, what is being offered is much more than just these elements. First of all, the bread and wine symbolize the self-offering of Christ, following on Jesus' words at the Last Supper: "This is my body. . . . This is my blood . . . given for you." Thus the gifts are offered up to God, and God offers Himself back to us in the form of bread and wine.

The elements also represent the work of our hands: the bread comes from the wheat workers have sown and harvested, ground into flour, and baked into bread; the wine from the grapes vinedressers have grown, pressed, and made into wine. In the industrial era, and even more so in our present, post-industrial age, this direct connection often is lost: we think of bread as something ready-made we buy in a supermarket, and wine in a liquor store. In our era, the most direct symbol of our labor is the money we earn, which in turn enables us to acquire life's necessities (symbolized by the bread), as well as luxuries (represented by the wine, "to gladden the

---

[11]See for example, D. J. Constantelos, *Poverty, Society and Philanthropy in the Late Medieval Greek World* (New Rochelle, N.Y.: A.D. Caratzas, 1992).

[12]Cf. T. S. Miller, *The Birth of the Hospital in the Byzantine Empire* (Baltimore, Md.: Johns Hopkins University Press, 1985).

[13]Indeed, the opening section of Byzantine matins is a prayer office for the emperor. It consists of fixed opening prayers, Pss 19–20, troparia in honor of the emperor ("O Lord, save your people"), and a brief litany interceding for the local authorities. This service originated in monasteries founded by the emperor and was eventually attached to the morning office.

heart of man" [Ps 104.15]). Whether directly or indirectly, however, the bread and wine clearly represent both God's gift to us and our own offering to God of the work of our hands.

The bread and wine represent creation, freely given by God to humanity and now offered back to God by His people. As we learn from the creation narrative in Genesis, humanity is given dominion over creation. Dominion, however, does not grant a license to use and abuse creation for purely selfish purposes. Rather, it means sharing in God's creative power by "naming" all things (Gen 3.19–20). It means also being held accountable for the gifts that God has given us, as is evident in the parable of the talents (Mt 25.14–30; cf. also Lk 19.11–27). Finally, it means thanking God for the gifts we receive, as is taught in the story of the one out of ten lepers whom Jesus heals and who returns to praise God and to give thanks to Jesus. This leper, though a Samaritan, is the only one who is ultimately healed through his faith (Lk 17.11–19).

"OFFERING"

The Eucharist, then, is the paradigm for Christian life. As co-rulers with God over all creation, as stewards accountable to God, as persons who have, through baptism, been healed, "we praise, bless, and thank" God for all He has done for us. This is why these words come at the very center, at the climax of the eucharistic prayers of both John Chrysostom and Basil the Great. In this way, too, we fulfill our ultimate calling, which is to refer all things to God:

> Remembering therefore this our Savior's command and all that has been done for us: the Cross, the Tomb, the Resurrection on the third day, the Ascension into heaven, the Sitting at the right hand, the Second and glorious Coming again; *Offering*[14] you your own of your own—

[14]The contemporary Greek text, as well as most English translations, renders "offering" in the indicative "we offer." See, for example, the official text most commonly used in the Orthodox Church in America (*The Divine Liturgy According to St. John Chrysostom* [Russian Orthodox Greek Catholic Church of America, 1967], 59); in the Antiochian Orthodox Christian Archdiocese (*The Liturgikon* [Englewood, N.J.: Antiochian Orthodox Christian Archdiocese, 1989], 287); the Romanian Episcopate (*The Divine Liturgy According to Saint John Chrysostom* [Jackson, Mich.: The Romanian Orthodox Episcopate of America, 1975, rep. 1987, 1990], 83; and the Holy Cross faculty edition commonly used in the Greek Orthodox Archdiocese (*The Divine Liturgy* [Brookline, Mass.: Holy Cross Orthodox Press, 1985], 24. The original Greek text, as well as the Slavonic to the present, uses the participial form: προσφέροντες, Slavonic: *prino-*

in all things and for all things—We praise you, we bless you, we give thanks to you, O Lord, and we pray to you, our God.[15]

The chief action, expressed by the active verbs, is done by the entire assembly: "We praise . . . we bless . . . we give thanks . . . we pray." Few people today are even aware that this response is an integral part of the Eucharist prayer, and not simply a pious response sung while the clergy continue their (often silent) recitation of the anaphora. Nor are many today aware that the anaphora is the prayer of the entire assembly, even if the presiding bishop or presbyter pronounces it.

The first thing to note here is the importance of the gathered assembly, which consists of both clergy and laity acting as one. The presiding bishop or presbyter who proclaims these words is doing so in the name of the whole gathering. The "we," which is the grammatical subject of the sentence, includes all who gather, and not just the clergy. This is made all the more evident by the fact that the active verbs are sung by the people, or by the choir in their name. For most of the Church's history, the entire congregation would sing these responses, and it is only in recent centuries that choirs have taken over this function.

Second, as the grammatical structure indicates, we do these things precisely by "remembering" all the things that God has done for us. "Do this in memory of me," Jesus tells His disciples at the Last Supper. Each time that we celebrate the Lord's Supper, the Eucharist, we remember, we call to mind, God's saving activity. And as we remember all these things, we make them present, real, and effective for us today. Remembering, therefore, is an essential task for all Christians, for it is only by always keeping in mind that we are God's creatures and that He has done everything for us, including sending His own Son to die on the cross, that we can live. If we forget God, then we are cut off from the source of life, and like a flower separated from its roots, we quickly die.

Precisely because we remember everything that God has done for us, we offer to him that which is already His—"Your own of your own." This act of offering is central, because it is by remembering and offering that we are able to "praise, bless, and thank God." Here again, the gathered assembly, the liturgical "we," is the active agent. The offering is not done by the clergy,

siashche. Among recent English translations, only the Oxford edition cited in this chapter, as well as the recent SCOBA translation (unpublished), uses the original, participial form.

[15] The Divine Liturgy, 32–33.

but by the entire assembly, led by the bishop or presbyter who recites the prayer *in their name*. Thus the priestly function of offering is exercised by the entire priestly people. "You are a chosen race, a royal priesthood, a holy nation, God's own people," St Peter writes to the Christians of Asia Minor (1 Pet 3.9). By celebrating the eucharistic liturgy, by remembering God's saving activity, by making their offering, the people perform their priestly role, which has been given to them at baptism. Significantly, the term "priest" (ἱερεύς) is never used in the New Testament to refer to the ordained clergy, but only to Christ, who is the "high-priest" (cf. Heb 2.17; 3.1; 4.14; 5.5, 6, 10; 6.20; 7.26) and to the entire body of Christ, the Church, as in the passage cited above.[16] Christ, the high priest, has offered the once-for-all sacrifice for the expiation of our sins. Baptized Christians, who form the body of Christ, the Church, have the priestly task of carrying on Christ's mission to the world, "baptizing all nations in the name of the Father, the Son, and the Holy Spirit" (Mt 28.19). Just as Christ, they have the calling to lay down their lives for others, for the sake of the kingdom.

Liturgy is the work of the entire people of God (the *laos tou theou*), and not, as was the case in both Jewish and pagan antiquity, the task of a clerical caste. Liturgy, and this is implied by the Greek word *leitourgia*, is the common work of the people. The function of the ordained clergy is to lead the gathered assembly in performing their priestly function of praising and giving thanks to God, of offering prayers and intercessions on behalf of all creation. This is what is implied, for example, in the doctrine of recapitulation, according to which Jesus Christ is the New Adam, who brings humanity out of its fallen state and restores the communion between God and humanity that had been broken by sin. Through Christ, humanity can once again share in God's creating activity. Thus humanity, or at least those who hear Christ's message, receive new birth through baptism, and become members of Christ's body, is now able to resume its priestly role at the head of God's creation.[17] In baptism, every Christian comes to share in the priesthood that belongs to Christ.[18]

[16]Not until the fourth century is the term "priest" applied to the ordained clergy. See R. E. Brown, *Priest and Bishop: Biblical Reflections* (New York: Paulist Press, 1970). Clergy in the early Church were referred to as bishops (ἐπίσκοπος means "overseer") and presbyters (πρεσβύτερος means "elder").

[17]On the priesthood of the laity, see my article, "The Liturgical Path of Orthodoxy in America," *St Vladimir's Theological Quarterly* 40/1-2 (1996): 43–64, esp. 55–58.

[18]See A. Schmemann, *Of Water and the Spirit: A Liturgical Study of Baptism* (Crestwood, N.Y.: St Vladimir's Seminary Press, 1974), 94–99.

Among the tasks reserved for priests is the offering of sacrifices. In ancient times, the priests did this as intermediaries on behalf of the people. This is precisely what Christ did on behalf of humanity when He offered himself up, once for all, on the cross. In doing so He fulfilled, and therefore abolished, the Old Testament sacrificial order. As a result, Christian liturgy no longer contains the bloody sacrifices of old–it is now "spiritual and without the shedding of blood";[19] it is our "sacrifice of praise."[20] But it is a sacrifice nevertheless,[21] and sacrifices are the business of priests! Each time that we celebrate the Eucharist, therefore, we realize our priestly calling of offering sacrifices on behalf of all humanity and for all creation.

This priestly dimension is emphasized particularly in the Book of Hebrews, in which both the Jewish sacrificial cult, fulfilled by Christ, and the eucharistic assemblies of the early Christian Church form the backdrop. According to this book, Jesus is the high priest (4.14), who enters the sanctuary once for all (7.29) through His blood (9.12ff). Christ fulfills the Old Testament sacrifice by performing the sacrifice for sin (Yom Kippur) in accordance with the principle that there is no forgiveness of sin without the shedding of blood (9.22). Christ becomes a high priest with His glorification–the divine investiture (5.4) is the divine oracle: "Out of the womb before the morning star have I begotten you" (Ps 109.3 LXX). Christ's sacrifice assures our own entrance into the sanctuary (10.19–26). But since only priests can enter the sanctuary, this implies that we are all priests, and we are called to offer acceptable worship to God through Christ (12.29). Thus Christian life, the life of the priestly people of God, is itself sacrificial. The last chapter of Hebrews draws out the implications of this for Christian life:

We have an altar from which those who serve the tent have no right to eat. For the bodies of those animals whose blood is brought into the sanctuary by the high priest as a sacrifice for sin are burned outside the camp. So Jesus also suffered outside the gate in order to sanctify the people through His own blood. Therefore let us go forth outside the camp and bear the abuse He endured. For here we have no lasting city,

[19]From the opening words of the epiclesis (invocation of the Holy Spirit) in Chrysostom's liturgy.

[20]From the introductory dialogue to the anaphora.

[21]On the Eucharist as sacrifice, see particularly the fourteenth-century commentary of Nicholas Cabasilas, *A Commentary on the Divine Liturgy* (Crestwood, N.Y.: St Vladimir's Seminary Press, 1977), ch. 32, 80–82. Cf. also A. Schmemann, *The Eucharist*, 101–131.

but we seek the city which is to come. Through him then let us continually offer up a sacrifice of praise to God, that is, the fruit of lips that
acknowledge His name. Do not neglect to do good and to share what
you have, for such sacrifices are pleasing to God. (13.10–16)

Thus Christians share in Christ's sacrifice by accepting abuse; they share in
it by praising God; and they share in it by doing good and sharing their
belongings. The language here is totally sacrificial—note the constant references to "altar," "altar food," a "sacrifice of praise." These are all terms coming from the communion sacrifices in the Old Testament, now fulfilled in
the eucharistic liturgy of the Christian Church. Particularly notable in these
and other New Testament texts is the integration between liturgy and life.
Christians are called to do in their everyday life exactly what they do in the
Church's liturgy.

Conclusion

Through baptism, Christians are incorporated into Christ's body, the
Church. Through the eucharistic liturgy which they celebrate at least every
Sunday, Christians live out their membership in this body. They "put on
Christ" in baptism, they receive Christ by partaking of His Body and Blood
in the Eucharist. And in so doing they also become sharers of the priesthood of Christ. Thus they are called in this world to do exactly what Christ
did: become signs of the kingdom; restore the communion between God
and creation that was lost as a result of human sin; bring God's love and
healing to the world; entrust themselves, one another, and their whole lives
to God; and offer back to God all that God has given them. In the second
century, St Irenaeus says the following about the relation between the
Eucharist and our sacrifice:

> For it behooves us to make an oblation to God, and in all things to be
> found grateful to God our Maker, in a pure mind, and in faith without
> hypocrisy, in well-grounded hope, in fervent love, offering the first-
> fruits of His own created things. And the church alone offers this pure
> oblation to the Creator, offering to him, with giving of thanks, [the
> things taken] from His creation.[22]

[22]*Against Heresies* IV.18, 4 (*Ante-Nicene Fathers*, vol. 1 [Grand Rapids, Mich.: Eerdmans, 1973],
485). All of IV.18 deals with Christian offering and does so within a liturgical, eucharistic context.

Thus the offering we make at the eucharistic liturgy becomes the paradigm for the way in which we are called to offer all that we have to God with gratitude and thanksgiving:

> They (the Jews) had indeed the tithes of their goods consecrated to him, but those who have received liberty [Christians] set aside all their possessions for the Lord's purposes, bestowing joyfully and freely not the less valuable portions of their property, since they have the hope of better things [hereafter]; as that poor widow acted who cast all her living into the treasury of God.[23]

Stewardship in the sense of material support for the Church and, indeed, for anyone who needs assistance, therefore, is an integral part of the Christian message as reflected in Scripture, tradition, and liturgy. As we have seen, it is one expression of the priestly ministry of all the baptized. In the liturgy, we are taught who we are as members of Christ's body and where we stand in relation to God. The central act of the liturgy, which consists of praising God and thanking him for everything He has done for us, includes our freely offering back to God of everything He has freely given to us:

> Remembering therefore this our Savior's command . . . offering you your own of your own—in all things and for all things—we praise you, we bless you, we give thanks to you, O Lord.[24]

This is the priestly task of all the faithful, and it does not cease when they step out of the Church, but continues in every moment of their life, whether at home, at work, or at play. In this way the faithful can carry out St Paul's concluding instructions to the Thessalonians:

> Rejoice always, pray constantly, give thanks in all circumstances; for this is the will of God in Christ Jesus for you. (1 Thess 5.16–18)

[23]Ibid., IV.18, 2 (*ANF* 1, 485).
[24]*The Divine Liturgy*, 33.

ETHICS AND STEWARDSHIP

STANLEY SAMUEL HARAKAS*

Both terms in the title of this chapter are widely and ambiguously used. This chapter will begin by indicating briefly their contextual meanings. This will be followed by an equally brief treatment of some theological foundations for stewardship as an ethical behavior. The primary ethical dimensions of stewardship as defined will then be outlined. The balance of the chapter will deal with two dimensions of the ethics of stewardship: stewardship as money raising and stewardship accountability by the recipients of stewardship giving.

STEWARDSHIP CONTEXTS

A survey of recent theological literature dealing with the term "stewardship" finds that the term is used in widely different contexts. By far, in modern theological literature, the term is used most frequently in reference to ecological concern.[1] It is also used in reference to science,[2] medicine and

---

*The Very Rev Stanley Samuel Harakas, Th.D, D.D. is the Archbishop Iakovos Professor of Orthodox Theology *Emeritus* at Holy Cross Greek Orthodox School of Theology, Brookline, MA.

[1]Cf. M. C. Paternoster "Thy Humbler Creation," *Church Quarterly* 3.3 (1971): 204–214; Laurel Kearns, "Saving the Creation: Christian Environmentalism in the United States," *Sociology of Religion* 57.1 (1996): 55–70; Calvin DeWitt, "The Church's Role in Environmental Action," *Word and World* 11.2 (1991): 180–185; Fred G. Van Dyke, "Planetary Economics and Ecologies: The Christian World View and Recent Literature," *Journal of the American Scientific Affiliation* 40.2 (1998): 66–71; Gary Roche, "Some Reflections on the Stewardship of Creation," *Melasian Journal of Theology* 6.2 (1990): 22–25. Included in such use of stewardship concepts in reference to ecology and the protection of the environment are the three seminars organized by the Ecumenical Patriarchate on "Religion & the Environment": "The Environment and Religious Education, at Halki, Istanbul," 1994; "The Environment and Ethics, at Halki, Istanbul," 1995; and "Symposium II: The Black Sea in Crisis," 1997. See Internet site http://www.patriarchate.org or http://www.epnet.gr for texts in English.

[2]E.g., Calvin B. DeWitt, "Christian Environmental Stewardship: Preparing the Way for Action," *Perspectives on Science and Christian Faith* 46.2 (1944): 80–89.

health issues,[3] economics,[4] genetic engineering,[5] multicultural society,[6] missiology,[7] the mind,[8] salary setting at Christian colleges,[9] and other referents. So, it is important to understand that stewardship is an attitude and behavior that is much broader than financial support for ecclesial bodies, even though this is the main interest of this volume. We need to be alert to meanings of stewardship that transcend our parish and jurisdictional needs and concerns.

The basic idea of stewardship is rooted empirically in economic organization and practice. The English word is traceable to the fifteenth century. But it is based on a translation of the Greek words οἰκονομία, οἰκονομεῖν, and οἰκονόμος. The term refers originally to the ancient organization and management of the household, in which the master or owner assigned management responsibilities for the running of the household to a steward, or οἰκονόμος. Thus, the dictionary definition: "the conducting, supervising, or managing of something; *especially*: the careful and responsible management of something entrusted to one's care (*stewardship* of our natural resources)."[10]

So, in the historical order of things, stewardship has organizational, managerial, and economic foundations. These functions are exercised on behalf of another, precisely on behalf of the owner of the property, which

[3]E.g., John F. Peppin, "The Health Care Institution-Patient Relationship: Paradigm Lost," *Ethics and Medicine* 14.2 (1998): 41–45; Dennis Holinger, "Theological Foundations for Death and Dying Issues," *Ethics and Medicine* 12.3 (1996): 60–65; Robin Crawford, "The Presbyterian Church in the United States of America: A History of Concern for Addictions," *Journal of Ministry in Addiction and Recovery* 4.2 (1997): 69–79.

[4]E.g., Denis Goulet, "Catholic Social Doctrine and New Thinking in Economics," *Cross Currents* 42.4 (1993): 504–520; Christopher J. H. Wright, "God or Mammon: Perspectives on Economics in Conflict," *Mission Studies* 12.2 (1995): 145–156.

[5]E.g., Darryl Macer, "Genetic Engineering: Catastrophe or Utopia?" *Evangelical Review of Theology* 15.2 (1991): 148–165.

[6]E.g., Sharon E. Sutton, "Learning Stewardship in a Multicultural Society," *Liturgy* 9.2 (1990): 57–61.

[7]E.g., Daniel C. Van Zyl, "Cosmology, Ecology, and Missiology: A Perspective from Genesis 1," *Missionalia* 1 9.13 (1991): 203–214.

[8]E.g., Robert Wild, "The Stewardship of the Mind," *Word and Spirit* 13 (1991): 132–147.

[9]E.g., C. Stephen Layman, "Should Faculty Salaries Differ by Discipline?" *Christian Scholar's Review* 25.3 (1996): 260–272; Frank Anthony Spina, "Problematic of Faculty Remuneration in the Christian College," *Christian Scholar's Review* 25.3 (1996): 273–278; Todd P. Steen, "Stewardship in Salary Setting: A Reply to C. Stephen Layman," *Christian Scholar's Review* 25.3 (1996): 279–287; C. Stephen Layman, "Reply to Steen and Spina," *Christian Scholar's Review* 25.3 (1996): 288–296.

[10]Entry in *Merriam-Webster Dictionary CD*, 1996.

the steward is assigned to manage. Stewardship, as originally conceived, is delegated authority to be practiced on behalf of the interests of another.

An interesting biblical example of this is related to the stewardship responsibilities of the wife in a Jewish household. The well-known passage from Proverbs 31.10–31 does not use the term "steward," but in many ways praises "the good wife," for her stewardship of the household. Of course, this passage reflects the traditional relationship of spouses in antiquity, in which the husband is the absolute head of the household, the legal owner of its property, and the person through whom the property is conveyed to heirs. Nevertheless, in many ways, praise is accorded to the wife precisely because of her stewardship and managerial skills in managing her husband's property. Thus, those skills are valued because they further the interests of her husband. Thus, the section begins:

> A good wife who can find? She is far more precious than jewels. The heart of her husband trusts in her, and he will have no lack of gain. She does him good, and not harm, all the days of her life. (Prov 31.10–12)

Several elements regarding stewardship are present in this introductory passage: trust, profit, effective management ("good, and not harm"), and long-term consistency.

The wife as steward and manager is resourceful, energetic, and anticipates tasks and needs:

> She seeks wool and flax, and works with willing hands. She is like the ships of the merchant, she brings her food from afar. She rises while it is yet night and provides food for her household and tasks for her maidens. (Prov 31.13–16)

As the household steward, she negotiates purchases, improves the productivity of family resources, develops capabilities, and produces profit:

> She considers a field and buys it; with the fruit of her hands she plants a vineyard. She girds her loins with strength and makes her arms strong. She perceives that her merchandise is profitable. (Prov 31.16–18a)

As a steward and manager, she is hard-working, diligent, and "hands on" in her work:

Her lamp does not go out at night. She puts her hands to the distaff, and her hands hold the spindle. (Prov 31.18–19)

As a steward and manager, however, she is not only concerned with profit and the material advancement of her household. She cares for others, the poor, as well as those in her immediate family and staff. There is balance and wholeness in her stewardship, as she maintains a dignified stance and appearance for herself, meeting her own personal needs, as well:

She opens her hand to the poor, and reaches out her hands to the needy. She is not afraid of snow for her household, for all in her household are clothed in scarlet. She makes herself coverings; her clothing is fine linen and purple. (Prov 31.20–22)

The passage continues in the same vein in the final eight verses.[11] Two emphases can be noted that contribute to an understanding of stewardship. The first is that the woman's husband and children are honored by her skills, so that her talents reflect well upon others, as well as herself. Effective exercise of stewardship is praiseworthy and worthy of emulation:

Her husband is known in the gates, when he sits among the elders of the land (Prov 31.23) . . . Her children rise up and call her blessed; her husband also, and he praises her (Prov 31.28) . . . and let her works praise her in the gates. (Prov 31.31)

A second, notable aspect of this passage is that this exemplary practitioner of effective and productive stewardship is described as a person who is rooted in piety and reverence for God, which produces consequences. Her faithful stewardship is to be rewarded:

[11]Prov 31.23–29: "Her husband is known in the gates, when he sits among the elders of the land. She makes linen garments and sells them; she delivers girdles to the merchant. Strength and dignity are her clothing, and she laughs at the time to come. She opens her mouth with wisdom, and the teaching of kindness is on her tongue. She looks well to the ways of her household, and does not eat the bread of idleness. Her children rise up and call her blessed; her husband also, and he praises her: 'Many women have done excellently, but you surpass them all.' Charm is deceitful, and beauty is vain, but a woman who fears the Lord is to be praised. Give her of the fruit of her hands, and let her works praise her in the gates."

Charm is deceitful, and beauty is vain, but a woman who fears the Lord is to be praised. Give her of the fruit of her hands. (Prov 31.30-31)

Clearly, what we have in this passage is a description of the proper exercise of stewardship by a confident, skilled, and effective steward of the property of another. It is a perfect illustration of the practice of stewardship in an essentially economic context, completely in harmony with the dictionary definition presented above. The religious reference at the end of the passage would seem to be more of a character reference than the central theme or the primary motivation for the excellence of the woman's stewardship skills.

ETHICAL CONTEXTS

Nevertheless, this biblical passage forms a natural bridge to the ethical dimension of stewardship. Just as is the case with the concept of stewardship, there are different understandings and, one might add, misunderstandings of the meaning of ethics.

On a general popular level, the term "ethics" is used to describe, rather, what is more properly termed morals or morality. "Morals" and "morality" are descriptive terms. Thus, it would be appropriate, on the basis of particular ethical criteria, to say that "John has bad morals," or that "prostitution is immoral." Morals and morality refer to overt behavior, or to actual motivations and intents in individuals or as embodied in social agencies. These terms are Latin in origin.

Their Greek equivalents are ἦθος (*ethos*) and ἠθικότης (*ethikotes*), terms that describe a style of life that is observable and may be judged and evaluated according to standards and criteria that may determine a particular ethos as either good or evil. Some modern, Greek Orthodox theologians and philosophers, and other Orthodox following them, have confused "ethos" with "ethics," to the point of rejecting "ethics" in favor of "ethos."[12]

The linguistic source of the confusion of *ethos* (ἦθος) with *ethics* (ἠθική) is obvious. However, *ethics* is very different from *ethos*. While *ethos*

---

[12]E.g., see the writings of Chestos Giannaras, especially his book Ἡ Ἐλευθερία τοῦ Ἤθους, published in English as *The Freedom of Ethos* (Crestwood, N.Y.: St Vladimir's Seminary Press, 1984), a work that is rooted in an essentially existential philosophical stance and not on Orthodox Christian theological presuppositions. For more on this, see Stanley S. Harakas, *Toward Transfigured Life: The* Theoria *of Eastern Orthodox Ethics.* Minneapolis, Minn.: Light and Life Publishing Co., 1983, 59-65.

is descriptive, the task of *ethics* is to prescribe what *ought to be done*, on the basis of certain criteria. Thus, ethics is not descriptive. It is normative. Its two basic questions are: what determines the good, right, and fitting; and, what ought to be done in a given circumstance under those criteria.

The answer may come in at least three different forms. Sometimes, the response comes in the form of "what is *right*." In this case, it usually is very specific, such as, "Do not bear false witness." It is concrete and most often cast in legal or rule language. Thus, a question such as "What is the right thing to do in this situation?" invites a specifically defined response: "The right thing is to return the stolen money."

Not all ethical language, however, is that specific. More often than not, the ethical question is more general, pointing to values, rather than to concrete actions. Thus, a question such as "What is the best thing to do in this situation?" may imply conflicting values. What is at stake is "*the good*." How is the good to be maximized and evil minimized? Thus, an answer might be "Act so that as much good as possible can be realized in this situation and minimize the potential evil in it." Though much less specific than "right" ethics, it may be more useful and practical, since it is more capable of balancing values and goods in complex situations in which there are multiple and conflicting ethical claims.

This leads to the third dimension of ethical reflection, that of relationships. Here, the holistic approach is dominant. The ethical response tends to be cast in terms of "fitting" and "appropriate." "Why is killing of one's own father—patricide—worse than killing a stranger?" Clearly, while homicide is evil, the unique relationship between parent and child make it totally inappropriate (not fitting, not harmonious) with the very idea of the child's relationship to parents. On the other hand, "fitting" and "appropriate" can be guiding concepts for defining suitable and seemly actions and attitudes.

Thus, ethics expresses its normative, "ought" imperatives in different ways.

But the substance of what is considered "right," "good," or "fitting" varies according to different worldviews and understandings of the nature of things. Thus, a materialist worldview embodied, for instance, in the *laissez faire* capitalist system may lead to a disregard of the needs of the poor. The dialectical materialism of communism may equally consider it ethically justified to violate the property rights of certain persons. Hedonism as a philosophy directs action through an ethic of selfish pleasure seeking. There are many ethical approaches possible.

Thus, we should not expect all ethical systems of thought to have a supportive stance toward the practice of stewardship. The ethical imperatives that flow from the Christian worldview, or to say it better, from the Orthodox Christian faith tradition will point toward an ethic of stewardship that will reflect values and claims unique to the Orthodox Christian Church. Orthodox ethics derives from the Orthodox faith tradition—from the Creed, worship, spiritual tradition, and theological presuppositions of the Orthodox Church.

The norms of Orthodox Christian ethics regarding stewardship, thus, will be derived from the Orthodox Christian faith and way of life. They will sometimes take the form of "what is right." Other times, the stewardship norms will be cast as "good and bad values." And other times, the norms of Orthodox Christian ethics will take the form of proscriptions or prescriptions that will be expressed in terms of what is "fitting and appropriate," or "unfitting and inappropriate."

THREE THEOLOGICAL CONTEXTS

What theological affirmations of Orthodox Christianity, then, serve to inform Orthodox ethical reflection on the issue of stewardship? For the sake of simplicity, we can highlight three: the Trinitarian God as Creator and Provident; the image and likeness doctrine of human existence; and the eucharistic, sacramental life.

Theological questions are foundational. They respond to some of the most profound and deep human perplexities. In a presentation that I made regarding Orthodox theology and the environment, I raised some of these issues:

> And so we ask, what is the Orthodox theological vision of reality? What is the nature of reality? How did it come into being? Is matter all that is? Or is everything really spiritual? Or is the "stuff" of the world both material and spiritual? What is the meaning of life? Why do we exist and for what purpose do we live? What is our human condition? Do we need to do anything about it? If so, what? Do we do it alone? Do we need help? And the questions go on and on. Many seek to answer such questions: theologians, philosophers, scientists, politicians, artists,

poets, novelists, people of every faith and religion, and every ordinary man and woman on some level or another.[13]

The first and most fundamental Orthodox theological affirmation is that the only ultimate reality is God. The only uncreated reality is God. All else that exists is the consequence of the creative work of the Triune God. "In the beginning, God created . . ." (Gen 1.1). Unlike God, the creation is, precisely, *created*. This means it is contingent and dependent upon the sustaining energies of God. Theologically, that means that the created world does not have an existence based on its own self-sufficiency; what exists, exists only under the conditions of existence granted by God. Everything that exists that is other than God was not created out of the being of God; it was not created out

> of pre-existing matter; it did not emanate from God. It was created literally "out of nothing," so that it will always be different from God, who brought it into being. God is one reality; the creation is totally and irrevocably different. The creation came into existence in a process of development. It includes every spiritual and material reality that exists that is not God. So the hundred or so elements that are the building blocks of the creation and the hundreds of thousands, if not millions of forms in the creation ultimately depend upon God to sustain them in their existence. The Son, the Bible says, upholds "the universe by his word of power." (Heb 1.3)[14]

From a clear Orthodox theological perspective, ownership of the creation belongs to no one but God.

> The Prophet Isaiah affirms it for us in several places. In chapter 40 he challenges us: "Have you not known? Have you not heard? The Lord is the everlasting God, the Creator of the ends of the earth . . ." (Is 40.28). In chapter 45, the Lord affirms his creative acts "I made the earth, and created man upon it; it was my hands that stretched out the heavens, and I commanded all their host" (Is 45.12). In chapter 48 God speaks and

[13] "'The Earth Is the Lord's': Orthodox Theology and the Environment," *Greek Orthodox Theological Review* 44. 1–4 (1999): 149–162.

[14]Ibid., 151–152.

declares "I am he, I am the first, and I am the last. My hand laid the foundation of the earth, and my right hand spread out the heavens" (Is 48.12–13). We cannot evade the conclusion. We need to change our fundamental attitude in the way we deal with the earth. It is not ours, it is God's. All else will flow from that changed perspective.[15]

Consequently, the Psalmist declares, "The earth is the Lord's and the fullness thereof, the world and those who dwell therein" (Ps 24.1). It follows that the primary and essential theological foundation for any discussion of stewardship is the creative action of the Triune God and our total dependency on that reality. He owns everything. The most we can claim for ourselves is that we are stewards of what he owns. And even then, "We are unworthy servants; we have only done what was our duty" (Lk 17.10).

Similarly, our creation as human beings in the image and likeness of God contains a stewardship dimension. Since we are not creators in the strict sense, we are not owners of anything in the strict sense. But, as God is provident and caring for the created world, our calling in the "likeness" (καθ' ὁμοίωσιν) is to grow dynamically to achieve God-likeness in many ways. In reference to this discussion, all human beings are called to God-likeness, in serving the ultimate owner of all in the role of stewards. If God himself is judicious and attentive to his Creation, overseeing its welfare as a Provident God, then we too, are called to be provident and caring as household stewards of our own Master's property.

One of the most profound expressions of the understanding of the Incarnation—that the Son of God, the Second Person of the Holy Trinity, took on a concrete and particular human nature in a particular and concrete historical time and place—is the doctrine and liturgical practice of the Holy Eucharist in the Orthodox tradition. Much has been preached and written about eucharistic theology in the past three decades, to the point that it seems to have supplanted the very gospel itself as the core of the Orthodox Christian faith.[16] Nevertheless, the sacramental and eucharistic focus of Orthodox theology is essential to its wholeness. It is a response to the redemptive and sanctifying work of the Holy Trinity, especially that of the death and resurrection of Jesus Christ, and the pentecostal

[15]Ibid., 160.
[16]See my comments on eucharistic theology, in "Reflections on the Ethical Dimensions of the Topics of the Great and Holy Synod," *Greek Orthodox Theological Review* 24 (1979): 131–157.

sanctification of the Holy Spirit in the process of fulfilling the divine image and likeness in human existence.

Humanity is created in the image and likeness of God of both material and spiritual components: from the earth and by the breath of life from God. So, human beings were thus created to stand as a connecting link between heaven and earth, as a "microcosm" joining the spiritual and the material together into one. But precisely because we are called to realize the image and likeness of God in us, we have the concurrent divine-like freedom and self-determination to choose or not to choose to assume our role as stewards. An authentic stance of stewardship cannot be forced; it must be assumed and practiced freely, as a personal and corporate offering to the Creator, as an act of communion with Creator that embodies the liturgical words and *praxis*: "Τά Σά ἐκ των Σων, Σοί προσφέρομεν"–"The things that are Yours from the things that are Yours, do we offer to you." This passage not only acknowledges God's "ownership" of all things (including economic goods), but also the free offering of those things back to their Giver, God, by those who acknowledge his ownership, in a spirit of gratitude for the blessings that God has bestowed upon them. Stewardship is a theologically grounded concept for the Orthodox Christian's life in spiritual growth toward God-likeness.

God now awaits our response to his loving work of creation, providence, redemption, and salvation. Human beings–especially Orthodox Christian believers–now are called to offer back to God what he has given to us, but to do so freely and gratefully, in Christ,[17] and with the grace of the Holy Spirit empowering us.[18] We not only offer praise, glory, and worship. We offer "λογική λατρεῖα"–a rational worship that is in accord with God's will as the right thing to do, as the expression of the good, and as the most fitting and appropriate response to the truth of the Master's ownership of all that exists and the place we have as servants of our Savior and Redeemer.

---

[17]"I am the vine, you are the branches. He who abides in me, and I in him, he it is that bears much fruit, for apart from me you can do nothing. If a man does not abide in me, he is cast forth as a branch and withers; and the branches are gathered, thrown into the fire and burned" (Jn 15.5–7).

[18]"But you shall receive power when the Holy Spirit has come upon you" (Acts 1.8); "And I was with you in weakness and in much fear and trembling; and my speech and my message were not in plausible words of wisdom, but in demonstration of the Spirit and of power, that your faith might not rest in the wisdom of men but in the power of God" (1 Cor 2.3–5).

THE RELATIONSHIP OF ETHICS AND STEWARDSHIP

Stewardship as responsibility for the management of what belongs to another is the basis of New Testament uses of the term. Thus, St Paul understands his ministry in terms of being a steward of the "mysteries of God," adding that "it is required of stewards that they be found trustworthy" (1 Cor 4.1–2). He understands his care of the Gentile, Ephesian Christians in this same framework, when he speaks of "the stewardship of God's grace that was given to me for you" (Eph 3.1–2).

The Gospels also present the steward as a person managing household events, such as a marriage feast (Jn 2.8–10), or mismanaging household affairs and being condemned for it (Lk 16.15–9). The Parable of the Vineyard Workers presents the steward as fulfilling the commandments of the owner of the vineyard: "When evening came, the owner of the vineyard said to his steward, 'Call the laborers and pay them their wages, beginning with the last, up to the first' "(Mt 20.8).

Stewardship is a responsibility that can be exercised either properly or improperly in the well-known passage in Luke 12.41–48. The faithful steward is rewarded with praise and increased responsibilities: "And the Lord said, 'Who then is the faithful and wise steward, whom his master will set over his household, to give them their portion of food at the proper time? Blessed is that servant whom his master when he comes will find so doing. Truly, I say to you, he will set him over all his possessions.' "

On the other hand, the irresponsible and evil steward who takes advantage of his position and violates his accountability is subject to punishment. The parable continues: "The master of that servant will come on a day when he does not expect him and at an hour he does not know, and will punish him, and put him with the unfaithful."

The parable has another application, as well. The rewards and the punishments are proportional. Thus, unfaithfulness to the extent that it is based on understanding and knowledge is proportionally rewarded or punished: "And that servant who knew his master's will, but did not make ready or act according to his will, shall receive a severe beating. But he who did not know, and did what deserved a beating, shall receive a light beating. Every one to whom much is given, of him will much be required; and of him to whom men commit much they will demand the more."

Further, according to 1 Peter, stewardship is to be exercised in accordance with each person's particular gifts. Stewardship, thus, is based on resources available, as well as on the reality of personal community with others. For the Christian, the source of all these resources is God. Thus we read: "Practice hospitality ungrudgingly to one another. As each has received a gift, employ it for one another, as good stewards of God's varied grace: whoever speaks, as one who utters oracles of God; whoever renders service, as one who renders it by the strength which God supplies; in order that in everything God may be glorified through Jesus Christ" (1Pet 4.9–11).

In particular, the leadership of the church is called to a special kind of stewardship, one of the church's mysteries that must, of course, also be extended to all aspects of ministry. Thus, Titus describes the stewardship of the overseer of the life of the church, the ἐπίσκοπος. "For a bishop, as God's steward, must be blameless; he must not be arrogant or quick-tempered or a drunkard or violent or greedy for gain, but hospitable, a lover of goodness, master of himself, upright, holy, and self-controlled; he must hold firm to the sure word as taught, so that he may be able to give instruction in sound doctrine and also to confute those who contradict it" (Titus 1.7–9).

What we see here are sets of "oughts" and sets of "ought nots"; precisely the kind of language that is appropriate to the ethical dimension of stewardship. Thus, there are attitudes and behaviors that are right or wrong according to the Christian faith that relate to the exercise of stewardship. In addition, there are attitudes and behaviors that express good values and bad values that relate to the exercise of stewardship. And there are attitudes and behaviors that are either fitting and appropriate, or unfitting and inappropriate that relate to the exercise of the Orthodox Christian's practice of stewardship. So we can safely say that the decision to serve and be a steward, the practice of functioning as a steward of the Lord, and the inner dispositions associated with being a conscientious steward of the "things that are (his)" for the Orthodox Christian have a decidedly ethical dimension. How *ought* Orthodox Christians to exercise their stewardship? What *ought* *they not to do* in the exercise of their stewardship as Orthodox Christians? These are the ethical questions that address the *praxis of stewardship.*

The Ethics of Stewardship-Giving

As we have seen, stewardship, even within the Christian context, is a broad and inclusive dimension of the Christian life. In this sense, Orthodox ethicist Vigen Guroian is correct, as we shall see immediately below, that when the focus turns to the Christian as a steward of the blessings he or she has received in life, the economic model moves to the background. In the framework of ecology, Guroian connects ecological stewardship with the redemptive vocation of the church. In his explication of an ecclesial-based stewardship, he elevates the concept into the sphere of gift and blessing: that is, the redemptive relationship of the church and Christians to the Trinitarian God, while minimizing the property stewardship approach.[19] In short, Guroian fosters the idea that Orthodox Christians ought to transform and transfigure the managerial model into the context of blessing and grace. Stewardship no longer functions only as a managerial dimension of the Christian life in the allocation and distribution of funds and talents, but becomes an expression and means of the life in the Spirit, embodied in the ascetic, liturgical, and sacramental life of the church.

We see this approach expressed clearly and succinctly in a biblical meditation presented on the Internet by *Dynamis for Orthodox Christians* on 2 Corinthians 9.6–11 for October 21, 2000.[20] This meditation provides a fresh look at the ethical dimensions of stewardship giving. It identifies seven areas of stewardship motivation and action that are ethical in character. In the balance of this section, I will present these seven meditation portions as they were written originally in italics and follow each of the passages with some comment expanding on the theme of "Ethics and Stewardship."

Godly Giving: 2 Corinthians 9.6–11, especially vs. 10, *"Now may he who supplies seed to the sower, and bread for food, supply and multiply the seed you have sown and increase the fruits of your righteousness." Today's passage from the Apostle Paul encourages us to look deeply into our motives for giving. His words are greatly illumined when read in terms of seven prescriptions for godly giving, each of them derived directly from the Apostle's words and intent.*

As seen from the title, the theme of this meditation is "Godly Giving," placing it in the framework of the stewardship practices of individual

[19]Vigen Guroian, "Toward Ecology as an Ecclesial Event: Orthodox Theology and Ecological Ethics," *Communio: International Catholic Review* 18.1 (1991): 89–110.

[20]DYNAMIS for October 21, 2000. DYNAMIS provides daily meditations on Scripture for Orthodox Christians. It is produced and sponsored by St George Orthodox Cathedral (Antiochian Archdiocese) 7515 E 13 Street N, Wichita, Kans. 67206–1223. Phone 1-316-636-4676 to obtain printed copies. The email address is a3dynamis@aol.com. To enroll for daily email reception of DYNAMIS, send an email to: orthodoxdynamis-subscribe@onelist.com. Permission has been granted to include portions of this meditation in this article by the author David Patton.

persons or family units in regard to their financial contributions to the church and to charities and to those in need. The meditation is on a classic passage for church stewardship reflection, 2 Corinthians 9.6–11. The focus is on motives and intents, essential dimensions of Orthodox Christian ethics.[21] Critical aspects of ethical evaluation of behaviors are the nature and quality of the inner dispositions that guide actions. For Christianity, especially, according to the ethic of the Sermon on the Mount, inner dispositions are paramount.[22] The author rightly emphasizes this ethical dimension as the starting point for discussing how the Orthodox Christian "ought" to give in the practice of stewardship. Precisely because the meditation is about "godly giving," the discussion is placed within the framework of the Orthodox Christian understanding of growing in the image and likeness of God. Giving by Orthodox Christians ought to be reflective of the way God gives to us. Stewardship is an aspect of our growth toward God-likeness, or *theosis*.

> **Give with blessings** (vs. 6). *Most English translations contrast "sparingly" with "bountifully" or "generously" in the opening verse. In the original St Paul used the plural of the word "blessing" in contrast to "stingy." Hence, "one who sows stingily" differs utterly from "one who sows with blessings." For one like the Apostle, formed in the Hebraic mind, to speak of blessings always implies God, for, as the Psalmist says, "Blessed is the Lord, the God of Israel, Who alone doeth wonders" (Ps 71.19). Only God is blessed, and all "blessings" flow from Him. The Apostle's point is that our giving always is in the context of the giving of the Giver of life.*

This dimension is made particular and more specific with the discussion about giving with blessings. In the first instance, the very form of the passage is ethical, in the sense that it is normative. It instructs how the Christian *ought* to give: "Give with blessings." It also instructs how the Christian *ought not* to give: "stingily." The author, on the basis of the Hebraic understanding of things, accents what was affirmed several times earlier in this chapter, that the goods we enjoy—and from which we give— are ours only by derivation: "Only God is blessed, and all 'blessings' flow

---

[21]Harakas, *Toward Transfigured Life*, cf. ch. 9, "Ethical Decision-Making."
[22]For more on this, see my *Toward Transfigured Life*, ch. 7, "The Evangelical Ethic."

from Him." It is an affirmation of the fundamental Orthodox Christian ethical insight, that the source of all good is God.[23] Since God is the "Giver of Life," all other values and goods that are in the sphere of human choice and decision making are derivative.

> **Give from the heart.** *Of course the Apostle is speaking of the heart that is submitted to the Lord. A heart which belongs to the Lord neither grudges nor feels compulsion to give, but shares in the manner in which the Lord gives, "pressed down . . . and running over." (Lk 6.38)*

The ethical dimension is also evident in this passage that expands and gives content to the affirmation that inner dispositions form the important ethical aspect of stewardship. In Orthodox spiritual thought, the heart is central to the Christian life.[24] The heart that is in union with God "neither grudges nor feels compulsion to give," precisely because it has reached the level of true freedom to be itself. Orthodox ethics distinguishes between "free choice" or "self-determination" (αὐτεξούσιον) on the one had and the condition of ἐλευθερία, or true freedom, which is when there are no conflicting inner impulses toward action.[25] The goal is for Christians to act in God-like ways, not conflicted by temptations, insecurities, and mental reservations. Such stewardship behavior is free and outpouring and "shares in the manner in which the Lord gives." In all likelihood, such a high standard in the practice of stewardship is rarely achieved, but the ethical "ought" pointing to such unconstrained and unreserved motives remains valid and a sought after goal.

---

[23]This concept is treated at length in *Toward Transfigured Life*, ch. 2, "The Orthodox Christian Theological Foundation of Ethics."

[24]Kallistos Ware defines the heart, in part, as follows: "HEART (καρδία–*kardia*): not simply the physical organ but the spiritual centre of man's being, man as made in the image of God, his deepest and truest self, or the inner shrine, to be entered only through sacrifice and death, in which the mystery of the union between the divine and the human is consummated." G. E. H. Palmer, Philip Sherrard, and Kallistos Ware, tr. & ed., *The Philokalia: The Complete Text–Compiled by St Nikodimos of the Holy Mountain and St Makarios of Corinth*, vol II, (Boston: Faber and Faber, 1981), 383.

[25]"Usually, the Fathers reserve the term *eleutheria*, i.e., "freedom," for the condition reached in *theosis* where there is no conflict or struggle in acting in a fully human, divine-like fashion." Harakas, *Toward Transfigured Life*, 34.

Give from joy (2 Cor 9.7), or "Give merrily." *The key word is "merry" or "joyous," in the original "hilarion." One invariably gives happily from a consciousness awash in the glad tidings that "God was in Christ reconciling the world to himself" (2 Cor 5.19). To know the Lord removes all reluctance and constraint for he is the great treasure and ample food. Note how St Paul changed Proverbs 22.9 LXX, from "God 'blesses'... to "God 'loves' a cheerful giver."*

Note, also, the imperative, or normative "ought" language. What is normally not thought of as something that can be willed and made to occur—joy—is nevertheless commanded. How can this be? Ethically, the opposite of giving joyfully is to give with reluctant sadness. Giving becomes an unpleasant duty, fulfilled because somehow the stewardship giver is psychologically, morally, or spiritually coerced into giving. Clearly for the Christian such giving "ought not" to be associated with stewardship. Giving to the church "ought" rather to be perceived as a privilege and an opportunity to express one's faith in the loving and blessing God, and therefore an ethical act. Cheerful giving implies that the giver is happy and eager and fully willing to be a part of the effort to do the work of the Lord in the church. Genuine stewardship giving is fulfilling and satisfying and so produces a sense of well-being and emotional and spiritual fitness. Authentic stewardship giving is rewarding in its wholesomeness. To give as God gives is to become more human, more of what God has created human beings to be. To be an unconstrained and authentic steward is to incorporate giving into the wholeness of the Christian life growing toward God-likeness.

Give from the abundance received from God (2 Cor 9.8). *The Apostle promises to hearts that are united to God: "you always [will have] all sufficiency" (vs. 8). Hesitation to give freely, which is driven by the desire to "guarantee" one's own needs, is tempered by knowing God's abounding grace. Even those of very simple means, but who truly know the Lord, understand that they have a real measure of "abundance for every good work." (vs. 8)*

The ethical aspect of this confidence in the abundance of God's giving is evident, pointing to the core Christian sense of dependency of the Christian on God for all of his or her needs. The words of the Lord's Prayer are a constant reminder of this reality: "Give us this day our daily bread" (Mt 6.11). Ethically, the confidence that God will provide for each of us is liberating. As Zechariah, the father of St John the Baptist put it, praying "that we, being delivered from the hand of our enemies, might serve him without fear, in holiness and righteousness before him all the days of our life." (Lk 1.74–75). Confidence in the "abundance of the Lord" in store for us in this life and in the next does not lead to a disregard for material needs, but to an inner peace that the Provident God cares for us.[26] And in that confidence stewardship giving carries with it no anxiety or hesitancy. It is part of the genuine freedom, or ἐλευθερία, of the Christian's life.

Give to the poor (vss. 9, 10). *The noun here describing the needy or the poor is "penesin," cousin to our English, penury, but alludes to those who are reduced to working just for bread, that is, for the bare necessities. To give to the poor cooperates with God in answering the prayer, "Thy kingdom come. Thy will be done on earth, as it is in heaven." (Mt 6.10)*

Here, *will*, in the sense of choice and freely adopted self-determination, comes into play. The imperative or "ought" character of the words "give to the poor" is self-evident. It is a normative statement instructing the Corinthian Christians and every Christian by extension, to actively assist those in need. This means that direct giving to the poor, to agencies that assist those in need, and the church's efforts at assisting the poor are ethical requirements. Giving to the church for its own needs and requirements is certainly proper and necessary. It is an essential aspect of Christian stewardship in order to facilitate the ministries of the church in making possible worship, sacramental life, education, mission, and fostering the communion of the saints for the edification of the body of Christ. "Let all things be done for edification" (1 Cor 14.26), St Paul says. But every

---

[26]"And he said to his disciples, 'Therefore I tell you, do not be anxious about your life, what you shall eat, nor about your body, what you shall put on. For life is more than food, and the body more than clothing. Consider the ravens: they neither sow nor reap, they have neither storehouse nor barn, and yet God feeds them. Of how much more value are you than the birds! And which of you by being anxious can add a cubit to his span of life? If then you are not able to do as small a thing as that, why are you anxious about the rest? Consider the lilies, how they grow; they neither toil nor spin; yet I tell you, even Solomon in all his glory was not arrayed like one of these. But if God so clothes the grass which is alive in the field today and tomorrow is thrown into the oven, how much more will he clothe you, O men of little faith! And do not seek what you are to eat and what you are to drink, nor be of anxious mind. For all the nations of the world seek these things; and your Father knows that you need them. Instead, seek his kingdom, and these things shall be yours as well'" (Lk 12.22–31).

Christian personally and individually also is instructed to fulfill a moral duty to the poor and the needy. Stewardship is inclusive of the needs of others. This part of the meditation also refers to cooperating with God in fulfilling his purposes, in this case caring for the poor. It reflects the Eastern Orthodox doctrinal and ethical concept of "synergy," that is, aligning our personal wills and actions with the purposes, intents, and will of God.[27]

> **Give, trusting that God will multiply** (2 Cor 9.10). *Among the practices which some of the excellent, contemporary, charitable organizations, such as the International Orthodox Christian Charities, follow is giving to build greater self-sufficiency, "getting the destitute on their feet." The Apostle speaks of Godly giving as having its source in God Who supplies seed to the sower and bread for food. There are some needs, however, brought about by overwhelming events such as drought, famine, and war, which require us to supply basic seed and food, knowing and trusting that God will "increase the fruits of [our] righteousness."* (vs. 10)

The first part of this commentary connects stewardship as giving with trust that God brings the giving to fruition. We do a small part, and God through his grace multiplies the small measure of our giving. As the Parable of the Sower puts it, "And other seeds fell into good soil and brought forth grain, growing up and increasing and yielding thirtyfold and sixtyfold and a hundredfold" (Mk 4.8). An ethical implication of this affirmation is that the Christian steward cannot assess his or her giving in a prideful manner. God gave the resources to begin with; our giving is only proportionate to what we have been given, and it bears fruit not because of us but because of what others do with it, most of all, God. So giving should be a humbling experience, not a prideful one. Thus, the source of any righteousness that comes from giving is the grace of God; our righteousness is always contingent and always short of purity and fullness. Part of the increase is its association with the giving of others. The parish as an agent for the use of stewardship contributions, as well as church and other philanthropic organizations, do, indeed, multiply the effects of individual stewardship. Thus, stewardship is a corporate act, not individualistic.

---

[27]For more on the ethical aspects of this concept, see Harakas, *Toward Transfigured Life*, ch. 5: 82, 104, 232–233, 243, 263.

The meditation ends with a summary statement that connects steward-ship giving with thanksgiving as a virtue of the Christian life, in general, and with the sacramental offering of bread wine and us. Truly, "the things that are Yours, from the things that are Yours, do we offer to You."

> **Give eucharistically** (vs. 11). *As one gives to the poor merrily from the heart, out of the abundance provided to oneself by God, trusting in Him to multiply our efforts, one naturally gives with praise and thanksgiving to the Lord. The two concepts, "praise and thanksgiving," fully express the single Greek word, "eucharistia," which we use to describe the quality of the Prayer of the Anaphora in the Divine Liturgy, which also truly expresses the whole Christian life.*

What better expression of this eucharistic approach to life than the words of the anaphora, mentioned above?

> You brought us into being out of nothingness, and when we had fallen, raised us up again, leaving nothing undone until You could lead us to heaven and grant us Your future kingdom. For all these things we thank You and Your only-begotten Son and Your Holy Spirit: for all these blessings, both known and unknown, manifest or hidden, that have been bestowed on us.[28]

ETHICS OF STEWARDSHIP ACCOUNTABILITY

These observations lead to a further ethical consideration in regard to stew-ardship. This is in reference to those who are entrusted with the steward-ship gifts given for the Lord's purposes.

The Parable of the Talents is frequently interpreted as referring to skills, personal gifts, abilities, and "talents" in the narrow sense, leading to the familiar and valuable motto regarding "Stewardship of Time, Talent, and Treasure." But, literally, it deals with the proper and improper (ethical and unethical) stewardship management of money, while in its context in Matthew 25, it is the final teaching of Christ regarding being prepared for

---

[28]Divine Liturgy of St John Chrysostom. Prayer at the priest's intonation of the words, "Let us give thanks to the Lord." Translation as found in Spencer T. Kezios, ed., *The Liturgikon: In the Original Greek with a New English Translation by Dr Leonidas Contos, Archiman-drite* (Northridge, Calif.: Narthex Press, 1996), 84.

the General Judgment and its strong ethical message about choosing to do good for others or choosing not to contribute to the welfare of others.[29]

St John Chrysostom makes a strong ethical point in relationship with the use of money and in particular, wealth, which is the excess of material resources over basic needs. Chrysostom points to the ethical instrumental character of wealth. It is judged ethically precisely on how it is used. Chrysostom reasons as follows:

> There are good things, bad things and things that are indifferent. Some of the things that are indifferent people consider to be good or bad while in reality they are neither. I will give you an example, to explain my meaning more clearly.
>
> Poverty is in general thought to be an evil. Not so: if someone who is poor practices watchfulness and wisdom, poverty itself can completely overcome evil. On the other hand, wealth is regarded as a good thing by most people. But that is not entirely true: it depends how you use it. If wealth were a good thing in itself and on its own account, then everyone who possesses it ought to be good. Yet not all rich people are virtuous, only those who manage their money in a responsible way. Therefore wealth is not a good thing in itself; it is only an instrument for doing good.
>
> So with regard to indifferent things: they are either good or bad according to the use that is made of them.[30]

The ethical implication for the proper management of the stewardship giving to the church is easily drawn from this passage. On one level, we have come full circle to the understanding of stewardship as good management. This speaks to those in the church who are responsible for the use of stewardship funds given for God's purposes: hierarchs, jurisdictional bodies, boards of trustees of church-related institutions, priests of parishes with

---

[29]John F. Walvoord, "The Parable of the Talents," *Bibliotheca Sacra* 129.515 (1972): 206–210.

[30]John Chrysostom, *Commentary on Isaiah*, 3ff. (PG 56, 146). From *Drinking from the Hidden Fountain: A Patristic Breviary*, by Thomas Spidlik and tr. by Paul Drake. Cistercian Studies Series One Hundred Forty Eight. (Kalamazoo, Mich.: Cistercian Publications, 1994), 46.

their parish councils, and leaders of parish organizations (catechetical schools, choirs, philanthropic organizations, youth groups, and so forth).

The ethical imperative of stewardship as good management is, firstly, the same as that for any human institution entrusted with the money of others. Thus,

> for business ethics, the contribution of Eastern Orthodox Christianity is not to provide ethical guidelines for maximizing profit. Rather it seeks to provide a constant reminder that the system itself must respond to elementary moral guidelines as it functions in the process of creating wealth, and it must acknowledge a responsibility to address human need in the context of spiritual values.[31]

Honesty in handling money, diligent attention to fiscal and fiduciary practices, and careful administration of church funds in accordance to charter and by-laws procedures are ethical requirements of all those entrusted with the proceeds of the stewardship giving of others. This is basic, elementary, natural law ethics as embodied in the Decalogue.[32]

But for those in the church who are stewards of the stewardship gifts of the faithful, this simple ethic is deepened and enhanced qualitatively. The Christian sense of a stewardship expressed by God in his provident care of his creation, by the stewardship we are called to exercise for the "mysteries of God," and by the ethical imperative that "it is required of stewards that they be found trustworthy" (1 Cor 4.1–2) are causes for soul-searching and prayerful concern for those who are responsible for the stewardship giving of the faithful. This stewardship is sacramental. Church bodies entrusted with reverently using the stewardship gifts of others can oftentimes fulfill their spiritual mandate in these material concerns by seeking

[31]Stanley Samuel Harakas, "An Eastern Orthodox Perspective on Business Ethics," in Stewart W. Herman, *Spiritual Goods: Faith Traditions and the Practice of Business: A Society for Business Ethics Anthology* (Bowling Green, Ohio: Philosophy Documentation Center-Bowling Green University, 2001), 152. Business ethics can be wide-ranging especially when it is religiously inspired. An older survey indicated that those who consciously brought religious values to their business decision-making and practice included concerns such as social responsibility, stewardship, and at least an elementary sense of the applicability of faith to work-place situations. Thomas F. McMahon, "Religion and Business: Concepts and Data," *Chicago Studies* 28.1 (1989): 3–16.

[32]For the biblical and patristic background of this, see Harakas, *Toward Transfigured Life*, ch. 6, "The Natural Moral Law."

counsel, assistance, and direction from professional fund-raising and financial planning agencies if these are attuned to Orthodox Christian spiritual
values. The literature on this kind of administrative stewardship is quite
broad, at least among non-Orthodox writers, dealing with issues such as disposing of church property, the management of church-owned physical
property, programs and church mission, the organization and deployment
of pastoral resources, the social, ethical roles of church bodies, including
monasteries, and the misappropriation of church funds.[33] These issues, and
others like them, indicate that it is time for deeper and more theologically
and ethically based reflection on the Orthodox understanding regarding
"the stewardship of accountability."

---

[33]Some examples from non-Orthodox sources are: *disposing of excess church property* in
Michael Bourke's article "The Archdeacon's Dilemma," *Theology*, 92.747 (1989): 196–203; *the
management and use of physical property* in W. M. Pinson's "Stewardship of Total Resources and
the Local Congregation," *Southwestern Journal of Theology* 13.2 (1971): 59–72; *addressing the work
of mission* in Arthur B. Rutledge's "The Church as Steward," *Review and Expositor* 70.2 (1973):
207–217; *pastoral resources and their allocation* in Warren Vanhetioo's "Pastors and Their Chief
Shepherd," *Calvary Baptist Theological Journal* 6.1 (1990): 141–148; *socially problematic minority
parish situations* such as that in William Norvel's "The African American Parish. Part 1.
Responsibility and Stewardship: A Parish Agenda for Pastoral Ministry," *New Theology Review*
7.1 (1994): 45–51; *the stewardship of monastic life* in Judith Sutera's "Stewardship and the Kingdom in the Rule of St Benedict," *American Benedictine Review* 41:4 (1990): 348–356; and, finally,
the misappropriation of church funds in Martin Marty's "Fleecing the Flock," *Sightings Internet
Magazine*, November 27, 2000 (rjmoore@midway.uchicago.edu).

ORTHODOX AMERICA

Philanthropy and Stewardship

ANTHONY SCOTT*

To give away money is an easy matter . . . and in any man's power. But to decide to whom to give it, and how large and when, for what purpose and how, is neither in every man's power nor an easy matter. Hence it is that such excellence is rare, praiseworthy and noble.

—Aristotle

For you know how generous our Lord Jesus Christ has been: he was rich, yet for your sake he became poor, so that through his poverty you might become rich. (2 Cor 8.9)　　　　　　　　—Paul of Tarsus

INTRODUCTION

I n terms of individual giving and the volunteer impulse, America is the most philanthropic country in the world. Yet the vast majority of Orthodox Christians in America have not yet learned how to give. Why do some Orthodox philanthropists give millions to secular charities and so little to their own church? How does philanthropy as practiced in America compare with stewardship as understood by Orthodox Christians? What motivates people to give sacrificially and joyfully? What can be done to assist Orthodox Christians to discover the freedom and joy inherent in sacrificial giving? The answer to these questions will form the content of this chapter.

*The Very Rev Anthony Scott has served as a parish priest and as the chief development officer for St Vladimir's Orthodox Theological Seminary, and now is president of Stewardship Advocates, an Orthodox planning and church development organization.

It is important from the outset to distinguish between philanthropy and stewardship. Secular in origin, philanthropy is viewed as motivated by love of man rather than love of God. As used by classical Greek and Latin authors and as generally understood today, the word *philanthropy* refers to the practice of giving material assistance to those in need. In the ancient world where state-sponsored social security, Medicare, unemployment benefits, and food stamps did not exist, the private citizen was vested with the primary responsibility of caring for the poor and the needy. Primary motivations for philanthropy included honor (Aristotle, *Nicomachean Ethics*), integrity and nobility (Cicero, *De Officiis*, I, XX, 68), and the brotherhood of man (Seneca, *De Ben*, xxv, *passim*).

Whereas for pagans, philanthropy was understood as the exercise of dutiful compassion or an expression of nobility, Christians came to understand this term differently. God became a human being and identified himself with the poor. Christians were taught to see in the poor and the needy the presence of Jesus himself. In a representation of the teaching of Christ from Matthew 25.31–41 on the Last Judgment, a famous icon of the Orthodox Church shows compassionate care being given to one who is hungry, one who is thirsty, one who is naked, one who is sick, and one who is in prison. The face of each person who is receiving compassionate care is shown to be the face of Jesus Christ. Pagans might have looked upon the poor or the needy and thought, "There, *but* for the will of the gods, go I." Early Christians might have look upon the poor and the needy and thought," There, *by* the grace of God, goes Jesus." No pagan would have looked upon a suffering person and thought, "This is Zeus."

Christians understood that once they were spiritually poor and spiritually ignorant, held in thrall to sin and death through fallen human nature. However, in God's redeeming love for humanity, expressed by Jesus in his ministry of healing and more particularly in his death upon the cross, each Christian viewed himself or herself as the beneficiary of God's love for humanity, thereby receiving the gifts of a transformed nature in eternal communion with God. The primary impetus for Christian philanthropy therefore, is gratitude. St John of Kronstadt, in a famous passage from *My Life in Christ*, describes prayer as a "continually grateful frame of mind" (Grisbrooke, *Spiritual Counsels* 27). Likewise, Bishop Kallistos Ware describes the vivifying effect of gratitude:

If I do not feel a sense of joy in God's creation, if I forget to offer the world back to God with thankfulness, I have advanced very little upon the Way. I have not yet learnt to be truly human. For it is only through thanksgiving that I can become myself. Joyful thanksgiving, so far from being escapist or sentimental, is on the contrary entirely realistic–but with the realism of one who sees the world in God, as the divine creation. (Ware, *The Orthodox Way*, 44)

Stewardship is an ongoing response to God in thanksgiving. It is expressed in the sacrificial giving of time, talents, and treasure.

A second, less common meaning of stewardship is the good management and faithful maintenance of those values and goods temporarily given into one's keeping. In this regard St Paul refers to the apostles as "stewards of the mysteries" (1 Cor 4.11). In light of this, stewardship is referred to as the good management of lives and the things given to each person–possessions, children, spouses, friends, co-workers, the legacy of parents and grandparents, and, more particular to the subject of this article, the parish facilities and the mission of the Church.

AMERICAN PHILANTHROPY

Robert Payton, a leading scholar of philanthropy, wrote, "The most distinctive virtue of the American character is philanthropy" (*Philanthropy: Voluntary Action for the Public Good*). Those who framed the Constitution of the United States felt that individuals should accept primary responsibility for the civic and religious life of the nation. This belief is enshrined in the doctrine of separation of church and state. The common citizenry was expected to fund hospitals, libraries, universities, and religious institutions. That most secular saint of America, Benjamin Franklin, is still revered today for founding the first library and the first hospital in America. He also established the University of Pennsylvania and created its first endowment through a bequest upon his death.

Henry Rosso, the father of the modern science of nonprofit development described the role of Benjamin Franklin in constructing a church. This was 225 years before the multi-billion dollar campaigns conducted today by leading charitable institutions.

When the Reverend Gilvert Tennent sought Franklin's help to build a Presbyterian church in Philadelphia, Franklin declined direct help but offered wise counsel that has earned a precious place in the archives of fund raising: "In the first place, I advise you to apply to all of those whom you know will give something, next to those whom you are uncertain whether they will give anything or not and show them the list of those who have given, and lastly, do not neglect those whom you are sure will give nothing, for in some of them you will be mistaken." Tennent took his advice, Franklin reported, for he asked everyone and he obtained a much larger sum than he had expected. (*Rosso on Fund Raising*, 106–107)

Though the government now provides vast programs for assistance to the poor and needy, the nonprofit or independent sector, as it is sometimes called, remains a vibrant, visible, and essential aspect of civic life in America.

In the 1980s the scholarly community began to research and reflect upon the nonprofit sector—both from the point of view of philanthropy and fundraising. Up until that time, what was known was largely anecdotal consisting of published memoirs by those whose lives had been dedicated to nonprofit service. Now scores of books based upon an ever-growing body of scholarly research are published each year in this field. Numerous universities offer graduate degrees in nonprofit management and fundraising. It is even possible to earn a doctorate in philanthropy at the University of Indiana. What once was deemed 80 percent art and 20 percent science has now become 80 percent science and 20 percent art. In terms of fundraising or what is sometimes called "development" or "advancement," it is now possible to have an entire career in any of the following activities: annual giving, events, major giving, grant writing, prospect research, direct mail, major gifts, strategic planning, board development, capital campaigns, gift planning, and endowments.

Much is now known concerning how Americans practice philanthropy. According to the *Nonprofit Almanac*, an annual comprehensive survey published by the Independent Sector, there are 1.2 million independent sector organizations and religious congregations in the United States. Independent sector organizations consist of 501(c)3s, 501(c)4s, and religious congregations. Of these, approximately 56,000 are grant-making private foundations, doubling since 1987. Fifty-five percent of all Americans formally volunteered through a nonprofit organization. Seventy percent of all American households gave to charity. In the twenty years from 1977 to 1997 the percentage of those employed by the independent sector in America compared to the total United States employment increased from 5.3 percent to 7.1 percent. In the same period of time, the number of independent sector organizations increased from 739,000 to 1.2 million—a whopping 66 percent!

Total giving in America exceeded $200 billion in 2002. Of this amount, individuals gave 84 percent, foundations gave approximately 10 percent, and corporations gave approximately 6 percent. Paul G. Schervish, co-author of the 1999 report "Millionaires and the Millennium," estimates that "the intergenerational transfer of wealth in current dollars over the next fifty years will be between $41 trillion and $136 trillion, with $6 trillion to $25 trillion going to charitable bequests." Of each philanthropic dollar, Americans gave sixty cents to religious organizations—this does not include giving to parochial schools and faith-based human services.

It is widely held that the nonprofit sector, or the conglomeration of nongovernmental organizations (NGOs), as they are called outside of the United States, is an integral and necessary part of every democratic society, providing a healthy counterweight to government, commerce, and the military. Many countries seek to emulate the philanthropic and volunteer culture of America. In the years 2000–2003, Germany, the United Kingdom, and France all enacted legislation to encourage charitable giving and the establishment of charitable foundations. Many of the measures were a conscious copying of the American way of charity including raising limits on the tax deductibility of donations, allowing deductions to be spread out over five years, increasing tax deductions for gifts by corporations, allowing greater flexibility in how foundations organize themselves, and lowering the administrative barriers that constrain giving (*The Chronicle of Philanthropy,* April 3, 2003).

Research confirms that those who participated regularly in religious worship were far more likely to give to charity and to volunteer than those who did not. Religious organizations, therefore, serve a vital need of society. Churches, synagogues, and mosques are schools where philanthropy and service is taught and practiced. It is the place where most people first experience nonsectarian giving and where most people learn to express concern for others who are not immediate family, friends, or members of the same ethnic group or confession of faith.

It is important for Orthodox Christians to understand the science of development not only because of the powerful tools it affords to the advancement of the mission of the Church but also because of the danger that the science of nonprofit institutional development presents to the Church. A nonprofit organization with a cause antithetical to Orthodox teaching and life, empowered through strategic planning, emboldened by an advocating board of directors, professionally managed, and adept at the challenging task of fundraising is as much a threat to the Church as militant atheism was to Orthodoxy in the twentieth century—perhaps even more so. Such a nonprofit is legally licensed by the state as a "charitable and philanthropic endeavor"—fully tax deductible, championing such human "rights" as abortion on demand, the legalization of certain drugs, euthanasia, and same-sex marriages. On this subject one Orthodox theologian quipped, "I am waiting for a murderers' rights group or a rapists' rights group to appear."

ORTHODOX *Philanthropia*

Why do Orthodox Christians give millions to universities, hospitals, and cultural institutions and relatively little to their own church? In addition to one particular Orthodox philanthropist who gives approximately $20 million per year to various institutions, during the past ten years the following gifts have been made by Orthodox Christians:

> Northeastern University—$6 million
> The Metropolitan Museum of Art—$13 million
> Emory University—a series of gifts totaling $6.1 million
> Tufts University—$12 million
> University of Illinois—$1.5 million
> Hampshire College—$2 million
> Grady Memorial Hospital—$4 million
> The University of Pennsylvania—$10 million
> American Red Cross—$15 million
> New York University—$5 million
> Library of Congress—$2 million
> Pennsylvania State University—$2.7 million
> Mercy General Hospital—$15 million
> Duke University—$25 million
> The University of Iowa—$10 million
> Five universities in Iowa—$5 million

Brown University–a series of gifts totaling over $35 million
Children's Hospital of Pittsburgh–$3 million
Johns Hopkins University–$2 million
Regional Trail Corporation of Pennsylvania–$2.25 million
Lawrenceville School–$8 million
Drexel University–a number of gifts totaling over $5 million
William Paterson College–$10.5 million
(*The Chronicle of Philanthropy, Philanthropy News Digest,* and
   Giving USA)

This is a fraction of the total number of gifts by Orthodox Christians
of $1 million or more, many of which were made anonymously or remain
unreported. Beyond giving money, Orthodox Christians have also chaired
national fundraising campaigns and have served as chairpersons of the
boards of universities, major hospitals, and eminent cultural institutions.
Orthodox Christians have established not less than fifty family foundations. As of 2003, the four largest of these foundations have assets exceed-
ing $165,000,000, $82,000,000, $65,000,000, and $48,000,000,
respectively. Surprisingly, these are not Greek-American. Another of these
fifty foundations makes grants exclusively to Orthodox 501(c)(3) charitable
institutions in a self-conscious effort to advance the Orthodox faith and
enhance Orthodox ministries of social service. Grants made by this foundation to Orthodox Christian projects include support of mission work,
orphanages, seminaries, cancer research, scholarly publications, monasteries, libraries, humanitarian concerns, abused and neglected children, prison
ministry, the homeless, Orthodox iconography, and the restoration of
ancient churches. In the ten-year period from 1993–2003, this foundation
has made grants totaling $4.5 million.

Recently, nascent efforts have been made to form an inter-Orthodox
alliance of foundations and philanthropists whose interests include Orthodox Church institutions and ministries. This intriguing prospect, which has
enormous potential to raise the standard of Orthodox philanthropy and
positively transform the manner in which Orthodox institutions are governed and managed, must be vigorously supported.

Interestingly, despite cynical observations that Orthodox make large
gifts to non-Orthodox institutions because these philanthropists seek a level
of recognition not attainable in the relatively small world of American

Orthodoxy, they do in fact fall into a national pattern that exists for all donors of major gifts, irrespective of their ethnic or religious background. In a study reported in the *Chronicle of Philanthropy*, April 17, 2003, in the years 1995–2000, 502 donors made gifts of $10 million or more that totaled $29.3 billion. Four out of every five of these philanthropic dollars went to the arts, education, and health institutions. Forty-three percent went to colleges and universities. Only one percent went to religion.

The director of the study, Gary A. Tobin, speculated that donors may be more inclined to give to large, prestigious organizations because they feel assured that their money will be used for its intended purpose and because those institutions have invested in sophisticated fund-raising offices that specifically seek big gifts.

Philanthropists feel a moral and fiduciary responsibility to accomplish as much good as possible with their limited ability to give. This is consistent with the Orthodox view of good stewardship. Furthermore, a philanthropist, like any other person, does not wish to be treated as the local ATM—walk up; put in the card; take out the money; turn and walk away. This may be the all-too-common method by which philanthropists are treated by representatives of the Church. This is certainly not the approach employed by the institutions listed at the beginning of this section of the chapter. At the best, this is ineffective fundraising. At the worst, it is a callous disregard for the sacrament of the human person.

Orthodox Christians do make significant gifts to their church, though not nearly on the same scale as they do to secular charities. Leadership 100, a philanthropic organization of the Greek Orthodox Archdiocese, in which members agree to contribute $100,000 to a restricted endowment fund in support of archdiocesan projects, programs, and occasionally, to charities sponsored by the Standing Conference of Orthodox Christians in America, lists more than 650 members. In the past ten years it is conservatively estimated that Orthodox churches, nationally and locally, have received between 40–45 gifts of $1 million or more.

It may be useful to know that philanthropists invest their charitable dollars in nonprofit institutions in precisely the same way that they make personal financial investments in for-profit businesses. Very few would make a sizeable investment in a company that consistently ran deficits, was poorly managed, had no vision for the future, trailed a history of accounting irregularities, and exhibited a spotty record of successes.

Orthodox Christians and the Local Practice of Stewardship

In the twentieth century, large populations of Orthodox Christians, almost entirely devoid of the Jeffersonian, democratic, and egalitarian experience of a voluntary society, immigrated to the United States. Since Constantine the Great and the establishment of Christianity as the official religion of the Roman Empire, these Orthodox Christians were accustomed to churches supported by endowments, income-producing properties, and state funding by means of involuntary taxation. Yet it was not always this way, for, as Professor Jaroslav Pelikan once remarked to me in passing, "Before Constantine, stewardship might have meant giving your life. After Constantine, stewardship consisted of paying your taxes." With the collapse of communism and the arrival of the Orthodox Church in the West, once again individual church members returned to the early apostolic practice of supporting the Church through their own material and voluntary support. This is one of the most positive developments in church life in many hundreds of years. And, as every parish priest and diocesan bishop would confirm, it is also one of the most daunting.

Unfortunately, the very antithesis of sacrificial giving is institutionally enshrined in many parishes by mandated minimal giving (dues or required minimal pledge amounts). Based on a recent national study, average annual giving as defined by "dues" or a "pledge" by Greek Orthodox Christians to their church in North America averages approximately $300 per year. And this from the Orthodox cultural group most often identified with material success! This is among the lowest per capita giving among all American faith traditions. Many parishes persist in leveraging dues though it is described as "stewardship." Simply changing the name of a practice does not change its nature. This is the nominalism that haunts sacramental realism.

To offset this poor performance in personal stewardship, Orthodox parishes have displayed enormous creativity and boundless energy in developing ancillary sources of funding. Most parishes take pride in extracting from the local community a substantial portion of the operating income of the parish through festivals. Months of parish life can be consumed by the enormous vortex that swirls in the midst of a parish during the preparation, execution, and recovery phases of a festival. Other parishes fund operating costs in a ceaseless round of fundraising events—bake sales, raffles, golf tournaments, Las Vegas nights, fashion shows, car washes, and so

forth. Additional ancillary fundraising methods may include leased park-
ing, state-funded schools, for-profit schools, apartment, home and office
rentals, microwave towers, health clubs, bars, hall rentals, food booths at
public gatherings, catering, real estate speculation, issuing church "bonds,"
day care, senior care, and retirement complexes.

Parishioners have been conditioned for generations to give miniscule
amounts to their church many times a year. One priest commented that he
once counted the number of times his parishioners were asked to give on
an average Sunday. It numbered 14 times. Each plea was for a very small
amount—candles, bulletin appeals, poor box, double tray passing, verbal
announcements of forthcoming fundraising events at the end of the service, bulletin board appeals, card tables set up to snag parishioners as they
left church for the maintenance fund, endowment, and youth group. Then,
in the every-Sunday parish luncheon that followed, numerous appeals for
relief for causes in the old country were made. He said that parishioners
had long ago learned to bring a roll of $1 dollar bills to drop in a few of
these multiple outstretched hands. He wondered what image the parish was
projecting to visitors and new members.

When Orthodox Christians do give, how do they give? What thoughts
shape their decisions and what values prompt their actions? Nonsacramen-
tal, nonsacrificial giving falls into several categories.

Herd giving: One of the saddest occasions of parish life is when that rare,
sacrificially giving Orthodox Christian leaves one parish environment
where proportionate giving is practiced by many people and enters into a
parish where the all too common experience of minimal giving predomi-
nates. They soon become aware that they give far above the mainstream
and make downward adjustments so as to conform to community standards. Rather than inspire others to give, they have been influenced to give
minimally, as others do in the local parish environment.

Comparative giving: Most Orthodox parishes have a number of parishioners whose church experience was shaped abroad. As is well known, most
new immigrants struggle with the American tradition of church and state
separation and the need for individual parishioners to support the work of
the Church. However, it is the giving of those born and raised in the United
States that is the issue. The nongiving or very poor giving of new immigrants often engenders in those born in the United States a smug superiority—even though their own giving is pitiful according to the teaching of

Holy Scriptures. The entire focus of the stewardship committee is to get the new immigrants or the loosely affiliated members who are "not doing their part" to give, thus allowing those born in America to conveniently overlook their own faint response to the Lord's injunction to give sacrificially.

Budgetary giving: Rather than reflect upon the immeasurable gifts and blessings from God and offer a sacrificial gift in gratitude, here the Orthodox Christian looks at the operating budget of the parish and makes a gift in relationship to the "needs" of the local parish. The problem is the budgetary process. Setting aside the issue of how many parishes are understaffed, how many parish operating budgets have ambitious line items for mission, evangelization, theological education, assistance to the poor and needy, monasteries, campus ministry or youth services? Operating budgets seem to be in response to the question "How little can the people be asked to give?" not to "What challenging new projects or efforts can be made in the coming year to expand ministries, contribute to mission, or further assist the poor and the needy?"

Averaged giving: Mathematics trump stewardship! The operating budget of the parish is $300,000. The number of giving families is four hundred. Subtracting the festival and ancillary income from other fundraising activities of $150,000, the figure of $150,000 is calculated, which is needed for this year's budget. Dividing four hundred into $150,000 means each family needs to give $375. If a family gives $400, the family feels that they are doing more than their share. Therefore, they are giving generously. This may be accurate mathematical formulation, but it is exceedingly poor stewardship. Conveniently forgotten are the uneven distribution of wealth, the uneven distribution of faith commitment, and the uneven distribution of the philanthropic disposition of parishioners.

Legal giving: The bane of stewardship! Here, in a desperate measure to shore up the crumbling finances of the parish, "minimal" giving standards are set. Unfortunately, minimal giving rapidly becomes maximal giving—people rarely giving beyond the legal requirements. If the Church is going to behave like the Internal Revenue Service, why should people respond any differently? Who voluntarily gives more in taxes than is absolutely necessary?

Disposable giving: This is the most common of all perfunctory giving. It is blithely assumed that all bills are unquestioned necessities and therefore automatically to be excluded from a determination of giving capability—mortgage payments, car payments, private tuition, utilities, restaurants, clothing, subscriptions, taxes, cosmetics, jewelry, vacations, renovations, investments, cable television, entertainment, furniture, appliances, health clubs, country clubs—every conceivable and self-indulgent whim. From the tiny amount that remains of disposable income, what further tiny percentage should be given to the Lord? What is the smallest gift that will allow a feeling of having fulfilled one's commitment?

The forms of giving described above relate to the operating budget of the parish. What of capital campaigns for property acquisition, renovation, construction, or endowment? It is reasonable to estimate that at any given time, one in every ten parishes of the approximately 2,000 Orthodox parishes in North America is planning or attempting to execute a capital campaign, averaging perhaps $1 million. (At a recent seminar on capital campaigns for thirty-four Orthodox parishes, the total amount sought by these parishes was over $90 million!) Combine this with the need of every parish to raise money for operations and the occasional effort to establish an endowment. Further add the fundraising efforts of church institutions—dioceses, seminaries, monasteries, and service organizations. The result is a vast enterprise totaling perhaps one half-billion dollars per year.

It must be acknowledged that church leaders receive no education or training to effectively shape these activities. Fortunately it's the rare Orthodox priest or bishop who feels his primary purpose is to manage fundraising enterprises. Yet, often the result is that priests and bishops spend a large portion of their time doing so. What is the effect of these uncritical approaches to funding operating budgets and capital needs upon the life of the parish?

The purpose of parish life is simple: confess the creed, worship God, and serve those in need. Yet an examination of how most parishes utilize volunteer resources reveals that a ceaseless round of fund raising activities has become the de facto purpose of parish life.

Granted, festivals and fundraising activities may provide additional benefits of weaving the fabric of community social ties or giving volunteer opportunities for new members to become integrated into the community. However, it must be asked if other activities would achieve the same purpose. Even a cursory reading of the New Testament reveals not one mention of the ubiquitous fundraising activities that fill parish social calendars.

Communal church activities that are revealed in the New Testament include worship, fellowship, mission, evangelization, study, and care for the poor and needy. How very different Orthodox parishes would be and how much more effective mission and evangelization efforts would be if the operating budget was fully pledged through sacrificial giving and community volunteer resources were dedicated to the activities described in Holy Scripture.

When faced with the occasional enormity of a capital campaign for property acquisition, renovation, construction, or building an endowment, parishes are often at a loss. The known methods of fundraising are insufficient to the task. With no consciousness of sacrificial giving, and decades of dues or the minimal giving many times a year mentality, people cannot begin to conceive of a five-, six-, seven-, or even eight-figure gift that is based not only upon annual income but also reflects the investments and appreciated assets accumulated through the years. How many families have been alienated from the Church due to a crass approach for a gift? Using earmarked contributions for a different purpose than the donor originally intended? A botched naming opportunity? A failed capital campaign? Mismanagement of funds? Promises not kept?

WHY PEOPLE GIVE

One of the most fascinating areas of philanthropic research today is termed donor motivation. It is an inquiry into what stimulates people to give generously and sacrificially. One clue may be found in a recent capital campaign conducted by St Vladimir's Orthodox Theological Seminary. The campaign raised over 22.5 million dollars in receipts and planned gifts. These funds were raised from every major Orthodox cultural group in America, from Orthodox faithful of every conceivable economic condition, parish environment, and region of the country. Yet of the more than 3,000 contributors to the campaign, only six requested naming opportunities. If not for recognition, then why did these people give? An understanding of donor motivation will shape the development of an effective program of fundraising.

First, a myth must be dispensed as to why people are motivated to make a major gift or to give sacrificially: Research shows that contrary to general public assumptions, the vast majority of those who make a large gift or give sacrificially do not do so to receive a tax deduction, nor for personal recognition, nor out of guilt, nor because there is a desperate fiscal crisis. Yet often this is the message and the approach.

Those who give sacrificially do so because *they identify with the mission of the parish or church organization.* They see in their contribution of time, talent, and treasure the extension, advancement, and perpetuation of their own life's values and goals. This begs the question: What do people understand the mission of the parish or church organization to be? How effectively is this communicated? Is a compelling vision of the Church as the manifestation of the kingdom of God on earth articulated? What efforts have been made to assist people to participate in the fulfillment of the mission of the parish? Is it assumed that parishioners understand and embrace the mission of the parish or church organization? What programs of the parish or church organization merit a major gift in the fulfillment of mission? Have major giving opportunities been described in this regard? Is there a reasonable plan to receive a major gift and utilize it responsibly? Will major donors be included as partners in the implementation phase of a major gift?

As stated earlier, major donors make large gifts just as they make personal investments. They give to corporations and they give to charitable organizations that are *well managed.* Would a person make a meaningful financial investment in a corporation that was poorly managed? One that was continually running budget deficits? One that was not following through on product development (church program definition and implementation)? One that never communicated with investors (donors)? One that could not cite a record of positive performance and success (changing lives and saving lives)? It is incumbent upon church leadership, therefore, to effectively lead and to effectively manage if sacrificial giving and major giving from appreciated assets and investments is requested.

Another significant motivating factor in precipitating major gifts and sacrificial giving comes from *the training and experience received at home in stewardship and giving.* People often give as their mothers and fathers gave, emulating their behavior. If parents practice good stewardship and teach their children to do so, there is an excellent possibility that this will be their behavior as adults. It must be acknowledged frankly that this is a major shortcoming in Orthodox households. The behavior of parents is often precisely the opposite—give as little as possible, wait for others to lead, or give as poorly as everyone else gives in the parish. If parents do not provide this example, the next best option is public teaching in the Church through programs designed to teach good stewardship to children and the youth and by means of the visible demonstration of exemplary giving by members of the church. Parishes sadly lack philanthropic mentors and exemplars of sacrificial giving. It is possible to observe the unending sacrifice of time from festival workers or parish volunteers, but the sacrament of stewardship is the sacrificial giving of time, talent, and treasure—all of the above, not one of the above.

Ideally, a person's entire motivation to give is a faith response in gratitude for life and communion with the living God. However, because humans are imperfect, the inner impetus that prompts sacrificial giving or a major gift is not always so simple or clear. People often give generously or make a very large gift because *they like or respect the person who is asking them for the gift.* They are investing in the representation of this person's values and vision of life. They trust the person who represents the institution that is asking for the gift. Is this not one of the main reasons why the apostles left all to follow Jesus? What does this imply for church leaders who seek gifts of this caliber? It requires humility, genuine acceptance of the donor, an ardent and effective articulation of the mission of the Church as it relates to the requested gift, a careful and thoughtful approach, and above all, honesty and integrity.

All indirect methods of engendering sacrificial giving and major gift giving are likely to prove ineffective. People give sacrificially and make major gifts because *they are personally asked to give sacrificially and to make major gifts.* Jesus was unafraid to ask people for meaningful personal sacrifice. Every teaching of the Lord was a call to repentance—to change—to give up one way of life for another. He even made what is called in the nonprofit world "the ultimate ask." To the rich young man he said: "Go and sell all that you have, distribute to the poor and follow me and you will have joy in heaven" (Mt 19.21). He called the apostles to leave family, homes, security, and jobs in order to follow him. Time and again, he asked the people who came into his presence to give up sin, darkness, ignorance, false gods, and willful disobedience so that they could accept the gift of eternal communion with God.

A number of years ago a research project investigated the donor intent of fifty philanthropists, each of whom had given at least one gift of $1 million or more. Each was personally interviewed. The interviewees cited a number of giving motivations, including many of those described above. Yet there was only one motivation that was universally present—*it was the desire to experience the joy in making the gift.* How encouraging this is when one considers the arduous task of raising the standard of giving in the parish or larger church environment. How elegantly this refutes the cynical observation that people make major gifts to glorify their own egos and receive public acclaim. How reassuring this is to those who ask people to make sacrificial or major gifts. The experience of making the gift, of making a difference in the life of a cherished parish or church organization, of changing lives and saving lives is really about deep spiritual joy.

WHAT CAN BE DONE?

If Orthodox churches and institutions wish to receive major gifts and the investment of trust that always precedes them, then hierarchs, governing boards, parish priests, and the staff of Orthodox organizations must emulate the behavior of major charitable institutions and organizations with sound strategic planning, willingness to be accountable, financial transparency, good management, a compelling vision of the future, a careful plan for the incorporation of a major gift within the vision, a committed and advocating governing board, a demonstrated record of success, and a professional approach to relationships with major donors. When this occurs, then it is likely that the Church, too, will begin to receive substantial monetary gifts.

One decisive factor may be the readiness for the Church to invest in professional development. Universities, eminent hospitals, and cultural institutions are institutionally prepared to spend 10 percent of the size of a major gift in order to secure the gift. Are leading Orthodox institutions and parishes prepared to do this? Or do they assume, perhaps arrogantly, that well-to-do Orthodox Christians should simply pray, pay, and obey? St Vladimir's Seminary spent $800,000 to conduct the multi-year capital campaign that concluded in 1997. Would most reasonable people concur that $800,000 was a worthwhile investment to receive a return in gifts and pledges of $22.5 million?

In many parishes a conspiracy of silence tyrannizes the entire process of giving. Never discuss money; never reveal what one's self is giving; never speak directly to any other person about giving; never sensitively and diplomatically announce a major gift publicly. Do not allow to those responsible for the stewardship ministry each year the necessary access to information on parishioner giving on a need-to-know basis. Some clergy proudly announce that they do not know, nor wish to know what anyone is giving lest it create a bias in pastoral care. If this is the case, perhaps they should not know how often people volunteer or attend church either, for fear of favoritism. One parish assigns numbers to families, like anonymous Swiss bank accounts, so as to preserve absolute secrecy. Other parishes mandate by general assembly legislation that the financial secretary must be a nonparishioner and that he or she alone is to know what people give. All of this reveals a profound confusion between confidentiality, which is necessary in a fallen world, and secrecy, which does not exist in the kingdom of God. The Holy Trinity, the angelic powers, and the communion of the saints are all witnesses to the most "private" thoughts and actions of each person. All that we think and do is done in community.

Stewardship is not about raising money. Stewardship is a powerful tool to engender *personal spiritual development*. Similarly, capital campaigns are not about constructing a hall or new church or establishing an endowment; capital campaigns are really about *community spiritual development*. People care about what they give to. When people give meaningfully, they care meaningfully. Conversely, when people do not give at all or when they give minimally, they do not care at all or care minimally.

The Lord understood human nature so very well when he taught: "Where your treasure is; there is your heart" (Mt 6.21). Jesus did not reverse this and say, "Where your heart is, there is your treasure." Who, having purchased stock in a company, bought a home, or acquired a car, does not monitor the stock regularly, attend to repairs in the home, or take the car in for regular maintenance? After a person has made a meaningful charitable investment in the life and mission of the parish, *that* church suddenly becomes *my* church. Those who have made personally significant gifts to the church tend to read the bulletin more assiduously, visit their *investment* more frequently, and listen more attentively when people talk about the church. Interestingly, most will tolerate no unjustified criticism of the church, because, after all, it has now become *their* church.

What should be the response to those who give sacrificially or to those who give very large gifts? Orthodox institutions may choose one of three responses to those who give in these ways. The first response is not to respond at all, which may convey arrogance or ignorance. In one sense the reason for the response makes no difference because the effect is the same— a negative and unpleasant experience for the donor. How does one feel when a gesture of love is met with unresponsiveness or uncaring passivity?

A second choice is complete and total responsiveness—this is fawning obsequiousness or worse—prostitution of the essential moral integrity of

the Church. The ultimate effect upon donors is a loss of respect and perhaps embarrassment that their gift engendered such a response.

There is a third choice. It is to be highly responsive—sensitive, courte-
ous, grateful, thoughtful, and faithful in the good management of the gift,
displaying scrupulous honesty and strict adherence to the purpose for
which the gift was made. This response seems to be most consistent with
the life of the Church.

Why are clergy largely ineffective in fundraising? The explanation is
simple: most people are not effective fundraisers. Therefore, most clergy are
not effective fundraisers. Yet there are other extenuating factors. Clergy fear
how they will be perceived in the community. "I don't want parishioners
to think that this is all I care about." "People might think that I have
favorites in the parish. I need to treat everyone equitably." "If I ask for a gift
and a parishioner responds positively, won't this mean that they have a
claim upon me for some future favor—something that might be in variance
with church policy?" "They might think that I care more about their bank
account than I do their soul."

Every Sunday and preaching opportunity clergy ask people to repent,
to give up coveted sins, to change their lives, to embrace life in the kingdom of God. What's so difficult about asking someone for a gift of time,
talent, and treasure? For most people these are far easier things to give than
substantive, personal inner transformation. Yet here is the mystery: the very
giving of time, talent, and treasure results in substantive personal inner
transformation. One cannot think one's way into good action, but one can
act one's way into good thinking.

Giving perceptions of church governing bodies and clergy are shaped
not by the potential of people to give, the desire of people to give, or the
need to fund ever-expanding growth in the ministries of service, but rather
by frustrating every-year struggles to get people to increase their stewardship
from a paltry $300 per year to an equally paltry $350 per year. Most efforts
to increase stewardship are directed in the largely ineffective attempt to
change the *corporate* behavior of the general parish membership. It is the top
leadership of the parish that first must embrace the vital necessity of personally significant giving. This becomes the leavening that results in many more
members following in a similar manner. People who discover the joy of sacrificial giving think: I give sacrificially and still have a great abundance of
life. Why shouldn't other people give sacrificially and also feel this joy?

A word to bishops, priests, deacons, and parish council members: all the stratagems, techniques, pithy bulletin one-liners, carefully crafted letters, closely reasoned sermons, and desperate pleading joined together will not affect the giving of church members in the positive manner that a simple, direct, one-on-one conversation on this subject will have in a quiet meeting with a parishioner. People change not because they see the light but because they feel the heat.

Every priest should have an awareness of the stewardship practice of his parishioners—how often and whether or not they honor their commitments. Stewardship ranks among the top factors composing the spiritual profile of a parishioner—along with confessing the creed, frequency of worship, fasting, personal prayer, reading Holy Scripture, and service to others.

Any Christian ministry that requires a "spiritual" antecedent is doomed to failure. If it is believed that first people must become "spiritual" before they can do mission, for example, it results in mission never being done. When do people become sufficiently "spiritual" so as to act with evangelizing fervor? It is exactly the opposite that it true. By going forward in mission, even though one feels inadequate to the task, one becomes spiritually alive. If it is assumed that fasting, prayer, participation in the sacraments, and an understanding of the Orthodox faith must precede sacrificial giving, then it is unlikely that sacrificial giving will ever occur because one never "arrives" spiritually. It is precisely in giving generously, together with all of these activities, that one receives the joy and freedom of a life in God.

Unfortunately, there is no direct linkage between piety and generosity. Witness the well-to-do parishioner who rarely participates in formal church life, yet often is very generous to secular charities and also to the Church. Conversely, witness the faithful and pious well-to-do church member who is extremely penurious. It's the difference between those who feel *richly blessed*, whose cup overflows with blessings and abundance and those who feel *deprived*, who feel they did not yet get their fair share in life. The impetus of the giving of the poor widow praised by Jesus and cited as an exemplar was gratitude for life in rich abundance—though she was in fact materially poor.

CONCLUSION

Good stewardship shapes the proper life of a Christian in the Church. It allows the Christian to stand before the Holy Trinity in a state of profound gratitude. Good stewardship also shapes the proper relationship between a Christian and his or her possessions. In the practice of good stewardship the Christian is freed from the debilitating fear of insufficiency and the avariciousness that results from feeling deprived. The joyful freedom of life in expanding, unending abundance is the gift of God to the good steward.

Corporate good stewardship in a parish improves the quality of spiritual life for the community. It allows the parish to fulfill its mission in fidelity to the gospel through a proper alignment of values and priorities. Corporate good stewardship in the Church is a means by which Christians learn to love the poor and the needy of the world and to actively transcend tribalism, ethnicism, racism, and all the other artificially divisive categories of human thought and behavior.

The practice of secular philanthropy is a tremendous force for good in the world. A very high percentage of secular philanthropy is completely consistent with life in the kingdom of God. Orthodox Christians who participate in the larger philanthropic enterprise in America are to be commended. It is incumbent upon the leadership of the Church to create giving opportunities and a responsible environment where Orthodox philanthropists may exercise similar beneficence in the Church.

SELECT BIBLIOGRAPHY

The Chronicle of Philanthropy. April 3, 2003. http://www.philanthropy.com. 1255 23rd St. N.W. Suite 700, Washington, D.C., 20037.

Grisbrooke, W. Jardine. *Spiritual Counsels of Father John of Kronstadt: Select Passages from* My Life in Christ. Crestwood, N.Y.: St Vladimir's Seminary Press, 1989.

Havens, John J., and Schervish, Paul G. "Millionaires and the Millennium: New Estimates of the Forthcoming Wealth Transfer and the Prospects for a Golden Age of Philanthropy." *Report from the Boston College Social Welfare Research Institute,* October 19, 1999.

Philanthropy News Digest, a publication of The Foundation Center, 79 Fifth Avenue/16th Street, New York, N.Y. 10003-3076.

Rosso, Henry A. *Rosso on Fundraising: Lessons from a Master's Lifetime.* San Francisco, Calif.: Jossey-Bass, 1996.

Giving USA, researched and written at The Center on Philanthropy at Indiana University, 550 W. North St., Suite 301, Indianapolis, Ind. 46202-3272; and a joint publication of Indiana University and the American Association of Fund Raising Counsel (AAFRC), 10293 N. Meridian Street, Suite 175, Indianapolis, Ind. 46290.

Ware, Kallistos. *The Orthodox Way.* Crestwood, N.Y.: St Vladimir's Seminary Press, 2002.